Implementing Information Technology Governance:
Models, Practices, and Cases

Wim van Grembergen
University of Antwerp Management School, Belgium

Steven De Haes
University of Antwerp Management School, Belgium

IGI PUBLISHING

Hershey • New York

Acquisition Editor:	Kristin Klinger
Senior Managing Editor:	Jennifer Neidig
Managing Editor:	Sara Reed
Development Editor:	Kristin Roth
Copy Editor:	Katie Smalley
Typesetter:	Amanda Appicello
Cover Design:	Lisa Tosheff
Printed at:	Yurchak Printing Inc.

Published in the United States of America by
    IGI Publishing (an imprint of IGI Global)
    701 E. Chocolate Avenue
    Hershey PA 17033
    Tel: 717-533-8845
    Fax: 717-533-8661
    E-mail: cust@igi-pub.com
    Web site: http://www.igi-global.com

and in the United Kingdom by
    IGI Publishing (an imprint of IGI Global)
    3 Henrietta Street
    Covent Garden
    London WC2E 8LU
    Tel: 44 20 7240 0856
    Fax: 44 20 7379 0609
    Web site: http://www.eurospanonline.com

Library of Congress Cataloging-in-Publication Data

Van Grembergen, Wim, 1947-
  Implementing information technology governance : models, practices and cases / Wim van Grembergen & Steven DeHaes.
    p. cm.
  Summary: "This book presents insight gained through literature reviews and case studies to provide practical guidance for organizations who want to start implementing IT governance or improving existing governance models, and provides a detailed set of IT governance structures, processes, and relational mechanisms that can be leveraged to implement IT governance in practice"--Provided by publisher.
  Includes bibliographical references and index.
  ISBN 978-1-59904-924-3 (hardcover : alk. paper) -- ISBN 978-1-59904-926-7 (ebook : alk. paper)
  1. Information technology--Management. I. DeHaes, Steven. II. Title.
  HD30.2.V363 2008
  658.4'038--dc22
                       2007022425

British Cataloguing in Publication Data
A Cataloguing in Publication record for this book is available from the British Library.

All work contributed to this book is new, previously-unpublished material. The views expressed in this book are those of the authors, but not necessarily of the publisher.

Implementing Information Technology Governance:
Models, Practices, and Cases

Table of Contents

Foreword...v

Preface..ix

Chapter I
Strategies and Models for IT Governance..1
    IT Governance Explained..*1*
    The Goal of IT Governance: Strategic Alignment......................*12*
    IT Governance Structures, Processes, and Relational
        Mechanisms...*24*
    Measuring the IT Governance Process.....................................*53*
    IT Governance Implementation Status.......................................*64*
    Conclusion...*68*
    References...*69*

Chapter II
Leveraging COBIT 4.0 as IT Governance Framework....................76
    The COBIT Framework..*76*
    COBIT Control Objectives...*83*
    COBIT Management Guidelines...*86*
    COBIT Maturity Models...*93*
    Adapting COBIT to Your Organisation.....................................*95*

COBIT and Compliancy for Sarbanes-Oxley..............................96
Other COBIT Products 98
Conclusion 99
References 100

Chapter III
Leveraging the IT Balanced Scorecard as Alignment
Instrument 101
Case Company Introduction: A Tri-Company 101
The Tri-Company IT Merger..102
IT BSC Project and Its Organization 104
Building the IT BSC 106
Maturity of the Developed IT BSC...108
Lessons Learned...113
Details on the Measures of the IT Strategic Scorecard..............115
Conclusion 123
References 124

Chapter IV
IT Governance in Practice: Six Case Studies 125
Introduction..125
Case Study: KBC..127
Case Study: AGF Belgium 145
Case Study: Vanbreda...163
Case Study: CM 181
Case Study: Huntsman..196
Case Study: Sidmar – Arcelor..217
Conclusion Pilot Studies...234
References 236

Chapter V
IT Governance Implementation Guide 238
Introduction..238
Nine Guidelines for Better IT Governance 239
References 248

About the Authors..249

Index...252

Foreword

During the 40 plus years that I have been involved with information technology (IT), the use of IT has become pervasive, and organisations and individuals have become increasingly dependent on IT. At the same time, the way that we use IT has changed. We have evolved from automating pre-existing, relatively simple, labour intensive and repetitive work through the provision of information to enable better decision-making to fundamentally transforming the nature of organisations and how they work. Along with this evolution comes potentially higher value, but also significantly increased costs and risks. All too often the potential value has not been realized. It is this failure to realize value, along with the increasing costs and risks that has led to the current focus on IT governance.

Early in this book, the authors reference the IT Governance Institute's five main focus areas for IT governance: value delivery, strategic alignment, resource management, risk management, and performance management. I would argue that, regardless of the nature of the investment in IT, value delivery is, or should be, the primary focus area. Strategic alignment is actually a fundamental objective of value delivery. Resource management is the key to ensuring that value is delivered at an affordable cost. Risk management is necessary to ensure that value is delivered with an acceptable level of risk. Performance management is required to ensure that objectives are being met and, when not, that appropriate corrective actions are taken.

We need to understand that value does not miraculously come from technology projects. Technology provides a capability. Value is only realized when this capability is applied and managed as part of a comprehensive program of business change. In the early days of automation, the amount of business change was limited, and the realisation of value was relatively simple. As we have evolved from automation through information to transformation, the extent and complexity of business change has grown dramatically, and now includes changes to business strategy, business processes, how people work, organizational structure, and technology.

Organisations cannot continue to respond to the increasing scope and dynamic nature of business change, and the complexity that it introduces with simple or, more often, simplistic solutions—solutions that are focused too much on the technology, and not enough on the complexities of business change. Only when complexity is understood and managed can simplification occur. Recognising, accepting, and managing complexity is today's leadership challenge. In a world where the only constant is change, where strategy must be dynamic, and where we must expect the unexpected, most current governance processes are woefully inadequate in this regard.

Inadequate governance processes result in a lack of shared understanding of the desired outcomes, unclear or inappropriate roles, responsibilities, and accountability, not knowing what to measure, not surfacing and tracking assumptions, and not sensing and responding to changing internal and external circumstances in a timely or well-considered manner. Many organizations are just hoping that it will get better. And many are still looking for that elusive silver bullet. This could prove a costly and risky pursuit.

We need to think beyond IT governance in isolation to the business governance of IT. Most decisions related to IT are today business decisions, not technology decisions.

The scope and complexity of business change alters the nature of investment decisions, how they are made, who should make them, and how they should be monitored. Governance provides the essential framework for making these decisions. It includes leadership, processes, with clear roles, responsibilities, and accountabilities, relevant metrics, and supporting organizational structures and tools.

A much more disciplined approach to governance is now needed. An approach that is comprehensive, complete, coherent, consistent, and encompasses new ways of creating the additional value sought—one that requires and facilitates engagement and partnership between the IT function and the other parts of the business. Without such an approach, we will continue to waste hundreds of billions of dollars a year on failed attempts to create additional value.

The frameworks covered in this book, including COBIT™[1] (and, by inference, the recently released *Val* IT™[2] extension to COBIT), and the IT Balanced Scorecard, provide a solid foundation for such an approach to effective governance. The cases included demonstrate that these are not theoretical frameworks—they are practical tools that can and have been adopted by organisations to improve their value creation performance.

Organisations must, however, recognize that selection of such an approach is only the beginning. Effective governance is the result of broad adoption, focused implementation, and continuous improvement of the approach. Organizations must evolve their processes to a governance system that is: value driven, business outcome based, enterprise-wide, dynamic, inclusive, and flexible. In the private sector, how well this is done will play an increasingly significant role in determining market valuation. In the public sector, the mandate, public perception, and viability of the organization may well hinge on the clarity with which its actions and investments can be tied to value.

Ten years ago, when, together with Fujitsu, I started writing *The Information Paradox*[3], the term "IT governance" was rarely used. Today, a Google search on the term yields over 67 million hits. Not a day passes without new articles on IT governance, and there are an increasing number of books and conferences on the topic. While, overall, this increased attention to IT governance is a good thing, there is still much confusion about what IT governance is, how it relates to enterprise and corporate governance, the difference between governance and management, and where and how to get started. This book makes a valuable contribution to providing clarity around the topic.

Adopting and implementing an effective governance approach is not easy. It requires vision, discipline, and the courage to stay the course. It represents a fundamental change in how we think, manage, and act. It is however only with such a change that we will truly realize value. I hope that this book will help you, your organization, or the organizations that you work with successfully undertake the necessary changes and realize and demonstrate the value of IT's contribution to business change.

John Thorp
Author, The Information Paradox

Endnotes

---

[1]   *Control Objectives for Information and related Technology* (COBIT), from the IT
Governance Institute, is an internationally accepted standard for IT management
processes. The latest edition, COBIT 4.0, was released in December, 2005

[2]   For more information about Val IT, refer to *Enterprise Value: Governance of IT Invest-*
ments, The Val IT Framework, which can be downloaded from www.isaca.org, and is
also available from the ISACA Bookstore, *www.isaca.org/bookstore.*

[3]   *The Information Paradox*, written by John Thorp jointly with Fujitsu, first published
by McGraw Hill in 1998 with a revised edition published in 2003.

Preface

IT governance is a concept that recently emerged and became an intergral aspect within the complex realms of information technology (IT). IT governance consists of the leadership and organisational structures and processes that ensure that the organisation's IT sustains and extends the organisation's strategy and objectives. IT governance is closely related to enterprise governance. In fact, the IT Governance Institute states that IT governance should be an integral part of enterprise governance. This implies that IT governance impacts all layers in the organisation, from operational management to senior and executive management, and finally the board of directors. This also suggests that IT governance is fundamentally different from IT management. IT management is focused on the effective and efficient internal supply of IT services and products and the management of current IT operations. IT governance in turn is much broader, and concentrates on performing and transforming IT to meet present and future demands of the business (internal focus) and its customers (external focus).

In market surveys (e.g., Gartner, Forrester, etc.), CIOs highlight IT governance as being an important management priority, together with the related theme for better business/IT alignment. Indeed, different studies have proven that a better alignment between the business and IT have resulted in a better IT service for the business an ultimately in better business performance.

The authors are not sure as to when the IT governance concept surfaced. However, Gartner introduced the idea of "improving IT governance" for the first time in their Top-ten CIO Management Priorities for 2003 (ranked third). In 1998, the IT Governance Institute was founded to generate awareness of the IT governance concept. In academic and professional literature, articles mentioning IT governance in the title began to emerge in 1999, for example Sambamurthy and Zmud with "Arrangements for information technology governance: A theory of multiple contingencies," and Van Grembergen, in 2000, with "The IT balanced scorecard and IT governance." We, therefore, conclude that the IT governance concept emerged in the late nineties, but that a lot of the underlying elements of the strategic alignment discussion attracted attention many years before.

IT governance has become an important discussion topic within most organisations. Some corporations and government agencies have started with the implementation of IT governance in order to improve the fusion between business and IT and to obtain the needed IT involvement of senior management.

To obtain more insight in these implementations, and to provide practical guidance for organisations, Microsoft Belgium and the Information Technology Alignment and Governance (ITAG) Research Institute (www.uams. be/itag) of the University of Antwerp Management School (UAMS) decided to set up a joint research project on Information Technology Governance practices.

Based on IT governance theories and frameworks, this book has studied a selection of large organisations in order to obtain practical insight into the IT governance issue and to come up with an answer to the following questions:

- Which IT governance structures, processes, and mechanisms are used in reality within organisations?
- Does the implementation of these structures, processes, and mechanisms result in a better fusion between business and IT?
- Will it contribute to the organisations bottom-line?
- What are the influencing factors on the IT governance practice?
- Which contingencies are to be taken into account?
- What is the maturity level of the IT governance effort?
- How will one try to get to the next level?

The target audience for this book is executive management and IT management who are searching for answers to the aforementioned questions. The presented IT governance models and the description of how they are applied in the reviewed organisations may assist the readers of this book in implementing their own specific IT governance structures, processes, and relational mechanisms. Still, it is important to note that what can work in one enterprise, can be less effective in other organisations. This book can also be used by master students majoring in MIS and MBA. Both will benefit from the IT governance concepts in the text and will certainly learn from the presented cases.

The case research presented in this book was conducted during the 2003-2005 period and the results are published in this book. Besides an extensive overview on the available theoretical concepts and models of IT governance and IT governance practices in corporate environments, this book concentrates on a practical approach based on the observed best practises implemented at the studied organisations. This should allow to develop new insights in the complex matter of IT governance and to provide practical guidance for organisations that are implementing IT governance practices.

This book is organised around five main chapters.

Chapter I records and interprets some important existing theories, models, and practices in the IT governance and strategic alignment domain. IT governance will be defined and its relationship with corporate governance and IT management clarified. A separate section is devoted to the concept of strategic alignment, one of the key elements of IT governance. Finally, a detailed set of IT governance structures, processes, and relational mechanisms is discussed that can be leveraged to implement IT governance in practise. Two important IT governance processes, COBIT and the balanced scorecard, are discussed in more detail in chapters 2 and 3.

Chapter II focuses on how COBIT can be leveraged as an instrument to implement IT governance. All the components of the COBIT framework are explained and guidance is provided on how COBIT can be adapted to or applied in a specific organisation. This chapter also makes reference to some other publications that can support IT governance professionals in using COBIT in practice.

Chapter III addresses the IT balanced scorecard as a possible measurement and management tool to support the achievement of strategic alignment. In this chapter, the application of the balanced scorecard is illustrated in more detail through a case study of a major Canadian financial group, where the balanced scorecard was adopted in its full scope.

In order to obtain an understanding on how large organizations implement IT governance in a pragmatic way, Chapter IV describes six case studies from different sectors. Case research is particularly appropriate for research within the IT domain because researchers in this field often lag behind practitioners in discovering and explaining new methods and techniques. This is certainly true for the concept of IT governance. The purpose of this case study research is to look for different IT governance elements in use and to determine how they contribute to better IT governance within the organisation.

Based on prior research and complemented with the observed best practices captured from the case study research, a set of guidelines and ideas is compiled in Chapter V, which should help an organization in achieving better IT governance. From this collection of practical guidelines and best practices, the reader can pick those that best suit a specific environment.

Acknowledgment

We would like to thank all involved in participating in our research and writing this book, without whose support this project could not have been satisfactorily completed. We gratefully acknowledge the business and IT managers who shared their insights and practices on IT governance and provided the material for the cases in this book. These managers include: Carl Tilkin-Franssens, Martine Allaert, Rudi Vanhaeren, Jan Vanhevel, Philippe Meerschaut and Paul Lietaert at KBC; Rudy Duyck and Marc Simons at AGF; Erik Cuypers, Bert Van Hove and Jan Desmet at Vanbreda; Kurt De Ruwe and Patrick Thomas at Huntsman; Luc Verhelst, Jos Muyshondt and Bert Loos at CM; Ghislain Claeys and Hugo Vercammen at Sidmar.

We are especially grateful to Bruno Segers and Dirk Tombeur of Microsoft Belgium for sponsoring this project. At every stage of our research they showed a great interest by sharing their insights and criticisms.

We appreciated support provided for this project by the business faculty of the University of Antwerp (UA) and the University of Antwerp Management School (UAMS). We also would like to thank our master and executive students who provided us with many ideas on the subject of IT governance and its related mechanisms.

A special note of thanks goes to Yves Hendrickx and An De Bie, researchers at the IT Alignment and Governance Research Institute, who did the interviews with the case companies and wrote a first draft of the cases. A very special acknowledgment goes to Senior Researcher Hilde Van Brempt from whom we've received great support during the development of the final manuscript. We greatly appreciated Hilde's research insights and feedback on the manuscript.

We would also like to thank our colleague, Mehdi Khosrow-Pour, who showed great interest in our research and invited us to write this book. A special word of thanks goes to Kristin Roth, Jan Travers, and Michelle Potter of IGI Global who both supported us in managing this project.

Finally, last but not least, we would like to thank our families. Wim would like to extend his gratitude to Hilde, Astrid, and Helen who always supported and helped him with every project including this book. Steven whishes to thank Brenda, Ruben, and Charlotte for their support and patience and would like to dedicate this book to his father who unexpectedly passed away prior to the completion of this book.

Wim Van Grembergen
Steven De Haes
Antwerpen, May 2007

Chapter I

Strategies and Models for IT Governance

This introductory chapter records and interprets some important existing theories, models, and practices in the IT governance and strategic alignment domain. IT governance will be defined and its relationship with corporate governance and IT management clarified. A separate section is devoted to the concept of strategic alignment, one of the key elements of IT governance. Finally, a detailed set of IT governance structures, processes, and relational mechanisms is discussed that can be leveraged to implement IT governance in practise. Two important IT governance processes, COBIT and the balanced scorecard, are discussed in more detail in separate chapters.

IT Governance Explained

Why IT Governance?

Information technology (IT) has become pervasive in current dynamic and often turbulent business environments. While in the past, business executives could delegate, ignore, or avoid IT decisions, this is now impossible in most sectors and industries (Peterson, 2003; Duffy, 2002a; Van Der Zee & De Jong, 1999). To emphasise this **pervasiveness of IT**, Broadbent and Weill (1998) refer to three layers of the *New Infrastructure*: local IT for business processes, firm IT infrastructure, and public IT infrastructures (Figure 1).

The *Public Infrastructure* and the *Firm Information Technology Infrastructure* are the foundations of the firm's *Information Technology Portfolio*. The *Public Infrastructure* links the firm to external industry infrastructures, such as the Internet, EDI networks, and so forth, which enables the firm to communicate and do business with customers, suppliers, partners, and so forth. Together with the *Firm Information Technology Infrastructure*, such as e-mail, customer databases, and so forth, the New Infrastructure is constructed. The *New Infrastructure* plus the local IT needed to perform business processes are the firm's *Information Technology Portfolio*.

Figure 1. The new infrastructure (Adapted from Broadbent & Weill, 1998)

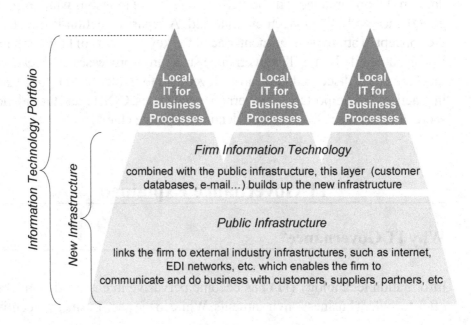

The dependency on IT becomes even more imperative in our **knowledge-based economy**, where organisations are using technology in managing, developing, and communicating intangible assets, such as information and knowledge (Patel, 2003). Corporate success can of course only be attained when information and knowledge, very often provided and sustained by technology, is secure, accurate, reliable, and provided to the right person, at the right time, at the right place (ITGI, 2003; Kakabadse & Kakabadse, 2001).

This major IT dependency implies **a huge vulnerability** that is inherently present in IT environments (ITGI, 2003; Duffy, 2002b). System and network downtime has become far too costly for any organisation these days as doing business globally around the clock has become the standard. Take, for example, the impact of downtime in the banking sector or in a medical environment. The risk factor is accompanied by a wide spectrum of external threats, such as errors and omissions, abuse, cyber crime, and fraud.

IT of course not only has the potential to support existing business strategies, but also to shape new strategies (Guldentops, 2003; Henderson, Venkatraman, & Oldach, 1993; Henderson & Venkatraman, 1993). In this mindset, IT becomes not only a success factor for survival and prosperity, but also an opportunity to differentiate and **to achieve competitive advantage**. Information technology also offers a means for increasing productivity. Leveraging IT successfully to transform the enterprise and to create products and services with added value has become a universal business competency (Guldentops, 2003). In this viewpoint, the IT department moves from a commodity service provider to a strategic partner as illustrated by Venkatraman (1999) (Figure 2).

Information technology often entails **large capital investments** in organisations, while companies are faced with multiple shareholders that are demanding the creation of business value through these investments. The question of the 'productivity paradox,' why information technologies have not provided a measurable value to the business world, has puzzled many practitioners and researchers (Brynjolfsson, 1993; Brynjolfsson & Hitt, 1998; Duffy, 2002b; Henderson & Venkatraman, 1993; ITGI, 2003; Kakabadse & Kakabadse, 2001; Lie, 2001; Strassman, 1990).

All these issues point out that the critical dependency on information technology calls for a specific focus on IT governance. This is needed to ensure that the investments in IT will generate the required business value and that risks associated with IT are mitigated.

Figure 2. IT as service provider or as strategic partner (Adapted from Ven-katraman, 1999)

IT as a service provider	as opposed to	IT as a strategic partner
IT is for efficiency		IT is for business growth
Budgets are driven by external benchmarks		Budgets are driven by business strategy
IT is separable from the business		IT is inseparable from the business
IT is seen as an expense to control		IT is seen as an investment to manage
IT managers are technical experts		IT managers are business problem solvers

However, not everybody seems to agree with the increasing strategic importance of information technology. In his article "IT doesn't matter," Carr (2003) makes the comparison between commodities such as water and gas, and information technology. He states:

As information technology's power and ubiquity have grown, its strategic importance has diminished. [...] By now, the core functions of IT—data storage, data processing, and data transport—have become available to all. Their very power and presence have begun to transform them from potentially strategic resources into commodity factors of production. They are becoming costs of doing business that must be paid by all but provide distinction to none. (Carr, 2003)

After Carr's article, a debate started between opponents and proponents of his ideas. In this book, it is acknowledged that some parts in the IT domain are standardised and became a commodity, but still many systems and technologies are very complex and IT investments and the way IT is used needs to be governed properly. Or, as the General Motors CIO Ralph Szygenda points out as a reaction on Carr's article in the May 19 *Information Week*:

Nicholas Carr may ultimately be correct when he says IT doesn't matter... [But] business-process improvement, competitive advantage, optimization, and business success do matter and they aren't commodities. To facilitate these business changes, IT can be considered a differentiator or a necessary evil. But today, it's a must in a real-time corporation. [...] I also agree on spending the minimum on IT to reach desired business results. Precision investment on core infrastructure and process-differentiation IT systems is called for in today's intensely cost-conscious business versus the shotgun approach sometimes used in the past. (Evans, 2003)

IT Governance Definition

Information technology, and its use in business environments, has experienced a fundamental transformation in the past decades. Since the introduction of IT in organisations, academics, and practitioners conducted research and developed theories and best practices in this emerging knowledge domain (Peterson, 2003). This resulted in a variety of IT governance definitions of which some are formulated in Figure 3.

Figure 3. Definitions of IT governance

IT governance is the responsibility of executives an the board of directors, and consists of the leadership, organisational structures and processes that ensure that the enterprise's IT sustains and extends the organisation's strategy and objectives. (ITGI, 2005)
IT governance is specifying the decision rights and accountability framework to encourage desirable behaviour in the use of IT. (Weill & Woodham, 2002)
IT governance is the organisational capacity exercised by the board, executive management and IT management to control the formulation and implementation of IT strategy and in this way ensure the fusion of business and IT. (Van Grembergen, 2000)

Although these definitions differ in some aspects, they focus on the same issues, such as achieving the link between business and IT and the primary responsibility of the board. In Van Grembergen's definition it is indicated that IT management should also be involved in the IT governance processes. As explained later, there is a clear difference between IT governance and IT management. The definition from the IT Governance Institute states that IT governance is an integral part of enterprise or corporate governance. Indeed, to make sure that corporate governance matters are covered, IT needs to be governed properly first.

As indicated by Van Grembergen's definition, IT governance is situated at multiple layers in the organisation (see Figure 4): at a strategic level where the board is involved, at a management level within the C-suite layer and finally at the operational level with IT and business management. This implies that all these levels, business as well as IT, need to be involved in the IT governance process and they have to understand their individual roles and responsibilities within the framework.

Figure 4. Three layers of IT governance responsibility (Van Grembergen, De Haes, & Guldentops, 2003)

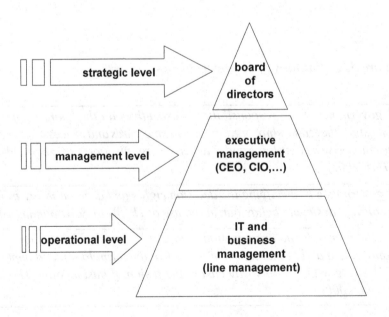

Focus Areas of IT Governance

The IT Governance Institute (ITGI, 2003) states that: *Fundamentally, IT governance is concerned about two things: IT's delivery of value to the business and mitigation of IT risks. The first is driven by strategic alignment of IT with the business. The second is driven by embedding accountability into the enterprise. Both need to be measured adequately.* This leads to five main focus areas for IT governance, all driven by stakeholder value:

- Value delivery
- Strategic alignment
- Resource management
- Risk management
- Performance management

Figure 5. Focus areas of IT governance (ITGI, 2003)

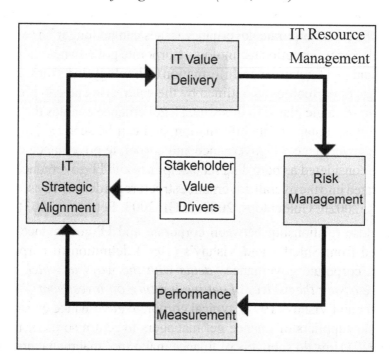

The relationship between the three drivers, strategic alignment, resource management, which overlays them all, and performance measurement and the two outcomes, value delivery and risk management, is visualised in Figure 5. This picture shows a continuous life cycle, which can be entered at any point. Usually one starts with the strategy and its alignment throughout the enterprise. Then implementation occurs, delivering the value the strategy promised and addressing the risks that need mitigation. At regular intervals (some recommend continuously) the strategy needs to be monitored and the results measured, reported and acted upon.

IT Governance vs. Corporate Governance

The definition of IT governance as proposed by the IT Governance Institute (Figure 3) expresses that "*IT governance is the responsibility of the board and executive management*" and that IT governance "*should be an integral part of enterprise governance.*" The term "enterprise governance" is somewhat broader than "corporate governance" and refers not only to businesses, but also to other organisations such as government agencies. Throughout this book, the more common term "corporate governance" will be used.

Corporate governance is the system by which organisations are directed and controlled. The business dependency on information technology has resulted in the fact that corporate governance issues can no longer be solved without considering information technology. Corporate governance should therefore drive and set IT governance. Information technology, in its turn, can influence strategic opportunities as outlined by the enterprise and can provide critical input to strategic plans. In this way, IT governance enables the enterprise to take full advantage of its information, and can be seen as a driver for corporate governance. IT governance and corporate governance can therefore not be considered as pure distinct disciplines and IT governance needs to be integrated into the overall governance structure, as denoted by several authors (Duffy, 2002b; Guldentops, 2003; ITGI, 2003; Peterson, 2003).

The close relationship between corporate and IT governance can also be derived from Shleifer and Vishny's (1997) definition of corporate governance: corporate governance "*deals with the ways in which suppliers of finance assure themselves of getting a return on investment.*" According to Shleifer and Vishny (1997), typical corporate governance questions are: (1) How do suppliers of finance get managers to return some of the profits to them? (2) How do suppliers of finance make sure that managers do not steal the capital they supply or invest it in bad projects? (3) How do suppliers of finance control managers? The business dependency on IT means that the corporate governance issues can not be solved without considering information technology. This relationship can be made more eloquent by translating the corporate governance questions into specific IT governance questions (Figure 6), which discloses that corporate governance issues can not be addressed, without considering IT governance issues.

As IT governance becomes an integral part of corporate governance, it falls under the responsibility of the board of directors. The composition of the board varies widely from organisation to organisation, but generally involves a mix of members representing the shareholders, independent members appointed from outside the business and representing the other stakeholders and the firm, and often executive directors. Although it is often the case that executives are also board members, this is not a good governance practice because the segregation between the board and executive management is an important governance requirement. There are also important differences between countries regarding the role, composition, and modus operandi of the board. These differences naturally lead to variations in expectations,

Figure 6. Corporate governance and IT governance (Adapted from Shleifer & Vishny, 1997)

Corporate governance questions	⊠	IT governance questions
How do suppliers of finance get managers to return some of the profits to them?	$\Rightarrow$	How do the board and executive management get their CIO and IT organisation to return some business value to them?
How do suppliers of finance make sure that managers do not steal the capital they supply or invest it in bad projects?	$\Rightarrow$	How do the board and executive management make sure that their CIO and IT organisations do not steal the capital they supply or invest it in bad projects?
How do suppliers of finance control managers?	$\Rightarrow$	How do the board and executive management control their CIO and IT organisation?

emphasis, and so forth, but the fundamental responsibilities of the board do not change and attention should be paid to the close link between technology management and the achievement of business goals (Duffy, 2002b). Moreover, market analysts state that investors are willing to pay more for the shares of a well-governed company. Although hypothetical premiums are difficult to measure, there is little questioning that good governance makes a difference to corporate value (Duffy, 2002b; ITGI, 2003).

IT Governance vs. IT Management

An important and implicit concern in the provided IT governance definitions is certainly the link between information technology and the present and future business objectives. There is not always a clear distinction between IT governance and IT management, which is visualised in Figure 7.

Figure 7. IT governance and IT management (Peterson, 2003)

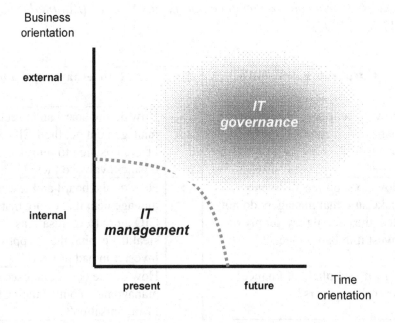

IT management is focused on the effective and efficient internal supply of IT services and products and the management of present IT operations. IT governance, in turn, is much broader and concentrates on performing and transforming IT to meet present and future demands of the business (internal focus) and business customers (external focus).

This does not undermine the importance and complexity of IT management, [...] but whereas elements of IT management and the supply of (commodity) IT services and products can be commissioned to an external provider, IT governance is organisation specific, and direction and control over IT can not be delegated to the market. (Peterson, 2003)

Sohal and Fitzpatrick (2002) differentiate between the concept of governance and the concept of management as illustrated in Figure 8. In doing so, Sohal

Figure 8. Governance versus management (Adapted from Sohal & Fitzpatrick, 2002)

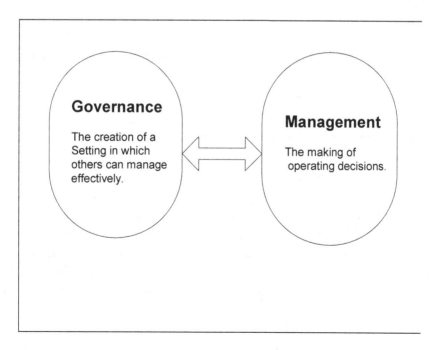

and Fitzpatrick (2002) confirm Peterson's (2003) insights that governance has a wider time dimension and looks further than the organisation as such.

The Goal of IT Governance: Strategic Alignment

The definitions in Figure 3 underline that the ultimate outcome of IT governance is the alignment of information technology with the business, often referred to as strategic alignment. Strategic alignment is an important driving force to achieve business value through investments in IT (Guldentops, 2003; ITGI, 2005). This section will discuss the strategic alignment concept in more detail.

Strategic Alignment Model (SAM)

What does "strategic alignment between the business and IT" exactly mean? Duffy (2002a) formulated the following definition: "*the process and goal of achieving competitive advantage through developing and sustaining a symbiotic relationship between business and IT.*" The idea behind strategic alignment is very comprehensive, but the question is how organisations can achieve this ultimate goal. Henderson and Venkatraman (1993) were the first to clearly describe the interrelationship between business strategies and IT strategies in their well-known Strategic Alignment Model. Many authors used this model for further research, including Luftman and Brier (1999), Burn and Szeto (2000) and Smaczny (2001).

The concept of the model, pictured in Figure 9, is based on two building blocks: "strategic fit" and "functional integration." *Strategic fit* recognizes that the IT strategy should be articulated in terms of an external domain (how the firm is positioned in the IT marketplace) and an internal domain (how the IT infrastructure should be configured and managed). Strategic fit is of course equally relevant in the business domain. Two types of *functional integration* exist: strategic an operational integration. Strategic integration is the link between business strategy and IT strategy reflecting the external components, which are important for many companies as IT emerged as a source of strategic advantage. Operational integration covers the internal

Figure 9. Strategic alignment model (Adapted from Henderson & Venkatraman, 1993)

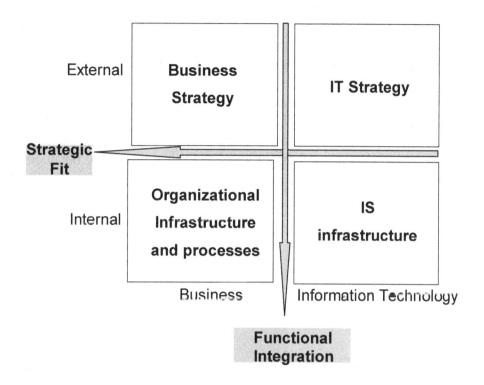

domain and deals with the link between organizational infrastructure and processes and IT infrastructure and processes.

Henderson and Venkatraman (1993) argue that the external and the internal domain are equally important, but that managers traditionally think of IT strategy in terms of the internal domain, since historically IT was viewed as a support function that was less essential to the business. Relating this to the difference between IT governance and IT management, as referred to in Figure 8, the historical internal view coincides with the IT management perspectives which are focused on the internal domain—while the IT governance perspective is focused on both the internal and the external domain.

An important premise of the strategic alignment model is that effective governance of IT requires a balance among the choices made in all the four domains of Figure 9. Henderson and Venkatraman (1993) describe two cross-domain relationships in which business strategy plays the role of driver, and two relationships where IT strategy is the enabler (Figure 10). The "strategic execution alignment" perspective is probably the most widely understood as it is the classic, hierarchical view of strategic management. The perspective starts from the premise that business strategy is articulated and that this strategy is the driver for the choices in organisational design and the design in IT infrastructure. The "technology transformation alignment" perspective also starts from an existing business strategy, but focuses on the implementation of this strategy through appropriate IT strategy and the

Figure 10. Strategic alignment domains (Adapted from Henderson & Venkatraman, 1993)

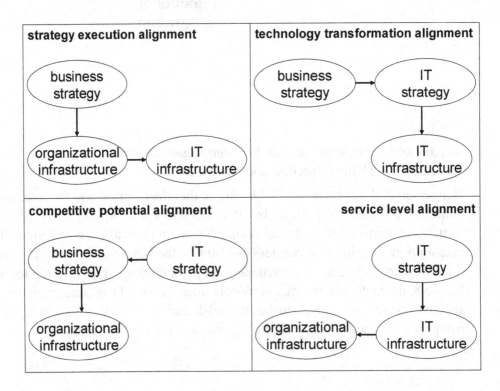

articulation of the required IT infrastructure and processes. The "competitive potential alignment" perspective allows the adaptation of business strategy through emerging IT capabilities. Starting from the IT strategy, the best set of strategic options for business strategy and a corresponding set of decisions regarding organisational infrastructure and processes are determined. The "service level alignment" perspective focuses on how to build a world-class IT service organisation. This requires and understanding of the external dimensions of IT strategy with the corresponding internal design of the IT infrastructure and processes.

In their research results, Henderson and Venkatraman (1993) warn of the problems that may surface when a bivariate approach is undertaken with respect to balancing across the four domains—IT strategy, business strategy, IS infrastructure, and organisational infrastructure—is used. For instance, when only external issues—IT strategy and business strategy—are considered, a serious underestimation of the importance of internal issues, for example, the difficulty or even risks of redesigning key business processes, might occur. Therefore, the strategic alignment model calls for the recognition of multivariate relationships, which will always take into consideration at least three out of the four defined domains.

Extensions to and Interpretations of the Strategic Alignment Model

As mentioned before, many authors have used this model for further research and have provided comments and additional insights. In the Figure 11, a limited list of research work and their conclusions is provided. For reasons of conciseness, only some of these works are discussed in more detail in this section.

Maes (1999) developed an interesting extension to the strategic alignment model of Henderson and Venkatraman. The basic idea is that the 2*2 dimensions of the strategic alignment model (see Figure 9) is an oversimplification of reality and needs to be extended to a 3*3 model.

In the first place, the internal domain of the strategic alignment model (bottom row of Figure 9) is subdivided into two separate areas: a structural and an operational level. This results from the observation that the former plays an essential role in the tuning of long-term strategic vision (which is set in the external domain, the top row of Figure 9) and the latter serves the short-term

Figure 11. Summary of important contributions to the strategic alignment model

Author(s)	Subject of study / added value
Bergeron et al. (2003)	Link between strategic alignment and business performance
Broadbent and Weill (1998)	Enablers and barriers in achieving alignment
Burn and Szeto (2000)	Factors contributing to successful strategic alignment
Croteau and Bergeron (2001)	Relationships between business strategy, technological deployment, and organisational performance
Feurer et al. (2000)	IT strategy as a driver for alignment
Hirschheim and Sabherwal (2001)	Link between alignment profile and business strategy
Luftman and Brier (1999)	Organisational assessment using the strategic alignment model and six-step approach for achieving strategic alignment
Luftman and Brier (1999)	Factors contributing to versus factors hindering strategic alignment
Maes (1999)	Extension of the strategic alignment model: 3*3-matrix
Sabherwal and Chan (2001)	Mapping business strategies to IT strategies
Smaczny (2001)	Fusion between IT and the business
Teo and Ang (1999)	Study on critical success factors for IS/business alignment
Van Grembergen et al. (2005)	Linking business goals to IT goals

operational transformation. The IT domain in turn (left column in Figure 9), is being reshaped into an information/communication level and a technology level. The split of the IT domain results from the observation that "*the vast majority of all information and communication processes in organisations are ICT (Information and Communication Technology)—independent*" (Davenport & Prusak, 1997, cited in Maes, 1999) and therefore need to be regarded

Figure 12. The generic framework of Maes: An extension of SAM (Adapted from Maes, 1999)

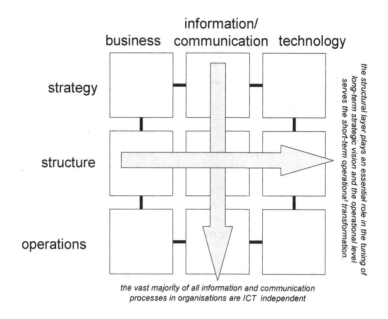

the vast majority of all information and communication
processes in organisations are ICT independent

separately. This results in a 3*3 matrix, as shown in Figure 12, as opposed to the 2*2 matrix first presented by Henderson and Venkatraman (1993).

The extended model of Maes clearly demonstrates the complexity of the alignment challenge. To assist practitioners in achieving a better alignment, Luftman and Brier (1999) executed valuable research concerning enablers, inhibitors and critical success factors for alignment. The enablers and inhibitors defined by Luftman and Brier (1999) are summarised in Figure 13. Executives should work towards minimising those activities that inhibit alignment and maximising those activities that bolster it (Luftman & Brier, 1999).

It is not surprising that the level of congruence between these enablers and inhibitors and the results of Teo and Ang's (1999) and Burn and Szeto's (2000) studies on critical success factors, is significant. The study of Burn and Szeto (2000) revealed that only 50 percent of the business managers and 60 percent of IT managers indicated that the matching of business and IT strategies in their companies was either successful or highly successful. In

Figure 13. The enablers and inhibitors of strategic alignment (Luftman & Brier, 1999)

Strategic alignment enablers	Strategic alignment inhibitors
Senior executives support for IT	IT/business lack close relationship
IT involved in strategy development	IT does not prioritise well
IT understands the business	IT fails to meet its commitments
Business-IT partnership	IT does not understand the business
Well prioritised projects	Senior executives do not support IT
IT demonstrates leadership	IT management lacks leadership

Figure 14. Critical success factors in business/IS planning alignment (Teo & Ang, 1999)

Critical Success Factor	
1.	Top management is committed to the strategic use of IT
2.	IS management is knowledgeable about business
3.	Top management has confidence in the IS department
4.	The IS department provides efficient and reliable services to user departments
5.	There is frequent communication between user and IS departments
6.	The IS staff are able to keep up with advances in IT
7.	Business and IS management work together in partnership in prioritising applications development
8.	Business goals and objectives are made known to IS management
9.	The IS department is responsive to user needs
10.	Top management is knowledgeable about IT
11.	The IS department often comes up with creative ideas on how to use IT strategically
12.	The corporate business plan is made available to the IS department
13.	There is a set of organisational goals and objectives for the IS department
14.	User departments view IS staff as competent
15.	The IS management actively participates in IS planning
16.	Top management actively participates in IS planning
17.	The planning horizons for business and IS plans are similar
18.	Users actively participate in IS planning

the Burn and Szeto study, the key success factors for alignment were identified as *top management selections of appropriate alignment approach to accomplish business objectives* and *matching the internal IT with external market*. Figure 14 shows the critical success factors for strategic alignment, based on a survey of Teo and Ang (1999) in 169 firms in different sectors with top ranked factors being *management commitment to strategic use of IT* and *IT management business literacy*.

Broadbent and Weill (1998) continue in this domain by describing a number of difficulties (barriers) that organisations have experienced while aligning business with IT. The *expression barriers* arise from the organisation's strategic context and from senior management behaviour, including lack of direction in business strategy. This results in insufficient understanding of and commitment to the organisation's strategic focus by operational management. *Specification barriers* arise from the circumstances of the organisation's IT strategy, such as lack of IT involvement in strategy development and business and IT management conducting two independent monologues. This ends up in a situation where business and IT strategies are set in isolation and are not adequately related. The nature of the organisation's current IT portfolio creates *implementation barriers,* which arise when there are technical, political, or financial constraints on the current infrastructure. A good example of this last barrier is the difficult integration of legacy systems.

Another valuable piece of research is that of Sabherwal and Chan (2001). These authors tried to define IT strategies that map best on specific business strategies. Those business strategies were defined based on the Miles and Snow typology (Miles & Snow, 1978), which identifies different types of business strategies: defenders (aiming to reduce costs, maximising efficiency and effectiveness of production, and avoiding organizational change), prospectors (seen as leading innovators, reacting first on signals of change in their market) and analysers (closely watching competitor's activities and carefully evaluating organisational changes). Figure 15 demonstrates which IT strategies align best with specific business strategies. "IT for efficiency" is oriented towards internal and inter-organisational efficiencies and long-term decision making and maps well on the defender's business strategy. "IT for flexibility" focuses on market flexibility and quick strategic decisions which maps on the prospector's business strategy. "IT for comprehensiveness" enables comprehensive decisions and quick responses through knowledge of other organisations which complies with the analyser's business strategy.

Figure 15. Mapping IT and business strategies (Adapted from Sabherwal & Chan, 2001)

Business Strategy IT Strategy	Defenders	Prospectors	Analysers
IT for efficiency	High	Low	Low
IT for flexibility	Low	High	Low
IT for comprehensiveness	Low	Low	High

Figure 16. Business goals driving IT goals

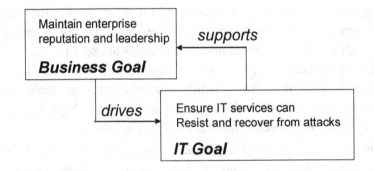

A more concrete translation of these insights, at a level of business and IT goals instead of business and IT strategies, was realised during a research project by the University of Antwerp Management School and the IT Governance Institute (Van Grembergen, De Haes, & Moons, 2005). This research is primarily focused on how business goals drive IT goals and vice versa, as visualised in Figure 16. If "maintaining the enterprise reputation and leadership" is an important business goal, a supporting IT goal could be: "ensuring IT services can resist and recover from attacks."

In eight different industries, interviews were conducted with both business and IT managers. Based on the outcome, a list of 20 generic business goals and 28 generic IT goals were established, including indications of how those IT goals support the achievement of business goals. These goals are now the core of the COBIT 4.0 framework (ITGI, 2005). Chapter II provides a more detailed overview of IT and business goals.

Maturity Models for Strategic Alignment

Insight into the key success factors, barriers, enablers and inhibitors, the linkage between business and IT strategies and goals, can be very helpful when an organisation strives for a more mature strategic alignment process. To be able to measure its alignment maturity, organisations can use a maturity model. This is a method of scoring that enables the organisation to grade itself from non-existent (0) to optimised (5). This tool offers an easy-to-understand way to determine the "as-is" and the "to-be" (according to enterprise strategy) position, and enables the organisation to benchmark itself against best practices and standard guidelines. In this way, gaps can be identified and specific actions can be defined to move towards the desired level of strategic alignment maturity (Guldentops et al., 2002; ITGI, 2005).

Good examples of strategic alignment maturity models were developed by Luftman (2000), Duffy (2002a) and the IT Governance Institute (ITGI, 2005). Each of these models uses criteria, composed of a variety of attributes, to build different levels of maturity. Luftman (2000) defines five maturity levels using the criteria and attributes described in the first two columns of Figure 17. The last two columns indicate the characteristics or values of each attribute to obtain a level 1 or level 5 of the maturity model. When doing this maturity assessment, it is important to comply with the basic principles of maturity measurement: one can only move to a higher maturity level when all conditions, described in a certain maturity level, are fulfilled. This implies that, in order to obtain a maturity level 5, all attributes must have the values described in the last column of Figure 17.

Duffy (2002a) developed a similar maturity model (Figure 18), which is composed of four maturity levels. Although this maturity model differs from the previous example, it aspires to the same goal, which is, providing a tool to help management in their journey to align business and IT. This maturity model states that in level one, there is a fundamental disconnect between the technology executive and the rest of corporate management. A maturity level of four (the highest level in this model) however implies that IT and

Figure 17. The strategic alignment maturity levels of Luftman (Adapted from Luftman, 2000)

Criteria	Attribute	Characteristics level 1	Characteristics level 5
Communications	Understanding of business by IT	Minimum	Pervasive
	Understanding of IT by business	Minimum	Pervasive
	Inter/intra-organisational learning	Casual, ad-hoc	Strong and structured
	Protocol rigidity	Command and control	Informal
	Knowledge sharing	Ad-hoc	Extra-enterprise
	Liaison(s) breadth/effectiveness	None or ad-hoc	Extra-enterprise
Competency/value measurement	IT metrics	Technical, not related to business	Extended to external partners
	Business metrics	Ad-hoc, not related to IT	Extended to external partners
	Balanced metrics	Ad-hoc unlinked	Business, partner, & IT metrics
	Service Level Agreements	Sporadically present	Extended to external partners
	Benchmarking	Not generally practised	Routinely performed with partners
	Formal assessments/reviews	None	Routinely performed
	Continuous improvement	None	Routinely performed
Governance	Business strategic planning	Ad-hoc	Integrated across, external
	IT strategic planning	Ad-hoc	Integrated across, external
	Reporting/organization structure	Central/decentral, CIO report to CFO	CIO reports to CEO, federated
	Budgetary control	Cost centre, erratic spending	Investment centre, profit centre
	IT investment management	Cost based, erratic spending	Business value
	Steering committee(s)	Not formal/regular	Partnership
	Prioritization process	Reactive	Value added partner
Partnership	Business perception of IT value	IT perceived as a cost of business	IT co-adapts with business
	Role of IT in strategic business planning	No seat at the business table	Co-adaptive with business
	Shared goals, risks, rewards / penalties	IT takes risk with little reward	Risks and rewards shared
	IT program management	Ad-hoc	Continuous improvement
	Relationship/trust style	Conflict/minimum	Valued partnership
	Business sponsor/champion	None	At the CEO level
Scope and architecture	Traditional enabler / driver, external	Traditional (e.g. accounting, email)	External scope, business strategy driver/enabler
	Standards articulation	None or ad-hoc	Inter-enterprise standards
	Architectural integration	No formal integration	Evolve with partners
	Functional organization		Integrated
	Enterprise		Standard enterprise architecture
	Inter-enterprise		With all partners
	Architectural transparency, flexibility	None	Across the infrastructure
Skills	Innovation, entrepreneurship	Discouraged	The norm
	Locus of Power	In the business	All executives, including CIO
	Management style	Command and control	Relationship based
	Change readiness	Resistant to change	High, focused
	Career crossover	None	Across the enterprise
	Education, cross-training	None	Across the enterprise
	Attract and retain best-talent	No program	Effective program for hiring and retaining

Figure 18. The strategic alignment maturity model of Duffy (Adapted from Duffy, 2002a)

Maturity level one: "Uneasy alliance"	Maturity level two: "Supplier/consumer relationship"
In this stage, there is a fundamental disconnect between the technology executive and the rest of corporate management. IT responds to business demands with little understanding of how the technology can contribute to value. IT is viewed primarily as something to make the company more efficient. Business units have little understanding of technology and prefer to hold the IT organization accountable for the success and/or failure of any IT related project.	If IT has a strategic plan it is developed in response to the corporate strategy. IT is probably viewed as a cost centre and there is little appreciation for the value that IT contributes to corporate success. In this stage, IT is still not viewed as a strategic tool and IT executives are unlikely to be involved in developing corporate strategy.
Maturity level three: "Co-dependence/grudging respect"	**Maturity level four: "United we succeed, divided we fail"**
In this stage, the business is dependent on IT and there are early signs of recognition that it is a strategic tool. CIOs are becoming more knowledgeable about cross-functional business processes because of ERP, CRM, and so forth. The Internet and interest in e-business forces some level of IT/Business alignment. CEOs begin to recognize that IT is a competitive tool.	*In this stage, IT and business are inextricably entwined.* Business executives have less time to prove they can deliver. Business cannot continue without IT and IT has little real value if it is not to support the corporate strategy. There is only a single strategy and it incorporates both IT and business. Whether the business is a pure play Internet company, or a "bricks 'n clicks" company, IT and business move in lockstep.

business are inextricably entwined and there is only one single strategy that incorporates both business and IT.

IT Governance Structures, Processes, and Relational Mechanisms

The previous sections described what IT governance is about. However, having developed a high-level IT governance model does not imply that governance is actually working in the organisation. Conceiving the IT governance model is the first step, deploying it throughout all levels of the organisation is the next challenging step. In this section, an implementation framework is supplied, covering different possible mechanisms.

As will be illustrated in the case studies later in this book, the decision to implement an IT governance framework is sometimes initiated by a specific event or a major issue. In other cases different elements for implementing IT governance have been step-wise introduced.

IT Governance Implementation Framework

IT governance can be deployed using a mixture of various structures, processes and relational mechanisms (Peterson, 2003; Weill & Woodham, 2002). Some examples of these structures, processes and relational mechanisms are provided in Figure 19.

Structures involve the organisation, and location of the IT function, the existence of clearly defined roles and responsibilities and a diversity of IT/business committees. Processes refer to strategic decision making, strategic information systems planning (SISP) and monitoring, control, and process frameworks. The relational mechanisms finally complete the IT governance framework and are paramount for attaining and sustaining business-IT alignment, even when the appropriate structures and processes are in place. These mechanisms include business/IT participation, strategic dialogue, training, shared learning, and proper communication. The next sections will further elaborate on these three necessary elements of an IT governance framework: structures, processes, and relational mechanisms.

Figure 19. The necessary elements of an IT governance framework

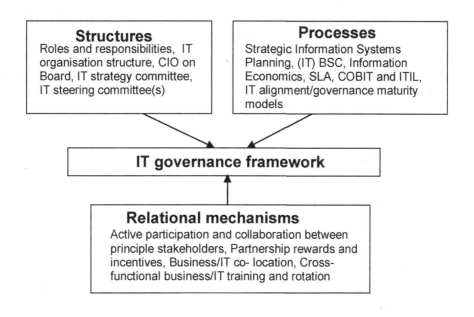

Each of these practices serve specific or multiple goals in the complex IT governance challenge. However, dividing the complex IT governance problem into smaller pieces, and solving each problem separately does not always solve the complete problem (Peterson, 2003). A holistic approach towards IT governance acknowledges its complex and dynamic nature, consisting of a set of interdependent subsystems that deliver a powerful whole (Duffy, 2002a; Patel, 2003; Peterson, 2003; Sambamurthy & Zmud, 1999). The necessary set for a successful IT governance implementation framework therefore consists of a mix of structures, processes and relational mechanisms (Figure 19).

When designing IT governance for an organisation, it is important to recognise that it is contingent upon a variety of sometimes conflicting internal and external factors. Determining the right combination of mechanisms is therefore a complex endeavour and it should be recognised that what works for one company does not necessarily work for another. For example, larger companies often have a broader budget to implement IT governance mechanisms compared to smaller companies, or need to have a richer mix of mechanisms because of organisational complexity. Industry can also be a determining factor. Organisations in the finance industry are more dependent upon IT compared to a cement factory, which probably requires the finance industry to have a more solid IT governance framework. Finally, geography can also have an impact. This means that different organisations may need a different combination of different structures, processes and relational mechanisms (Patel, 2003; Ribbers et al., 2002).

IT Governance Structures

Roles and Responsibilities

It is crucial and a prerequisite for an effective IT governance framework that the roles and responsibilities of the involved parties are clearly and unambiguously defined. It is the responsibility of the board and executive management to communicate these roles and responsibilities and to make sure that they are clearly understood throughout the whole organisation.

One of the roles that must have clear responsibilities defined in the IT governance process is that of executive management. Dependent on the strategic importance of IT within an organisation, management involvement may differ, but at least the charter must be clearly defined.

The CIO is an important but certainly not the only stakeholder in the IT governance process. The CEO has singular responsibility for carrying out the strategic plans and policies that have been established by the board, and he should ensure that the CIO is part of it and that he is accepted in the senior-level decision-making process. The CIO and the CEO should report on a regular basis to the board, while the board in its turn has to play the role of independent overseer of business performance and compliance. The board members should not only keep their knowledge of current business models, management techniques and information technology up-to-date, but also the potential risks and benefits associated with each of them (Duffy, 2002c). The IT Governance Institute (ITGI, 2003) identified in more detail the roles and responsibilities of the board of directors related to the five defined IT governance areas: strategic alignment, value delivery, risk management, resource management, and performance management (Figure 20).

Figure 20. Roles and responsibilities of the board of directors (ITGI, 2003)

Strategic alignment	Value delivery	IT resource management	Risk management	Performance management
Ensure management has put in place an effective strategy	Ascertain that management has put processes and practices in place that ensure IT delivers provable value to the business	Monitor how management determines what IT resources are needed to achieve strategic goal	Be aware about IT risk exposures and their containment	Assess senior management's performance on IT strategies in operation
Ratify the aligned business and IT strategy			Evaluate the effectiveness of management's monitoring of IT risks	
Ensure the IT organisational structure complements the business model and direction	Ensure IT investments represent a balance of risks and benefit and that budgets are acceptable	Ensure a proper balance of IT investments for sustaining and growing the enterprise		Work with the executive to define and monitor high-level IT performance

Ross and Weill (2002) very clearly illustrate the importance of these roles and responsibilities, specifically by describing the impact when executive management is ignoring their IT responsibilities (Figure 21).

According to Bill Gates, CEOs themselves must view IT as a strategic resource to help the business generate revenue. The CEO needs to learn about technology and include the CIO in management deliberations. Gates reminds us, *"If IT doesn't 'get' the business issues, and the CEO does not integrate*

Figure 21. What happens when senior managers ignore their IT responsibilities? (Adapted from Ross & Weill, 2002)

	IT decision	Senior management's role	Consequences of abdicating the decision
Strategy	How much should we spend on IT?	*Define the strategic role* that IT will play in the company and then determine *the level of funding* needed to achieve that objective.	The company fails to develop an IT platform that furthers its strategy, despite high IT spending.
	Which business processes should receive our IT dollars?	Make clear decisions about *which IT initiatives will and will not be funded.*	A lack of focus overwhelms the IT unit, which tries to deliver many projects that may have little company wide value or can't be implemented simultaneously.
	Which IT capabilities need to be company wide?	Decide which *IT capabilities* should be *provided centrally and* which should be developed *by individual businesses.*	Excessive technical and process standardization limits the flexibility of business units, or frequent exceptions to the standards increase the costs and limit business synergies.
Execution	How good do our IT services really need to be?	Decide *which features*—for example, enhanced reliability or response time—are *needed on the basis of their costs and benefits.*	The company may pay for service options that, given its priorities, aren't worth the costs.
	What security and privacy risks will we accept?	Lead the decision making on the *trade-offs between security and privacy on one hand and convenience on the other.*	An overemphasis on security and privacy may inconvenience customers, employees, and suppliers; an under-emphasis may make data vulnerable.
	Whom do we blame if an IT initiative fails?	*Assign a business executive to be accountable for every IT project*; monitor business metrics.	The business value of systems is never realized.

the CIO into important business decisions, then the fault is the CEOs. If IT doesn't 'get' the business issues, but the CEO does include the CIO in business strategy, then the fault is the CIOs" (Bill Gates, 1999, cited in Duffy, 2002c).

IT Organization Structure

Effective IT governance is also determined by the way the IT function is organised and where the IT decision-making authority is located within the organisation. Over the last years, several models were developed and implemented such as a centralised, decentralised, and federal IT organisation. The adoption of a particular model is influenced by different determinants and different variations of these models exist. A dominant model, though, in many contemporary enterprises is the federal structure. The federal structure is mostly a hybrid design of centralised infrastructure control and decentralised application control. This model tries to achieve 'the best of both worlds' (see Figure 22 and Figure 23). efficiency and standardisation for the infrastructure (centralised) and effectiveness and flexibility for the development of applications (decentralised)

IT organizations may run through different centralization and decentralization cycles. In order to better understand the complex dynamics underlying these IT organizational structures, Peterson (2003) identified some key determinants for centralised versus decentralised IT organisations: *"Centralised IT governance is associated with small-sized organisations following a cost-focused*

Figure 22. Tradeoffs and the best of both (Peterson, 2003)

Design Drivers	Centralized IT governance	Decentralized IT governance	Federal IT governance
Synergy	+	-	+
Standardization	+	-	+
Specialisation	+	-	+
Customer responsiveness	-	+	+
Business ownership	-	+	+
Flexibility	-	+	+

business (competitive strategy), and characterised by a centralised business governance structure, environmental stability, low information-intensive

Figure 23. The federal IT organisation: 'The best of both worlds' (Adapted from Rockart, Earl, & Ross, 1996)

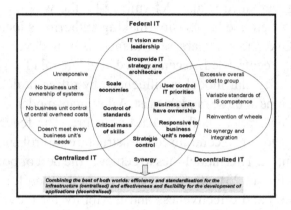

Figure 24. Key IT decision domains (Adapted from Weill & Ross, 2004)

IT principles decisions		
High-level statements about how IT is used in the business		
IT architecture decisions	**IT Infrastructure decisions**	**IT investment and prioritisation decisions**
Organising logic for data, applications, and infrastructure captured in a set of *policies, relationships, and technical choices* to achieve desired business and technical standardisation and integration	Centrally coordinated, shared IT services that provide the *foundation for the enterprise's IT capability*	*Decisions about how much and where to invest in IT,* including project approvals and justification techniques
	Business application needs	
	Specifying the business need for purchased or internally developed IT applications	

business products/services, and low business experience and competency in managing IT." The opposite is valid for decentralised IT governance.

Weill and Ross (2004) defined more detailed decision-making allocation models that go beyond the traditional centralised, decentralised, or federal approaches. They state that "an effective IT governance structure is the single most important predictor of getting value from IT." The findings in their book are based on different research projects, done in more than three hundred enterprises in over twenty countries. They studied how firms make decisions in five key interrelated IT domains. IT principles, IT infrastructure, IT architecture, business applications needs, and IT investments and prioritisation (Figure 24). In finding an answer on the question "Who should make governance decision?" they defined six IT governance archetypes or styles (Figure 25), describing who within the organisation has decision rights or provides input to IT decisions.

They found that the organisations in the study often showed different governance archetypes for different IT decision domains both for making decisions as for providing input to decisions. Figure 26 shows the percentages of organisations that use a specific style when taking decisions or providing input for specific IT decisions. The federal governance model is typically

Figure 25. IT governance styles (Adapted from Weill & Ross, 2004)

IT governance style	Who has decision or input rights?
Business monarchy	*A group of business executives* or individual executives (CxOs). Includes committees of senior business executives (may include CIO). Excludes IT executives acting independently.
IT monarchy	Individuals or groups of *IT executives*
Feudal	*Business unit leaders*, key process owners or their delegates
Federal	*C-level executives and business groups* (e.g., business units or processes); may also include IT executives as additional participants.
Duopoly	*IT executives and at least one other group* (e.g., CxO or business unit or process leaders)
Anarchy	*Each individual business process owner* or end user

Figure 26. How enterprises make IT decisions (Adapted from Weill & Ross, 2004)

Decision Style	IT Principles		IT Architecture		IT Infrastructure Strategies		Business Application Needs		IT Investment	
	Input	Decision	Input	Decision	Input	Decision	Input	Decision	Input	Decision
Business Monarchy	0	27	0	6	0	7	1	12	1	30
IT Monarchy	1	18	20	73	10	59	0	8	0	9
Feudal	0	3	0	0	1	2		18	0	3
Federal	83	14	46	4	59	6	81	30	93	27
Duopoly	15	36	34	15	30	23	17	27	6	30
Anarchy	0	0	0	1	0	1	0	3	0	1
No Data or don't know	1	2	0	1	0	2	0	2	0	0

■ *Most common input pattern for all enterprises.* ■ *Most common decision patterns for all enterprises*

The numbers in each cell are percentages of the 256 enterprises studied in 23 countries. The columns add to 100 percent.

used as input for the three more business related IT decisions (IT principles, business applications, and IT investments). Enterprises mainly rely on IT monarchies when choosing an IT architecture or making IT infrastructure strategy decisions, both seen as more technical.

This "typical" pattern follows generally accepted corporate governance guidelines—that is, encouraging broad-based inputs and at the same time firmly controlling decision rights to a small group of leaders—and reflects the stage of evolution of IT management in many firms. Weill and Ross also analysed the governance performance of these companies and they concluded that the federal style is the most effective for input to all five key IT decisions. Indeed, *the federal model for input provides a broad-based vehicle for capturing the tradeoffs between the desires of the senior corporate managers and the managers in the business units.* For making decisions, on the other hand, the federal model in general is experienced as less effective, mainly because of too much people involved, slowing down the decision-making process and creating too many compromises, which may block the real needs of the business. Top governance performers often used duopolies for both IT principles and investments, enabling joint decision making between the business leaders and IT professionals. Figure 27 portrays the three most successful combinations of archetypes (in terms of governance performance) used in IT decisions, balancing multiple performance objectives such as cost, growth and flexibility.

Further breakdown and refinement of governance is done taking into account the enterprise's strategy and its performance goals. For example, firms with higher growth in market capitalization typically had very decentralized IT

Figure 27. Archetypes of the top three governance performers (Adapted from Weill & Woodham, 2002)

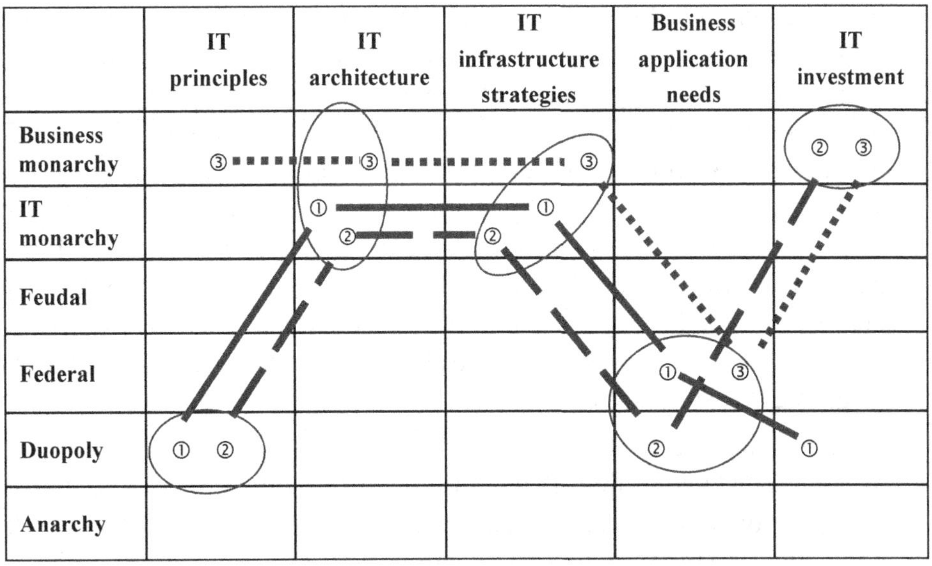

①②③ = *TOP three governance performers (achieving four performance objectives, weighted by importance)*

governance structures with a combination of a federal style for investment, feudal style for architecture and anarchy for IT principles, which encourages entrepreneurship with little regard to standardization. Top performers measured by return on asset improvements combined infrastructure and architecture decisions made by a centralized business monarchy with the pattern of a typical firm for the other decision domains, encouraging sharing, reuse, and asset utilization. Leading performers measured by profit margin or revenue per employee also prefer business monarchy over IT monarchy for decisions on IT principles. Another interesting finding of the study is the fact that "feudal structures" are used by top performing firms for infrastructure decisions, thereby maximising local responsiveness (Weill & Woodham, 2002).

IT Strategy Committee and IT Steering Committee

IT governance should be an integral part of corporate governance, and in this way a primary concern of the board of directors. Boards may carry out their governance duties through committees and they can consider the criticality of IT through an IT strategy committee. This IT strategy committee—composed of board and non-board members—should assist the board in governing and overseeing the enterprise's IT-related matters. This committee should ensure that IT is a regular item on the board's agenda, where it must be addressed in a structured way. The IT strategy committee should work in close relationship with the other board committees and with management in order to provide input to, and to review and amend the aligned enterprise and IT strategies (ITGI, 2003). The implementation of the IT strategy must be the responsibility of executive management assisted by one or more IT steering committees. Typically, such a steering committee has the responsibility for overseeing major projects and managing IT priorities, IT costs, and IT resource allocation. While the IT strategy committee operates at the board level, the IT steering committee is situated at executive level, which implies that they have different responsibility, authority and membership (Figure 28) (ITGI, 2003).

Similar, Nolan and McFarlan (2005) describe an IT governance committee as a board-level IT committee that is on par with the company's audit, compensation, and governance committees. Establishing a board-level IT committee is not, however a best practice for all companies. The way to involve the board in IT decisions is dependent upon a variety of contingencies. For example companies that require dependable systems and emerging technologies to

Figure 28. Comparison of typical IT strategy committee and IT steering committee responsibilities (ITGI, 2003)

	IT Strategy Committee	IT Steering Committee
Level	Board level	Executive level

Responsibility	• Provides insight and advice to the board on topics such as:
	  • The relevance of developments in IT from a business perspective
	  • The alignment of IT with the business direction
	  • The achievement of strategic IT objectives
	  • The availability of suitable IT resources, skills and infrastructure to meet the strategic objectives
	  • Optimisation of IT costs, including the role and value delivery of external IT sourcing
	  • Risk, return and competitive aspects of IT investments
	  • Progress on major IT projects
	  • The contribution of IT to the business (i.e., delivering the promised business value)
	  • Exposure to IT risks, including compliance risks
	  • Containment of IT risks
	• Provides direction to management relative to IT strategy
	• Is driver and catalyst for the board's IT governance practices
		• Decides the overall level of IT spending and how costs will be allocated
		• Aligns and approves the enterprise IT architecture
		• Approves project plans and budgets, setting priorities and milestones
		• Acquires and assigns appropriate resources
		• Ensures projects continuously meet business requirements, including re-evaluation of the business case
		• Monitors project plans for delivery of expected value and desired outcomes, on time and within budget
		• Monitors resource and priority conflict between enterprise divisions and the IT function, and between projects
		• Makes recommendations and requests for changes to strategic plans (priorities, funding, technology approaches, resources, etc.)
		• Communicates strategic goals to project teams
		• Is a major contributor to management's IT governance responsibilities

Authority	• Advises the board and management on IT strategy • Is delegated by the board to provide input to the strategy and prepare its approval • Focuses on current and future strategic IT issues	• Assists the executive in the delivery of the IT strategy • Oversees day-to-day management of IT service delivery and IT projects • Focuses on implementation
Membership	• Board members and (specialist) non-board members	• Sponsoring executive • Business executive (key users) • CIO • Key advisors as required (IT, audit, legal, finance)

hold their competitive position, have large IT expenditures and board level IT governance is critical for them (Nolan & McFarlan, 2005).

Luftman and Brier (1999) identified critical success factors for sustaining an IT steering committee (Figure 29). These critical success factors are important for both the strategic and more tactical and operational IT steering committees. Important for example is that the steering committee is responsible and accountable for its decisions made and that it has the authority to have decisions carried out.

In practice, the names used for these kinds of committees will be different in every organisation. The Canadian utility company NB Power, for example,

Figure 29. Critical success factors for sustaining IT steering committees (Adapted from Luftman & Brier, 1999)

Bureaucracy	Focus on reduction/elimination to expedite opportunities to leverage IT
Career building	Opportunities for participants to learn and expand responsibilities
Communication	Primary vehicle for IT and business discussions and sharing knowledge across parts of the organisation
Complex decisions	Do not get involved in 'mundane' areas
Influence / empowerment	Authority to have decisions carried out
Low hanging fruit	Immediate changes carried out when appropriate
Marketing	Vehicle for 'selling' the value of IT to the business
Objective measurements	Formal assessment and review of IT's business contributions
Ownership	Responsible/accountable for the decision made
Priorities	Primary vehicle for selecting what is done, when, and how much of resources to allocate
Relationships	Partnership of business and IT
Right participants	Cooperative, committed, respected team members with knowledge of the business and IT
Share risks	Equal accountability, recognition, responsibility, rewards and uncertainty
Structure, facilitator	Processes and leadership to ensure the right focus

Figure 31. Five SISP approaches summarised (Adapted from Earl, 1993)

	Business-led	Method-driven	Administrative	Technological	Organisational
Underpinning assumption	Business plans and needs should drive IS plans	Is strategies will be enhanced by use of a formal SISP method	SISP should follow and conform with the firm's management planning and control procedures	SISP is an exercise in business and information modelling	SISP is a continuous decision-making activity shared by business and IS
Emphasis of approach	Business leads IS and not vice versa	Selection of the best method	Identification and allocation of IS resources to meet agreed needs	Production of models and blueprints	Organisational learning about business problems and opportunities and the IT contribution
Major influence of outcomes	IS planners	Practitioners of the method	Resource planning and steering committees	Modelling method employed	Permanent and ad hoc teams of key managers, including IS

Business drives IS	Strategy Needs method	Follow the rules	IS needs blueprints	Themes with teams

Balanced Scorecard

An important part in the implementation process of strategic alignment is the performance measurement of IT and of IT related to the business. Kaplan and Norton (1992) introduced the balanced scorecard (BSC) as performance measurement tool at enterprise level. Their fundamental premise is that the evaluation of a firm should not be restricted to a traditional (i.e., financial) evaluation but it should be supplemented with measures concerning *customer satisfaction*, *internal processes*, and *the ability to innovate*. Results achieved within these additional perspective areas should assure future financial results and drive the organisation towards its strategic goals while keeping all four perspectives in balance. For this balanced measurement framework, Kaplan and Norton proposed a three-layer structure for each of these four perspectives: mission, objectives, and measures.

The BSC concept has been applied to the IT function and its processes (see, e.g., Van Grembergen, De Haes, & Guldentops, 2003). Recognising that IT is an internal service provider, the proposed perspectives of the IT balanced scorecard are described in Figure 32 (Van Grembergen, 2000). The *User Orientation* perspective represents the user evaluation of IT. The *Operational Excellence* perspective represents the IT processes employed to develop and deliver the applications. The *Future Orientation* perspective represents the

Figure 32. Balanced scorecard for the IT function (Van Grembergen, 2000)

USER ORIENTATION *How do the users view the IT department?*	CORPORATE CONTRIBUTION *How does management view the IT department?*
Mission To be the preferred supplier of information systems	*Mission* To obtain a reasonable business contribution of IT investments
Strategies * Preferred supplier of application * Preferred supplier of operations * Partnership with users * User-satisfaction	*Strategies* * Control of IT expenses * Provide new business capabilities * Business value of new IT projects
OPERATIONAL EXCELLENCE *How effective and efficient are the IT processes?*	FUTURE ORIENTATION *How well is IT positioned to answer future challenges?*
Mission To deliver effective and efficient deliver IT applications and services	*Mission* To develop opportunities to answer future challenges
Strategies * Efficient an effective software development * Efficient an effective operations	*Strategies* * Training and education of IT staff * Expertise of IT staff * Age of the application portfolio * Research into emerging information technologies

human and technology resources needed by IT to deliver its services. The *Business Contribution* perspective captures the business value of the IT investments.

Each of these perspectives has to be translated into corresponding metrics and measures that assess the current situation. These assessments have to be repeated periodically and have to be confronted with goals and benchmarking figures that have to be set beforehand. Example metrics for the future orientation perspective are provided in Figure 33.

To leverage the scorecard as a management instrument, it should be enhanced with cause-and-effect relationships between perspectives and measures. Within the perspectives, the relationships are articulated by two types of measures: outcome measures and performance drivers. A well developed scorecard should contain a good mix of these two metrics. Outcome measures without performance drivers do not communicate how they are to be achieved. And performance drivers without outcome measures may lead to significant investment without a measurement indicating whether the chosen strategy is effective. A good example of a cause-and-effect relationship, defined throughout the whole scorecard is showed in Figure 34: improved education of IT staff (future perspective) is an enabler (performance driver) for a better quality of developed systems (operational excellence perspective) that in turn is an

Figure 33. Measures for future orientation (Van Grembergen & Van Bruggen, 1997)

Permanent education of staff
* Number of educational days per person
* Education budget as a percent of total IT budget
Expertise of the IT staff
* Number of years of IT experience per staff member
* Age pyramid of the IT staff
Age of the Applications Portfolio
* Number of applications per age category
* Number of applications younger than 5 years
Research into emerging technologies
* Percent of budget spent on IT research

Figure 34. Cause-and-effect relationships within the IT strategic balanced scorecard

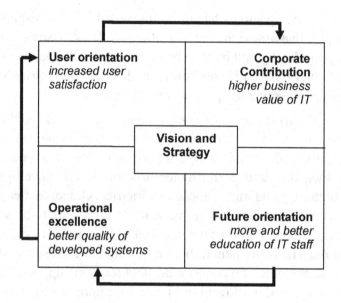

enabler for increased user satisfaction (user perspective) that eventually must lead to a higher business value of IT (business contribution perspective).

The proposed IT balanced scorecard links with the business, mainly through the business contribution perspective. The relationship between IT and business can be more explicitly expressed through a cascade of balanced scorecards (Van der Zee & De Jong, 1999). In Figure 35, the relationship between IT scorecards and the business scorecard is illustrated. The IT Development BSC and the IT Operational BSC both are enablers of the IT Strategic BSC that in turn is the enabler of the Business BSC. This cascade of scorecards becomes a linked set of measures that will be instrumental in aligning IT and business strategy and that will help to determine how business value is created through IT.

Van Der Zee and De Jong (1999) warn of some limitations of an integrated balanced business and IT scorecard approach. They acknowledge the barri-

Figure 35. Cascade of balanced scorecards (Van Grembergen, Saull, & De Haes, 2003)

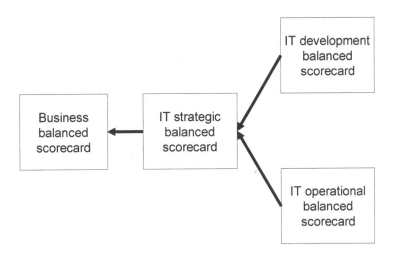

ers of an effective balanced scorecard implementation that were originally specified by Kaplan and Norton (1996):

• Visions and strategies that are not actionable
• Strategies that are not linked to departmental, team and individual goals
• Strategies that are not linked to long- and short-term resource allocation
• Feedback that is tactical, not strategic

However, the case studies performed by Van Der Zee and De Jong (1999) confirm that "the integrated balanced business scorecard approach, if applied intelligently and with awareness of its limitations, can successfully integrate business and IT planning processes."

In Chapter III of this book, a case study is presented where the balanced scorecards are employed as an IT governance alignment instrument.

Information Economics and Portfolio Management

The information economics method developed by Parker, Benson & Trainer (1988) can be used as an alignment/governance technique whereby both business and IT people score IT projects and in this way prioritise and select projects. In essence, information economics is a scoring technique resulting in a weighted total score based on the scores for the ROI and non-tangibles such as *"strategic match of the project"* (business evaluation) and *"match with the strategic IT architecture"* (IT evaluation) (see Figure 36). Typically scores from 0 to 5 are attributed whereby 0 means no contribution and 5 refers to a high contribution; the values obtain a positive score and the risks a negative score (Parker, 1995).

Figure 36. Information economics (Van Grembergen & Van Bruggen, 1997)

Traditional ROI (+)		
Value linking (+) Value acceleration (+)	Value restructuring (+) Innovation (+)	
Adjusted ROI	**Business Value**	**IT Value**
	Strategic match (+) Competitive advantage (+) Competitive response (+) Management information (+) Service and quality (+) Empowerment (+) Cycle time (+) Mass customization (+)	Strategic IT architecture (+)
	Business risk	IT risk
	Business strategy risk (-) Business organization risk (-)	IT strategy risk (-) Definitional uncertainty (-) Technical risk (-) IT service delivery risk (-)
VALUE (business contribution)		

Copyright © 2008, IGI Global. Copying or distributing in print or electronic forms without written permission of IGI Global is prohibited.

Figure 36 illustrates components of information economics. Most of the elements are self-explanatory; the others are explained hereafter using a generic e-business project as example. *Value linking* incorporates for instance interest savings due to an accelerated payment of invoices realised through electronic payment. *Value acceleration* contains the additional cash flows due to reduced time scale for e-business operations. *Value restructuring* refers to the efficiency and effectiveness of the employees. *Innovation* incorporates the additional cash flows arising from the innovation aspects of the e-business investment. *Strategic IT architecture* assesses the degree of value to which the project fits into the e-business plan. *Business strategy risk* and *IT strategy risk* respectively refer to the degree of risk in terms of how well the company or IT department succeeds in achieving its strategic objectives. Definitional uncertainty indicates the degree of risk in terms of how clearly the functional requirements and specifications have been agreed upon (Van Grembergen & Amelinckx, 2003).

Information economics fits into the broader discussion of portfolio management, as it provides a way to make prioritisations in the portfolio of IT investments. An interesting development in the context of portfolio management is the publication of VALIT, a framework put forward by the IT Governance Institute "for organisations to select and manage IT-related business investments and IT assets by means of investment programmes such that they deliver the optimal value to the organisation" (ITGI, 2006a).

The VALIT framework identifies three mains processes: value governance, portfolio management and investment management. In each of these processes, a set of key management practices is put forward (see Figure 37), addressing issues such as defining evaluations criteria per investment category (VG11), monitoring and reporting on portfolio performance (PM14) and developing a detailed programme business case (IM8).

The VALIT publication also states that "organisations generally are not good at developing and documenting comprehensive and comparable business cases" (ITGI, 2006b). Therefore, it provides a separate publication (ITGI, 2006b), in which guidance and templates are provided to build up a detailed business case for an IT enabled business investment. An eight-step business case development process is described, as visualised in Figure 38. The process starts with building a fact sheet with all the relevant data followed by analysis of the data concerning alignment, financial benefits, non-financial benefits and risk. This should result in the appraisal and optimisation of the risk/return of the IT-enabled investment represented by a structured record-

Figure 37. The VALIT framework (ITGI, 2006a)

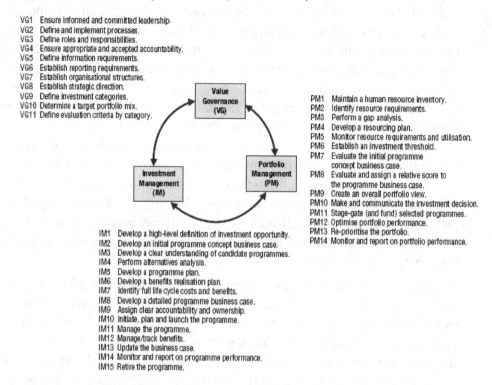

VG1 Ensure informed and committed leadership.
VG2 Define and implement processes.
VG3 Define roles and responsibilities.
VG4 Ensure appropriate and accepted accountability.
VG5 Define information requirements.
VG6 Establish reporting requirements.
VG7 Establish organisational structures.
VG8 Establish strategic direction.
VG9 Define investment categories.
VG10 Determine a target portfolio mix.
VG11 Define evaluation criteria by category.

PM1 Maintain a human resource inventory.
PM2 Identify resource requirements.
PM3 Perform a gap analysis.
PM4 Develop a resourcing plan.
PM5 Monitor resource requirements and utilisation.
PM6 Establish an investment threshold.
PM7 Evaluate the initial programme concept business case.
PM8 Evaluate and assign a relative score to the programme business case.
PM9 Create an overall portfolio view.
PM10 Make and communicate the investment decision.
PM11 Stage-gate (and fund) selected programmes.
PM12 Optimise portfolio performance.
PM13 Re-prioritise the portfolio.
PM14 Monitor and report on portfolio performance.

IM1 Develop a high-level definition of investment opportunity.
IM2 Develop an initial programme concept business case.
IM3 Develop a clear understanding of candidate programmes.
IM4 Perform alternatives analysis.
IM5 Develop a programme plan.
IM6 Develop a benefits realisation plan.
IM7 Identify full life cycle costs and benefits.
IM8 Develop a detailed programme business case.
IM9 Assign clear accountability and ownership.
IM10 Initiate, plan and launch the programme.
IM11 Manage the programme.
IM12 Manage/track benefits.
IM13 Update the business case.
IM14 Monitor and report on programme performance.
IM15 Retire the programme.

Figure 38. Business case development process (ITGI, 2006b)

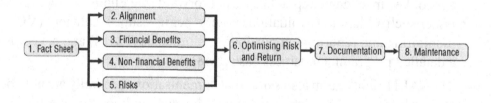

ing of the previous steps' results and documentation of the business case. Finally, a maintenance step is added addressing the review of the business case during the programme execution, including the entire life cycle of the programme results.

Service Level Agreements

In a maturing IT governance environment, service level agreements (SLAs) and their supporting service level management (SLM) process need to play an important role. A SLA is defined as *"a written contract between a service provider of a service and the customer of the service."* Some essential components of such a contract are summarised in Figure 39.

The functions of SLAs are: (1) to define what levels of service are acceptable by users and are attainable by the service provider, and (2) to define the mutually acceptable and agreed upon set of indicators of the quality of service.

Three basic types of SLAs can be defined: in-house, external, and internal SLAs. The differences between those types refer to the parties involved in the definition of the SLA. An in-house SLA is an agreement negotiated between an in-house service provider (e.g., the IT department) and an in-house client or department (e.g., marketing). External SLAs are SLAs between an external service provider (third party) and an organisation. Internal SLAs, finally, are used by a service provider to measure the performance of the groups within its own organisation (Sturm et al., 2000, in Van Grembergen et al., 2003). The negotiation of SLAs should be completed by an experienced and multi-disciplinary team that equally represents the user group and the service provider.

Figure 39. Some essential components of a service level agreement (Van Grembergen et al., 2003)

Parties in the agreement	Security procedures
Definitions of terminology	Audit procedures
Term / Duration	Roles & Responsibilities
Scope / Subject	Optional services
Limitations	Reporting
Service Level Objectives	Administration
Service Level Indicators	Review / Update
Non-performance Impact	Property
Maintenance	Legal
Pricing Mechanism	Approvals
Billing and Terms of Payment	

The SLM process includes the definition of a SLA framework, establishing SLAs including level of service and their corresponding metrics, monitoring, and reporting on the achieved services and problems encountered, reviewing SLAs, and establishing improvement programs. The major governance challenges are that the service levels are to be expressed in business terms and that the right SLM/SLA process has to be put in place (Van Grembergen et al., 2003).

COBIT and Complementary Frameworks

COBIT (control objectives for information and related technology), developed and issued by Information Systems Audit and Control Association (ISACA), is increasingly internationally accepted as a good practice for control over information, IT and related risks (www.isaca.org). COBIT delivers a control and security framework for IT, providing management with a better understanding of the risks and constraints of IT at all levels within their organisation. Since its first issuance in 1996, COBIT has been adopted in corporations and by governmental entities around the world and has become the de-facto standard for control over IT. The framework starts from the business with a simple and pragmatic premise: "In order to provide the information that the organisation needs to achieve its objectives, IT resources need to be managed by a set of naturally grouped processes." COBIT identifies 34 IT processes and describes a framework for control management and audit for each of the processes.

Previous edition, COBIT 3.0, issued in 2000 consists of three volumes: control objectives, management guidelines, and audit guidelines. In December, 2005, COBIT 4.0 was released, in which the control objectives and management guidelines were improved and integrated into one volume. This edition of COBIT is discussed in detail in Chapter IV.

Several standards and best practices, issued by both international standardisation organisations and private organisations, exist in addition to COBIT for managing the different aspects of IT. When implementing IT control and IT governance, it may be important to know how these different standards and best practices relate.

Figure 40 shows a non-exhaustive list of standards, identified by ITGI as the main guidance for IT governance (ITGI, 2006e).

In an ITGI study (2006e), COBIT was compared to other standards. While COBIT does address the full spectrum of IT governance duties, several other

Figure 40. Overview of IT governance standards/guidance

Guidance	Goals	Target Audience
COBIT	IT control objectives for day-to-day use	Management, users, and auditors
CMMi	Providing guidance to use when developing processes.	Systems and software developers-managers
COSO	Improve the ways of controlling enterprises by defining an integrated control system	CxOs, users, and internal auditors
ISO/IEC 17799:2005	Guidance for implementing information security	People responsible for information security
ISO/IEC TR 13335	Guidance on aspects of IT security management	Senior management, individuals responsible for security measures
ISO/IEC 15408:2005	Definition of criteria for evaluation of IT security	Consumers, developers and evaluators
ITIL	Vendor-independent approach for service management	People responsible for IT service management
NIST 800-14	Baseline for establishing and reviewing IT security programs	Parties responsible for IT security in government organizations
PRINCE2	Definition of a project management method	Organisations of varying sizes (project managers)
PMBOK	A common lexicon for discussing, writing and applying project management.	Anyone interested in the profession of project management.
TickIT	QMS for software development and certification criteria	Customers, suppliers and auditors

standards may describe the IT governance duties in a more comprehensive manner. Figure 41 places the different standards and guidelines in a completeness classification diagram, using the vertical dimension for the detail of the standard/guidance in terms of technical and operational profundity

Figure 41. Completeness classification of IT governance standards (ITGI, 2006e)

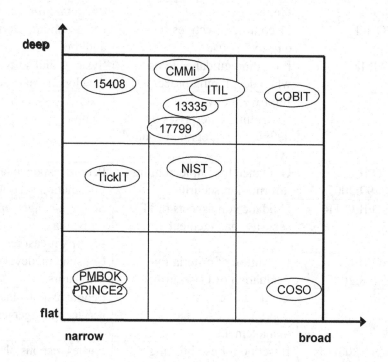

and the horizontal dimension for the completeness of the standard/guidance with respect to COBIT.

The IT Governance Institute provides more guidance for practitioners on how COBIT maps onto other standards. More information can be found at *www.itgi.org*.

IT Governance Relational Mechanisms

"I've been with several companies where, when they talk to each other or to me, they always refer to 'your side, my side.' That's wrong. It should be

'we.' Everything should be 'we' or 'us.' I don't like it when IT calls the people who use IT services 'end-users' or 'customers' or 'clients.' They're not any of these. They're partners. [...]" (Luftman, 2002).

Relational mechanisms are very important. It is possible that an organisation has all IT governance structures and processes in place, but that it does not work out because business and IT do not understand each other and/or are not working together (Luftman, 2002; Reich & Benbasat, 2000; Weiss & Anderson, 2004). Or it may be that there is little business awareness on the part of IT or little IT appreciation from the business side. So, to reach effective IT governance, a two-way communication and a good participation/collaboration relationship between the business and IT people is needed. Horovitz called this the social dimension of IT governance, with a focus on the people in the alignment process (Reich & Benbasat, 2000).

In this context, Reich and Benbasat (2000) investigated the impact of shared domain knowledge on short-term alignment within 10 business units of three life insurance companies. The concept of **shared domain knowledge** is defined as the actual amount of IT experience among the business executives and the actual amount of business experience among the IT executives. For short term alignment, one of the outcomes confirmed that *managers within a business unit with high level of shared domain knowledge understand and respect each other's contribution and trust that each is given their best effort. Even in the presence of a seriously derailed major IT project, these units may exhibit high levels of communication and short-term alignment.* Ensuring ongoing knowledge sharing across departments and organisations is therefore paramount for attaining and sustaining business/IT alignment. It is crucial to facilitate the sharing and the management of knowledge by using mechanisms such as career cross-over (IT staff working in the business units and business people working in IT), continuous education, cross-training, and so forth.

The concept of social capital also provides some elements in an attempt to analyse the (complex) relational mechanisms. Social capital can be seen as the relationships that make organisations work effectively. Social capital is regarded as a multi-dimensional construct, which highlights the importance of strong networks across groups that provide the basis for trust, cooperation, and collective action. According to Napahiet and Ghosal (stated in Hatzakis, 2004), social capital consists of three dimensions: the structural dimension, the relationship dimension, and the cognitive dimension. The structural dimension describes the relationship network and the mechanisms needed for connecting people. The relational dimension describes the sense of trust that individuals have toward each other. The cognitive dimension describes the shared understanding, interest, or problems that holds the group together. The framework in Figure 42 shows the possible impact of social capital on organisational functioning and business value, resulting in productivity gains from IT investments. A recent study (Dedrick, 2003, stated in Hatzakis, 2004) report productivity gains of 20 percent for organisations that did invest in social capital, while organisation that did not, even showed productivity losses.

As an illustration of the importance of relational mechanisms, Dutta (1996) compared how senior management of two banks, Banco Comercial Português (BCP), and Continental Bank (CB)—tried to align IT with their businesses. They both adopted a drastically different approach in their alignment attempt: in-house IT (BCP) versus complete outsourcing of IT (CB). What really differentiates the two banks (prior to outsourcing of IT by one of them) is "the will of senior management to participate on a regular basis and get involved in the management of IT" (Dutta, 1996). An important lesson learned from the study, is that *"the high level of awareness about IT issues at all levels within BCP is enhanced by frequent rotations of the IT staff within the business units. Not only are some IT technical staff resident in the different business units,*

Figure 42. Framework for understanding the contribution of social capital to IT investments (Adapted from Hatzakis, 2004)

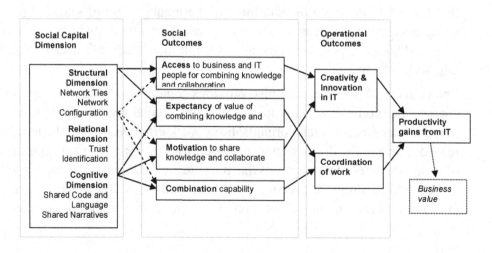

but IT staff are also moved into business management positions once they reach the project manager level within the IT division. All incoming staff is trained in the use of IT systems and the relation between BCP's IT systems and its business capabilities" (Dutta, 1996). It needs not be elucidated that BCP's adoption of relational mechanisms such as cross-functional training and cross-functional (IT) job rotation largely contributed to *"the most successful story in European banking within the last decade."*

Measuring the IT Governance Process

Building an IT Governance Balanced Scorecard

Today many organizations are in the process of implementing a combination of IT governance structures, processes and relational mechanisms. An important aspect of the IT governance implementation process is the measuring and evaluation part. It makes sense for CIOs, executive managers and board members to oversee the IT governance status: how well it is doing and how it can be improved. Van Grembergen and De Haes (2005) developed a balanced scorecard (BSC) as a performance measurement system for this IT governance process, enabling strategies for further improvement. Figure 43 displays the mission statements, objectives and corresponding measures for the four dimensions of the balanced scorecard: corporate contribution perspective, stakeholder's perspective, operational excellence perspective, and future perspective. The BSC is not only a performance management system but also provides a management system when causal relationships between metrics are properly implemented. The ultimate goal of the development and implementation of an IT governance process is the attainment of a better alignment between business and IT and consequently achieving better financial results. It is therefore logical that the IT governance balanced scorecard starts with a corporate contribution perspective. As shown in Figure 43, the other three perspectives have a cause relationship with corporate contribution and among each other cause-and-effect relationships. An illustration of these coupled metrics in a cause-and-effect relationship is: overall completed IT governance education (future orientation) may enhance the level of IT/business planning (operational excellence), which in turn may improve stakeholders' satisfaction (stakeholders orientation), and have a positive

Figure 43. IT governance scorecard perspectives and its cause-and-effect relationships (Van Grembergen & De Haes, 2005)

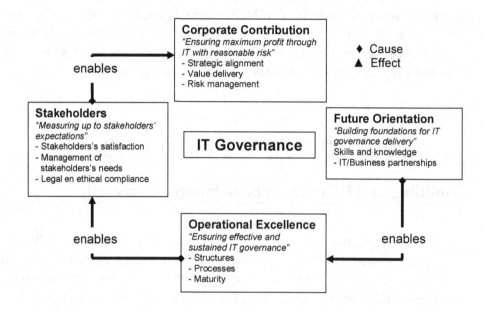

effect on the strategic match of major IT projects (corporate contribution). The metrics of the main elements of IT governance—structures, processes, and relational mechanisms—can be found in the operational excellence and future perspective dimensions.

Metrics for an IT Governance Balanced Scorecard

The corporate contribution dimension evaluates the performance of the IT governance process: a well balanced IT governance process must enhance business profit through IT while mitigating the risk related to IT (mission). The three key objectives, as depicted in Figure 44, are strategic alignment, value delivery and risk management, and are seen by the IT Governance Institute (2003) as main concerns of IT governance. The main measurement challenge is within the area of *strategic alignment*. As an overall metric, a weighted governance performance measure as developed by Weill and Ross

(2004) is proposed. This governance performance measure is based on the scores of a quick self-assessment of at least ten senior managers. They have to score on a scale from 1 (not successful) to 5 (very successful) how important a particular governance outcome is, and how well the IT governance process contributed in achieving that outcome. The outcomes that are scored include cost effective use of IT, effective use of IT for growth, effective use of IT for asset utilisation and effective use of IT for business flexibility. Based on the given scores, a weighted governance performance is calculated. Strategic match of major IT projects, percentage of development capacity engaged in strategic projects, and percentage of business goals supported by IT goals are specific strategic alignment concerns. Measuring the strategic match of IT projects can be done through a scoring technique as introduced by information economics (Parker, 1995): typical scores are attributed from

Figure 44. Corporate contribution (Van Grembergen & De Haes, 2005)

Perspective	Corporate Contribution	
Mission	Ensuring maximum profit while mitigating IT related risks	
Objectives	*Strategic Alignment*	
	Measures	Weighted governance performance
		Strategic match of major IT projects
		Percentage of development capacity engaged in strategic projects
		Percentage of business goals supported by IT goals
	Value Delivery	
	Measures	Business unit performance management
		Business value of major IT projects based on ROI, NPV, IRR, PB
		Ratio IT costs/total turnover
		IT costs charged back to the business
	Risk Management	
	Measures	Number of new implemented IT security initiatives and security breaches
		Attainment of disaster recovery plans
		Number of IT audits performed and reported shortcomings

0 tot 5 whereby 0 means no match at all and 5 a perfect match of the IT project with the business strategy. In the *value delivery* area, business unit performance measurement refers to the business results of the individual lines of business. Indeed, the ultimate responsibility for achieving and measuring the business value rests with the business units. Alternative metrics for value delivery assessment are the traditional financial evaluations such as the return on investment, net present value, internal rate of return, and pay back period (business value of major IT projects based on ROI, NPV, IRR, and PB). A major concern of senior management is the level of the IT costs and their recovery respectively measured through ratio IT costs/total turnover and percentage of IT costs charged back to the business. Regarding the *risk management* objective, a high level of security and disaster recovery should be attained and measured by the number of implemented IT security initiatives and security breaches and attainment of disaster recovery plans. The audit performance is measured through number of IT audits performed and reported shortcomings.

Figure 45 portrays the objectives of the **stakeholder's perspective:** stakeholders' satisfaction, management of stakeholders' needs and the legal/ethical compliance. This perspective evaluates the IT governance process from the stakeholders' viewpoint including the board of directors, CEO and executive management, CIO and IT management, business and IT users, customers, shareholders, and the community. It is important to point out that the scope of this stakeholder's perspective is much broader than the customer perspective of an IT Balanced scorecard (see Figure 32).

In relation to *stakeholders' satisfaction* the scores from satisfaction surveys (*stakeholders' satisfaction survey on fixed times*) for the aforementioned categories of stakeholders can be used. This can also be applied to the *number of complaints of stakeholders.* An overall specific metric for business users is *index of availability of systems and applications.* The *management of stakeholders' needs* are assessed through a set of performance metrics including measurements for the various stakeholder groups *(number of meetings with stakeholders),* more specific measurements for the board and CEO *(clear communication in place with CEO/board members* and *index of CEO/board involvement in new and major IT initiatives),* and specific measurements for the business users *(number of major IT projects within SLA).* Service level agreements (SLAs) as already pointed out in the previous section, are an important governance instrument for enforcing levels of IT service that are acceptable by users and are attainable by their IT department and/or external

Figure 45. Stakeholders (Van Grembergen & De Haes, 2005)

Perspective	Stakeholders Orientation	
Mission	Measuring up to stakeholders' expectations	
Objectives	*Stakeholders' satisfaction*	
	Measures	Stakeholders' satisfaction surveys on fixed times
		Number of complaints of stakeholders
		Index of availability of systems and applications
	Management of stakeholders' needs	
	Measures	Number of meetings with stakeholders
		Clear communication in place with CEO and board members
		Index of CEO/board involvement in new and major IT initiatives
		Number of major IT projects within SLA
	Legal and ethical compliance	
	Measures	IT adherence to Sarbanes-Oxley Act
		IT adherence to privacy regulations
		Adherence to IT code of ethics/ IT code of conduct

providers. The third objective within the stakeholder's perspective is the *legal and ethical compliance.* In their publication on the board balanced scorecard, Epstein and Roy (2004) state that *"the company's reporting strategy is a powerful driver of stakeholder satisfaction, so accountable companies should provide transparent reporting to their internal and external stakeholders, ..."* Accountability and transparency can be enhanced through the adherence to government and IT community regulations. The Sarbanes-Oxley (SOX) Act for example, focuses on the control and security of company's financial systems and consequently on its supporting IT processes (ITGI, 2006d). A crucial IT process in this context is "manage changes" as defined by COBIT, the international accepted IT control framework (ITGI, 2005). The business objective of the manage changes process is *"responding to business requirements in alignment with the business strategy, whilst reducing solution and service delivery defects and rework"* (ITGI, 2005) and in this sense is a crucial supportive mechanism for Sarbanes-Oxley compliance. A specific metric for IT adherence to SOX could be the maturity level of the manage changes process evaluated on the basis of the maturity model as defined in the management guidelines of COBIT (ITGI, 2005). Figure 46 illustrates maturity levels 0 and 5 for the manage changes process.

The **operational excellence** perspective identifies the key IT governance practices (structures and processes) to be implemented and their corresponding metrics. As defined previously, structures refer to the existence of responsible functions and committees, and processes to decision-making and monitoring. The operational excellence card of Figure 47 gives a variety of metrics for IT governance structures and processes including an overall IT governance maturity measurement. For the *structures* area three specific metrics regarding IT committees are retained: *number of meetings of IT strategy committee and IT steering committees, composition of IT committees,* and *overall attendance of IT committees.* Taking the criticality of IT into account, boards should manage IT with high commitment and accuracy as it does with other critical areas such as audit, compensation and acquisitions. An instrument for achieving this is an IT strategy committee that supports the board in carrying out its IT governance duties (ITGI, 2003). On the other hand, the detailed implementation of the IT/business strategies will be the responsibility of executive management assisted by a variety of steering committees overseeing

Figure 46. Maturity levels for 'Manage Change' process (COBIT 4.0) (ITGI, 2005)

Level 0: Non-existent
There is no defined change management process and changes can be made with virtually no control. There is no awareness that change can be disruptive for IT and business operations, and no awareness of the benefits of good change management.
Level 5: Optimised
The change management process is regularly reviewed and updated to stay in line with good practices. The review process reflects the outcome of monitoring. Configuration information is computer-based and provides version control. Tracking of changes is sophisticated and includes tools to detect unauthorised and unlicensed software. IT change management is integrated with business change management to ensure that IT is an enabler in increasing productivity and creating new business opportunities for the organisation.

major projects and managing priorities. Considering the importance of the IT strategy committee and the IT steering committees these committees need careful and close monitoring through the aforementioned measures. Besides the meeting frequency and the attendance, it should be monitored whether the right people are member, taking into account factors such as their profile and IT literacy. An ideal composition of an IT strategy committee would be: a board member as chairman, other board members, non-board independent members and ex-officio representation of key executives (ITGI, 2003). *CIO on board or member of executive management* is an indication of how important IT is considered within the organisation.

Figure 47. Operational excellence (Van Grembergen & De Haes, 2005)

Perspective	Operational Excellence	
Mission	Ensuring effective and sustained IT governance	
Objectives	*Structures*	
	Measures	Number of meetings of IT strategy committee and IT steering committees
		Composition of IT committees
		Overall attendance of IT committees
		CIO on board or member of executive management
	Processes	
	Measures	Level of IT strategy planning and business planning
		Number of hours spent on IT/business strategic issues
		Existence of an IT balanced scorecard and a business balanced scorecard
		Number of IT processes measured through a scorecard
		Number of IT processes covered by COBIT
		Number of IT processes covered by ITIL
		Maturity levels of IT processes
		Percentage of IT goals supported by IT processes
	Maturity	
	Measure	Overall level of the IT governance process maturity

The metric examples of the **processes** objective are focused on the level of and involvement in IT/business planning, the use of scorecards, the coverage by COBIT and ITIL, and the maturity levels of the IT processes. *Level of IT strategy planning and business planning* can be monitored by the effective use of strategic models such as the competitive forces model and the value chain of Porter (1998, 2001) and the strategic alignment model of Henderson and Venkatraman (1993). As already illustrated in previous section, the Balanced Scorecard can be an effective management instrument. The *existence of an IT balanced scorecard and a business balanced scorecard* is very supportive for achieving a linkage between IT and business objectives. Establishing such a cascade of scorecards with rolling-up and aggregating metrics of the IT scorecard in the business Balanced Scorecard may help to realise the ultimate link between IT and business. This cascade mechanism can also be used between the IT scorecard and scorecards on a lower level for the different IT processes (metric: *number of IT processes through a scorecard).* Outcome measures (key goal indicators) and performance drivers (key performance indicators) can be found in the management guidelines of COBIT (ITGI, 2005) for the 34 identified IT processes as well as the corresponding maturity models (metrics: *maturity levels of IT processes).* Based on a worldwide survey, it was found that the average maturity for the 34 COBIT IT processes was around 2.0 (Guldentops & De Haes, 2002). The control objectives of COBIT (ITGI, 2005) indicate what has to be accomplished for the different IT processes whereas other standards, such as the Information Technology Infrastructure Library, better known as ITIL (OGC, 2005), describe in detail how specific IT processes can be organised and managed. Regarding COBIT and ITIL two metrics are included: *number of IT processes covered by CO-BIT and ITIL. Percentage of IT goals supported by IT processes* is related to the corporate contribution measure "percentage of business goals supported by IT processes." A clear causal relationship between both metrics exists: if IT goals are not properly supported by IT processes, this may result in an insufficient IT support for the business. The operational excellence card concludes with an IT governance **maturity** evaluation. *Overall level of the IT governance process maturity* can be assessed through the IT governance maturity model of ITGI (2005). Such a maturity model provides a method for scoring that enables an organisation to grade itself from non-existent (level 0) to optimised (level 5). According to this model (see Figure 48), organisations that are situated in level zero are characterised by a complete lack of any recognisable IT governance process. To move up to level one, the organisation needs to at least recognise the importance of addressing

IT governance issues. Maturity level five at least implies an advanced and forward-looking understanding of IT governance issues and solutions, supported by an established framework and best practices of structures, processes and relational mechanisms. Maturity models such as the ITGI model and others such as the one developed by Luftman (2000), have to comply with the basic principles of maturity measurement: one can only go to a higher maturity when all conditions described in a certain level are fulfilled. The level that an organisation should target is of course dependent on the nature of the business: a business within the banking sector should probably strive to a higher IT governance level than a concrete factory.

Figure 48. IT governance maturity model (ITGI, 2003)

0 Non Existent. Complete lack of any recognisable processes. Organisation has not even recognised that there is an issue to be addressed.

1 Initial. There is evidence that the organisation has recognised that the issues exist and need to be addressed. There are, however, no standardised processes but instead there are ad hoc approaches that tend to be applied on an individual or case by case basis. The overall approach to management is chaotic.

2 Repeatable. Processes have developed to the stage where similar procedures are followed different people undertaking the same task. There is no formal training or communication of standard procedures and responsibility is left to the individual. There is a high degree of reliance on the knowledge of individuals and therefore errors are likely.

3 Defined. Procedures have been standardised and documented, and communicated through training. It is however left to the individual to follow these processes, and any deviations would be unlikely to be detected. The procedures themselves are not sophisticated but are the formalisation of existing practices.

4 Managed. It is possible to monitor and measure compliance with procedures and to take action where processes appear not to be working effectively. Processes are under constant improvement and provide good practice. Automation and tools are used in a limited or fragmented way.

5 Optimised. Processes have been refined to a level of best practice, based on the results of continuous improvement and maturity modelling with other organisations. IT is used in an integrated way to automate the workflow and provide tools to improve quality and effectiveness.

The **future orientation** scorecard reports on the building foundations for governance delivery focusing on relational mechanisms, the third leg of the IT governance tripod (Figure 19). Relational mechanisms, such as business/IT co-location, partnership rewards and incentives, shared understanding of business/IT objectives, cross-functional business/IT training, and cross-functional business/IT job rotation are of primordial importance. IT governance structures and processes may be in place, but when IT and business professionals do not understand each other and do not share the business/IT related problems, a successful fusion between both areas will not be achieved.   Implementing the right relational mechanisms will be the crucial enabler for better governance structures and processes (operational excellence perspective), higher stakeholders' satisfaction (stakeholder perspective), and ultimately a higher governance performance (corporate contribution perspective). Figure 49 displays the two distinct objectives of the future orientation perspective: skills and knowledge and IT/business partnership. Within the *skills and knowledge* area the cross-functional education and training metrics are predominant: *number and level of cross-functional business/IT training sessions, number of overall IT governance training sessions, percentage completed IT governance education per skill type.* A specific and important measure is the *number of IT governance presentations for CEO and board members* capturing the communication efforts between the IT management team and its business hierarchy. *Level and use of IT governance knowledge management system* refers to an intranet that all employees can access for seeking and sharing knowledge on the IT governance practices within the organisation. *IT/business partnership* objectives report on the IT and business literacy of respectively senior business managers (*percentage of senior manager IT literate*) and the IT team (*percentage of IT managers business literate*). The importance of these two metrics is confirmed by Teo and Ang's study (1999) where the knowledge ability of IT management and top executives concerning business and IT were found to be two crucial critical success factors in business/IT planning alignment. *Level of business perception of IT value* can be measured through scores indicating the level going from 1 (perceived as a cost) to 5 (IT seen as a driver/enabler) (Luftman, 2000).

The performance of the IT governance process can be visualised using this generic IT governance balanced scorecard. The corporate contribution perspective of this scorecard matches with the IT function's balance scorecard (Figure 32). Indeed, the ultimate goal for both scorecards is to obtain better corporate financial results. The main difference between both scorecards is

Figure 49. Future orientation (Van Grembergen & De Haes, 2005)

Perspective	Future Orientation	
Mission	Building foundations for IT governance delivery	
Objectives	***Skills and knowledge***	
	Measures	Number and level of cross-functional business/IT training sessions
		Number of overall IT governance training sessions
		Percentage completed IT governance education per skill type
		Number of IT governance presentations for CEO and board members
		Level and use of IT governance knowledge management system
	IT/business partnership	
	Measures	Percentage of senior managers IT literate
		Percentage of IT managers business literate
		Level of business perception of IT value

that the other perspectives focus completely on the IT governance process. Some of the metrics of the IT governance BSC will be, however, rolled-up and/or aggregated in the IT BSC. Additionally, the board BSC will certainly import some relevant IT governance measures. Improving the IT governance performance is the main reason for building and implementing an IT governance scorecard. It must be clear that just measuring is not enough; the scorecard must be implemented as a management system. When the measurements indicate that there are major problems with risk management (corporate contribution), a possible strategy may involve the improvement of the disaster recovery planning (DRP) through a COBIT and ITIL implementation of this process (operational excellence), which in turn may need a cross-sectional business/IT training in COBIT, ITIL and DRP (future orientation). With an IT governance balanced scorecard, organisations can empower their board, CEO, CIO, executive management, and the business and IT participants by providing them the necessary information to evaluate the IT governance success and act upon to achieve a better fusion between business and IT and consequently reach better results. In this sense, the IT governance scorecard can play an important role in an overall program that should be in place to enhance corporate governance. Currently, many organisations are introducing and implementing IT governance processes. Using this proposed generic IT governance BSC may help them to realise a successful implementation.

IT Governance Implementation Status

Previous sections provided various ways for aligning IT and business in the context of better IT governance. Let us now take a look at the actual status of IT governance implementation in today's businesses and the mechanisms, frameworks and best practices they have in place.

In a recent study, conducted by GAO (2005) the CIOs of 20 US leading private-sector organizations were interviewed about their responsibilities and about IT governance. The results were also compared with a similar study done earlier towards federal CIOs. In summary, most of the private-sector CIOs held responsibilities for nine of the 12 defined functional domains (Figure 50), with the top five responsibilities being: (1) systems acquisition, (2) IT capital planning, (3) information security, (4) IT human capital, and (5) e-commerce. Only in the areas of information dissemination and disclosure, information collection and statistical policy, fewer (half or less) CIOs held a responsibility. In most functional areas, there was little difference between the private and federal sectors. Only in the functional areas of enterprise architecture, strategic planning, information collection, and information dissemination and disclosure, the difference between the private- and federal-sector CIOs was greater; in each case, fewer CIOs in the private sector had these responsibilities.

In the same report the private-sector CIOs described four major challenges that they faced in their work:

- Aligning IT with business goals
- Implementation of new enterprise technologies
- Controlling IT costs and increasing efficiencies
- Ensuring data security and integrity

Aligning business and IT goals requires the development of IT plans that support the companies' business objectives. When asked to describe how the governance of information management and technology is carried out in their companies, 16 of the 20 private-sector CIOs reported they had an executive committee with the authority and responsibility for governing major IT investments. Some CIOs described using cross-organizational teams to drive broad collaborative efforts, such as the development and implementation of standards and enterprise wide business processes. Several spoke of the work they were doing in balancing between centralization and decentralization of their responsibilities and described their efforts to move between the two extremes while finding the right balance.

Another interesting benchmark is obtained from the "IT governance global status report" issued by the IT governance Institute and PricewaterhouseCoopers in 2006. This research was targeted to reach members of the C-suite (i.e., CEOs, CIOs, COOs, CFOs, and CTOs) to determine their sense of priority about IT governance and their needs for tools and services to help assure effective governance. Six hundred and ninety five interviews were

Figure 50. Comparison of the extent to which private-sector and federal CIOs are responsible for functional areas (GAO, 2005)

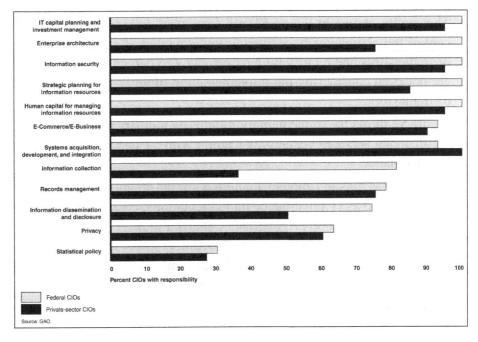

Figure 51. IT governance implementation status (ITGI, 2006c)

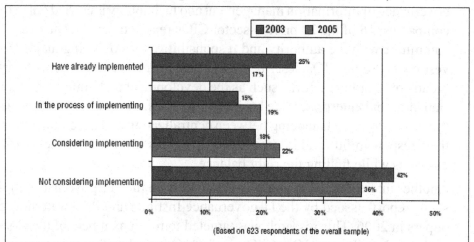

(Based on 623 respondents of the overall sample)

conducted from a random sample of companies with a representative distribution according to geography, size of the organisation, industry sector, and job function of the respondent.

The results, shown in Figure 51, are somewhat disappointing: only 17 percent of the companies have already implemented IT governance solutions or frameworks and a fairly high percentage (36 percent) of the respondents are not even considering the implementation of an IT governance solution or framework.

Figure 52 shows the implementation status by industry sector indicating that the financial services business is leading with 31 percent in implementing IT governance.

Some mechanisms and implementations within an organisation may not always be categorised as IT governance implementations, although in practice they do contribute to a good IT governance status. Figure 53 shows an overview of the implementation status of those 'partial' IT governance measures. As a result, this research found that only nine percent of the responding companies are not considering implementing any (partial) IT governance solution.

Figure 54 displays the IT governance frameworks which are selected by the

Figure 52. IT governance implementation status, by geographic region (ITGI, 2006c)

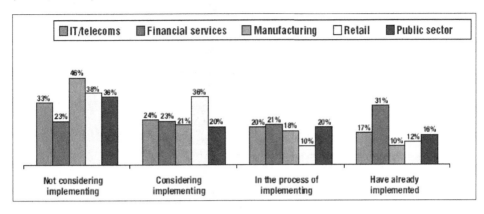

Figure 53. Implementation status of partial IT governance solutions (ITGI, 2006c)

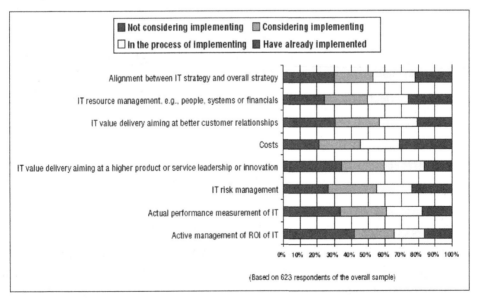

Figure 54. Selected IT governance framework (ITGI, 2006c)

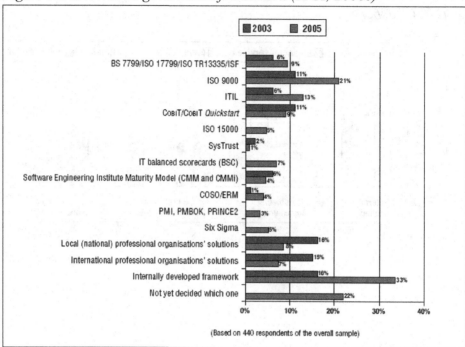

(Based on 440 respondents of the overall sample)

organizations that have implemented, are in the progress of implementing or are considering implementing an IT governance solution. About one-third of these companies use internally develop frameworks while the others use a variety of frameworks.

Conclusion

In this chapter, an overview of the definitions and different elements of IT governance was given, as well as its relationship with corporate governance and with IT management. A key element in IT governance is the alignment of the business and IT (strategic alignment) that must ultimately led to a better business value and/or better financial results. This high level goal can be achieved by acknowledging IT governance as a part of corporate governance and by setting up an IT governance framework with best practices. Such a framework and practices should be composed of a variety of structures, processes and relational mechanisms and what works for one organisation may not work for another organisation. Further, an approach for measuring the IT governance implementation process was described.

References

Bergeron, F., Raymond, L., & Rivard, S. (2003). Ideal patterns of strategic alignment and business performance. *Information & Management, 41*(8), 1003-1020.

Burn, J.M., & Szeto, C. (2000). A comparison of the views of business and IT management on success factors for strategic alignment. *Information & Management, 37*(4), 197-216.

Broadbent, M., & Weill, P. (1998). *Leveraging the new infrastructure: How market leaders capitalize on information technology.* Boston: Harvard Business School Press.

Brynjolfsson, E. (1993). The productivity paradox of information technology. *Communications of the ACM, 36*(12).

Brynjolfsson, E., & Hitt, L.M. (1998). Beyond the productivity paradox. *Communications of the ACM, 41*(8).

Callahan, J., & Keyes, D. (2003). The evolution of IT Governance at NB Power. In W. Van Grembergen (Ed.), *Strategies for information technology governance.* Hershey, PA: Idea Group Publishing.

Carr, N.G. (2003). IT doesn't matter. *Harvard Business Review, 81*(5), 41-49.

Croteau, A.M., & Bergeron, F. (2001). An information technology trilogy: Business strategy, technological deployment and organizational performance. *Journal of Strategic Information Systems, 10,* 77-99.

Duffy, J. (2002a). *IT/Business alignment: Is it an option or is it mandatory?* IDC document # 26831, IT and Business Alignment Advisory service.

Duffy, J. (2002b). *IT Governance and Business Value Part 1: IT Governance — An issue of critical importanc.* IDC document # 27291.

Duffy, J. (2002c). *IT governance and business value Part 2: Who's responsible for what?* IDC document # 27807.

Dutta, S. (1996). Linking IT and business strategy: The role and responsibility of senior management. *European Management Journal, 14*(3), 255-268.

Earl, J.M. (1993). Experiences in strategic information systems planning. *MIS Quarterly, 17*(1), 1-24.

Epstein, M.J., & Roy, M.J. (2004). How does your board rate? Now you can use a balanced scorecard to measure and improve corporate board performance. *Strategic Finance, February*, 25-31.

Evans, B. (2003). Business technology: IT is a must, no matter how you view it. *Information Week, May 19*, 74.

Feurer, R., Chaharbaghi, K., Weber, M., & Wargin, J. (2000). Aligning strategies, processes and IT: A case study. *Information Systems Management*, 23-34.

GAO (2005). *Chief information, responsibilities and information and technology governance at leading private-sector companies.* Retrieved from www.gao.gov

Guldentops, E. (2003). Governing information technology through COBIT. In W. Van Grembergen (Ed.), *Strategies for information technology governance*. Hershey, PA: Idea Group Publishing

Guldentops, E., & De Haes, S. (2002). COBIT 3rd Edition usage survey: Growing acceptance of COBIT. *Information Systems Control Journal, 6.*

Guldentops, E., Van Grembergen, W., & De Haes, S. (2002). Control and governance maturity survey: establishing a reference benchmark and a self-assessment tool. *Information Systems Control Journal, 6.*

Hammer, M., & Champy, J. (1993). *Reengineering the corporation. A manifesto for business revolution.* New York: Harper Business.

Hatzakis, T. (2004). *A social capital approach to IT relationship management evaluation.* Proceedings of the 37th Hawaii International Conference on System Sciences (HICSS).

Henderson, J.C., & Venkatraman, N. (1993). Strategic alignment: leveraging information technology for transforming organizations. *IBM Systems Journal, 32*(1).

Henderson, J.C., Venkatraman, N., & Oldach, S. (1993). Continuous strategic alignment: Exploiting iformation technology capabilities for competitive success. *European Management Journal, 11*(2), 139-149.

Hirschheim, R., & Sabherwal, R. (2001). Detours in the path toward strategic information systems alignment. *California Management Review, 44*(1), 86-108.

ITGI (2003). *Board briefing on IT governance* (2nd ed.). www.itgi.org

ITGI (2005). *COBIT 4.0*. Retrieved from www.itgi.org

ITGI (2006a). *Enterprise value: Governanace of IT investments, The Val IT framework.* Retrieved from www.itgi.org

ITGI (2006b). *Enterprise value: Governance of IT investments. The Business case*. Retrieved from www.itgi.org

ITGI (2006c). *IT Governance Global Status Report*. Report published by ITGI and PriceWaterhouseCoopers. Retrieved from www.itgi.org

ITGI (2006d). *IT control objectives for Sarbanes-Oxley* (2nd ed.). Retrieved from www.itgi.org

ITGI (2006e). *COBIT mapping: Overview of international IT guidance* (2nd ed.). Retrieved from www.itgi.org

Kakabadse, N. K., & Kakabadse, A. (2001). IS/IT governance: Need for an integrated model. *Corporate Governance, 1*(9), 9-11.

Kaplan, R., & Norton, D. (1992). The balanced scorecard: Measures that drive performance. *Harvard Business Review, 70*(1), 71-79.

Kaplan, R., & Norton, D. (1996). *The balanced scorecard: Translation vision into action*. Boston: Harvard Business School Press.

Lie, C. L. (2001). Modelling the business value of information technology. *Information & Management, 39*(2), 191-210.

Luftman, J. (2000). Assessing business-IT alignment maturity. *Communications of AIS, 4*(14).

Luftman, J. (2002). Achieving Alignment Détente. *CIO Insight, July.* Retrieved from http://www.cioinsight.com/article2/0,3959,325354,00.asp

Luftman, J., & Brier, T. (1999). Achieving and sustaining business-IT alignment. *California Management Review, 42*(1), 109-122.

Maes R. (1999). *Reconsidering information management through a generic framework*. PrimaVera Working Paper (pp. 99-15).

Miles, R.E., & Snow, C.C. (1978). *Organizational strategy, structure and process*. New York: McGraw-Hill.

Nolan, R., & McFarlan, F.W. (2005). Information technology and the board of directors. *Harvard Business Review, 83*(10), 96-106.

OGC (Office of Government Commerce). *About ITIL*. Retrieved May 2005, from www.ogc.gov.uk

Parker, M. (1995). *Strategic transformation and information technology*. London: Prentice Hall.

Parker, M., Benson, R., & Trainor, H. (1988). *Information economics: Linking business performance to information technology*. London: Prentice Hall.

Patel, N.V. (2003). An emerging strategy for e-business IT Governance. In W. Van Grembergen (Ed.), *Strategies for information technology governance*. Hershey, PA: Idea Group Publishing.

Peterson, R. R. (2003). Information strategies and tactics for information technology governance. In W. Van Grembergen (Ed.), *Strategies for information technology governance*. Hershey, PA: Idea Group Publishing.

Porter, M. (1985). *Competitive advantage: Creating and sustaining superior performance*. New York: Free Press.

Porter, M. (2001). Strategy and the internet. *Harvard Business Review, 79*(3), 62-78.

Reich, B. H., & Benbasat, I. (2000). Factors that influence the social dimension of alignment between business and information technology objectives. *MIS Quarterly, March*, 81-113.

Ribbers, P., Peterson, R., & Parker, M. (2002). *Designing information technology governance processes: Diagnosing contemporary practises and competing theories*. Proceedings of the 35th Hawaii International Conference on System Sciences (HICSS).

Rockart, J. (1979). Chief executives define their own data needs. *Harvard Business Review, 57*(2), 81-93.

Rockart, J. (1982). The changing role of the information systems executive: A critical success factors perspective. *Sloan Management Review, 245*(1).

Rockart, J.F., Earl, M.J., & Ross, J.W. (1996). Eight imperatives for the new IT organization: Guidelines for IT managers who are trying to respond to business and technological changes, assume new roles, and build relationships with line managers. *Sloan Management Review*, *38*(1), 43-55.

Ross, J.W., & Weill, P. (2002). Six IT decisions your IT people shouldn't make. *Harvard Business Review*, *80*(11), 84-92.

Sabherwal, R., & Chan, Y. (2001). Alignment between business and IS strategies: A study of prospectors, analyzers and defenders. *Information Systems Research*, *12*(1), 11-33.

Sambamurthy, V., & Zmud, R.W. (1999). Arrangements for information technology governance: A theory of multiple contingencies. *MIS Quarterly*, *23*(2), 261-290.

Shleifer, A., & Vishny, W. (1997). A survey on corporate governance. *The Journal of Finance*, *52*(2).

Smaczny, T. (2001). Is an alignment between business and information technology the appropriate paradigm to manage IT in today's organizations? *Management Decisions*, *39*(10), 797-802.

Sohal, A.S., & Fitzpatrick, P. (2002). IT governance and management in large Australian organisations. *International Journal of Production Economics*, *75*, 97-112.

Strassman, P. (1990). *The business value of computers*. New Canaan, CT: The Information Economics Press.

Teo, S.H.T., & Ang, J.S.K. (1999). Critical success factors in the alignment of IS plans with business plans. *International Journal of Information Management*, *19*, 173-185.

Van Der Zee, J.T.M., & De Jong, B. (1999). Alignment is not enough: Integrating business and information technology management with the balanced business scorecard. *Journal of Management Information Systems*, *16*(2), 137-156.

Van Grembergen, W. (2000). The balanced scorecard and IT governance. *Information Systems Control Journal*, *2*.

Van Grembergen, W. (2002). *Introduction to the minitrack: IT governance and its mechanisms*. In Proceedings of the 35th Hawaii International Conference on System Sciences (HICSS).

Van Grembergen, W., & Amelinckx, I. (2003). Measuring and managing e-business initiatives through the balanced scorecard. In W. Van Grembergen (Ed.), *Strategies for information technology governance*. Hershey, PA: Idea Group Publishing.

Van Grembergen, W., & Van Bruggen, R. (1997). *Measuring and improving corporate information technology through the balanced scorecard technique*. In Proceedings of the European Conference on the Evaluation of Information Technology, Delft, The Netherlands.

Van Grembergen, W., & De Haes, S. (2005). Measuring and improving IT governance through the balanced scorecard. *Information Systems Control Journal, 2*.

Van Grembergen, W., De Haes, S., & Amelinckx, I. (2003). Using COBIT and the balanced scorecard as instruments for service level management. *Information Systems Control Journal, 4*.

Van Grembergen, W., De Haes, S., & Guldentops, E. (2003). Structures, processes and relational mechanisms for IT governance. In W. Van Grembergen (Ed.), *Strategies for information technology hovernance*. Hershey, PA: Idea Group Publishing.

Van Grembergen, W., De Haes, S., & Moons, J. (2005). IT Governance: linking business goals to IT goals and COBIT processes. *Information Systems Control Journal, 4*.

Van Grembergen, W., Kritis V., & Van Belle, J.-L. (1997). *Bedrijfsveranderingen met informatietechnologie (Business transformations through information technology)*. The Netherlands: Kluwer, Deventer.

Van Grembergen, W., Saull, R., & De Haes, S. (2003). Linking the IT Balanced scorecard to the Business Objectives at a major Canadian Financial Group. *Journal for Information Technology Cases and Applications (JITCA), 5*(1).

Venkatraman, N. (1999). *Valuing the IS contribution to the business*. Computer Sciences Corporation.

Weill, P., & Ross, J. (2004). *IT governance: How top performers manage IT decision rights for superior results*. Boston: Harvard Business School Press.

Weill, P., & Woodham, R. (2002). *Don't just lead, govern: Implementing effective IT governance*. (CISR WP No. 326). Cambridge, MA: MIT Sloan School of Management.

- *Confidentiality* concerns the protection of sensitive information from unauthorised disclosure.

- *Integrity* relates to the accuracy and completeness of information, as well as to its validity in accordance with business values and expectations.

- *Availability* relates to information being available when required by the business process now and in the future. It also concerns the safeguarding of necessary resources and associated capabilities.

- *Compliance* deals with complying with those laws, regulations, and contractual arrangements to which the business process is subject, that is, externally imposed business criteria, as well as internal policies.

- *Reliability* relates to the provision of appropriate information for management to operate the entity and exercise its fiduciary and governance responsibilities.

Because these criteria are generic they can be applied in each organisation. On the other hand, the definitions may be too abstract, making it more difficult to translate the information criteria to a specific situation. In the context of further COBIT development, a more comprehensive research is conducted together with the University of Antwerp Management School (UAMS) in order to obtain a better view on business goals and IT goals and the way they support one another.

Based on this research, conducted in eight different industry segments, a set of generic business and IT goals was identified and an analysis was done how they are linked to each other.

Figure 1 presents a matrix on how IT goals can support the achievement of business goals for companies in the financial sector: "P" represents a primary link and "S" a secondary link. This figure shows for example that the IT goal "developing innovative IT services with a focus on information security" is important in supporting the business goals "improving competitiveness through IT" and "improving customer orientation and service."

This research resulted in the definition of 20 generic business goals and 28 generic IT goals that now serve as a base for COBIT 4.0 (see Figures 2 and 3). When combining both figures, they illustrate the relationship between business goals, IT goals, and IT processes. Figure 2 lists the 20 generic business goals, organised according the four perspectives of the business balanced scorecard, being *financial perspective, customer perspective, internal per-*

Figure 1. Linking business and IT goals in the financial sector (Van Grembergen, De Haes, & Moons, 2005)

Business Goals	Developing innovative IT services with a focus on information security	Fulfilling SLAs with business departments	Increasing IT department efficiency	Integration and consolidation of different IT departments	IT disaster recovery and business continuity	IT governance	IT strategic alignment	Lowering cost of transaction processing	Making IT measurable	Optimizing the IT infrastructure	Rapid development of new IT services	Reduce amount of IT insourcing	Standardizing IT systems	Tailoring IT measures to satisfy Basel II requirements
Achieving compliance with Basel II regulations				S									P	
Improving competitiveness through IT	P							S	P					
Improving customer orientation and service	P	S	P	S			P	S						
Post-merger integration and				P				S		S	S			
Reducing operational cost		P	P	S		P	P	P		P	P			
Reducing transaction cost		P	S			P	P	S			S			
Risk management	S	P	S	S	P		S			P	S			
Shortening service development							S		P					
Tailoring solutions for different target groups	P													

Figure 2. Business goals and IT goals (ITGI, 2005)

	Business Goals	IT Goals								Effectiveness	Efficiency	Confidentiality	Integrity	Availability	Compliance	Reliability
Financial Perspective 1	Expand market share.	25	28							✔	✔					
2	Increase revenue.	25	28							✔	✔					
3	Return on investment	24									✔					
4	Optimise asset utilisation.	14								✔	✔					
5	Manage business risks.	2	14	17	18	19	20	21	22				✔	✔		✔
Customer Perspective 6	Improve customer orientation and service.	3	23							✔						
7	Offer competitive products and services.	5	24							✔	✔					
8	Service availability	10	16	22	23					✔				✔		
9	Agility in responding to changing business requirements (time to market)	1	5	25						✔	✔					
10	Cost optimisation of service delivery	7	8	10	24						✔					
Internal Perspective 11	Automate and integrate the enterprise value chain.	6	7	8	11					✔	✔					
12	Improve and maintain business process functionality.	6	7	11						✔	✔					
13	Lower process costs.	7	8	13	15	24					✔					
14	Compliance with external laws and regulations.	2	19	20	21	22	26	27					✔		✔	
15	Transparency	2	18													✔
16	Compliance with internal policies	2	13										✔		✔	
17	Improve and maintain operational and staff productivity.	7	8	11	13					✔	✔					
Learning and Growth Perspective 18	Product/business innovation	5	25	28						✔	✔					
19	Obtain reliable and useful information for strategic decision making.	2	4	12	20	26				✔				✔		✔
20	Acquire and maintain skilled and motivated personnel.	9								✔	✔					

spective, and *learning and growth perspective.* Each business goal is linked to one or more IT goals that support the business goal. These are indicated by numbers, representing the IT goals of Figure 3.

For example, the IT goal *"ensure the satisfaction of end users with service offerings and service levels"* (3) supports the business goal *"improve customer orientation and service."* Additionally, for each business goal, the most relevant information criteria are indicated. The relevant information criteria for IT goals can be found in Figure 3, together with the IT processes, that support the IT goal. These are indicated with the process indices, explained later in the chapter. For example, the IT process DS1, which stands for *"define and manage service levels,"* may help achieving the aforementioned IT goal *"ensure the satisfaction of end users with service offerings and service levels."* In this way a cascade is formed from business goals to IT goals to IT processes.

Further, COBIT refers to four IT related resources that can be applied:

- *Information* refers to the data in all their forms handled by the information systems, in whatever form is used by the business.

Figure 3. IT goals and IT processes (ITGI, 2005)

IT Goals	Processes	Effectiveness	Efficiency	Confidentiality	Integrity	Availability	Compliance	Reliability
1 Respond to business requirements in alignment with the business strategy.	PO1 PO2 PO4 PO10 AI1 AI6 AI7 DS1 DS3 ME1	P	P		S	S		
2 Respond to governance requirements in line with board direction.	PO1 PO4 PO10 ME1 ME3	P	P					
3 Ensure the satisfaction of end users with service offerings and service levels.	PO8 AI4 DS1 DS2 DS7 DS8 DS10 DS13	P	P		S	S		
4 Optimise the use of information.	PO2 DS11			S	P			S
5 Create IT agility.	PO2 PO4 PO7 AI3	P	P		S			
6 Define how business functional and control requirements are translated in effective and efficient automated solutions.	AI1 AI2 AI6	P	P				S	
7 Acquire and maintain integrated and standardised application systems.	PO3 AI2 AI5	P	P				S	
8 Acquire and maintain an integrated and standardised IT infrastructure.	AI3 AI5	S	P					
9 Acquire and maintain IT skills that respond to the IT strategy.	PO7 AI5	P	P					
10 Ensure mutual satisfaction of third-party relationships.	DS2	P	P	S	S	S	S	S
11 Seamlessly integrate applications and technology solutions into business processes.	PO2 AI4 AI7	P	P		S	S		
12 Ensure transparency and understanding of IT cost, benefits, strategy, policies and service levels.	PO5 PO6 DS1 DS2 DS6 ME1 ME3	P	P				S	S
13 Ensure proper use and performance of the applications and technology solutions.	PO6 AI4 AI7 DS7 DS8	P	S					
14 Account for and protect all IT assets.	PO9 DS5 DS9 DS12 ME2	S	S	P	P	P	S	S
15 Optimise the IT infrastructure, resources and capabilities.	PO3 AI3 DS3 DS7 DS9	S	P					
16 Reduce solution and service delivery defects and rework.	PO8 AI4 AI6 AI7 DS10	P	P		S	S		
17 Protect the achievement of IT objectives.	PO9 DS10 ME2	P	P	S	S	S	S	S
18 Establish clarity of business impact of risks to IT objectives and resources.	PO9	S	S	P	P	P	S	S
19 Ensure critical and confidential information is withheld from those who should not have access to it.	PO6 DS5 DS11 DS12			P	P	S	S	S
20 Ensure automated business transactions and information exchanges can be trusted.	PO6 AI7 DS5	P			P	S	S	S
21 Ensure IT services and infrastructure can properly resist and recover from failures due to error, deliberate attack or disaster.	PO6 AI7 DS4 DS5 DS12 DS13 ME2	P	S		S	P		
22 Ensure minimum business impact in the event of an IT service disruption or change.	PO6 AI6 DS4 DS12	P	S		S	P		
23 Make sure that IT services are available as required.	DS3 DS4 DS8 DS13	P	P			P		
24 Improve IT's cost-efficiency and its contribution to business profitability.	PO5 AI5 DS6	S	P					S
25 Deliver projects on time and on budget meeting quality standards.	PO8 PO10	P	P		S			S
26 Maintain the integrity of information and processing infrastructure.	AI6 DS5	P	P		P	P		S
27 Ensure IT compliance with laws and regulations.	DS11 ME2 ME3 ME4			S	S		P	S
28 Ensure that IT demonstrates cost-efficient service quality, continuous improvement and readiness for future change.	PO5 DS6 ME1 ME3	P	P					P

- *Applications* are the automated user systems and manual procedures that process the information.

- *Infrastructure* includes the technology and facilities (hardware, operating systems, database management systems, networking, multimedia, etc., and the environment that houses and supports them) that enable the processing of the applications.

- *People* refers to the personnel required to plan, organise, acquire, implement, deliver, support, monitor, and evaluate the information systems and services.

The previous edition of COBIT refers to a fifth element, being *facilities*, which is now incorporated into the *infrastructure* resource.

Following the COBIT framework, information retrieved from IT systems is the result of a combined effort of IT related resources, managed by IT processes. It is important that IT processes are managed and controlled in an effective way, so that the delivered information satisfies the defined quality standards.

COBIT 4.0 defines 34 IT processes, categorised into four domains: planning and organisation, acquisition and implementation, delivery and support, and monitoring and evaluation (Figure 4).

The domain "*Planning and organisation*" concerns the identification of the way IT can best contribute to the achievement of the business objectives. Therefore it needs strategy and tactics for the information architecture, technology architecture, a good structured IT organisation, budget control and management, the way management objectives are communicated (such as awareness around security), IT human resource management, quality management, risk assessment and risk management, and project management.

The domain "*Acquisition and implementation*" is concerned with the identification of IT solutions (insourcing or outsourcing), the acquisition and/or development and maintenance of software applications, the acquisition and maintenance of hardware and system software, the production of documentation and training of users, the acquisition of the necessary IT, the process for managing application changes, and installing and accrediting solutions and changes.

The domain "*Delivery and support*" is concerned with the actual delivery of required services and contains those processes that deal with configuration management, problem management, data management, management of the

Figure 4. Thirty four IT processes of COBIT 4.0 (ITGI, 2005)

Planning and organisation (PO)	*Delivery and support (DS)*
PO1. define a strategic IT plan	DS1. define and manage service levels
PO2. define the information architecture	DS2. manage third party services
PO3. determine technological direction	DS3. manage performance and capacity
PO4. define the IT processes, organisation, and relationships	DS4. ensure continuous service
PO5. manage the IT investment	DS5. ensure systems security
PO6.communicate management aims and direction	DS6. identify and allocate costs
PO7. manage IT human resources	DS7. educate and train users
PO8. manage quality	DS8. manage service desk and incidents
PO9. assess and manage risk	DS9. manage the configuration
PO10. manage projects	DS10. manage problems
	DS11. manage data
	DS12. manage the physical environment
	DS13.manage operations
Acquisition and implementation (AI)	*Monitor and evaluate (ME)*
AI1. identify automated solutions	ME1. monitor and evaluate IT performance
AI2. acquire and maintain application software	ME2. monitor and evaluate internal control
AI3. acquire and maintain technology infrastructure	ME3. ensure regulatory compliance
AI4. enable operation and use	ME4. provide IT governance
AI5. procure IT resources	
AI6. manage changes	
AI7. install and accredit solutions and changes	

physical environment (data centre and other facilities), computer operations management and performance and capacity management of the hardware. This domain also holds the definition of service level agreements (SLAs) and the management of third party vendors, like outsourcers, the assurance for continuous service (like a disaster recovery plan), security management, the identification and allocation of costs, education and training of users and the support and assistance for end-users by means of a service desk.

The fourth domain, *"Monitor and evaluate,"* includes those processes that are responsible for the quality assessment in compliance with the control

Figure 5. Overall COBIT framework (ITGI, 2005)

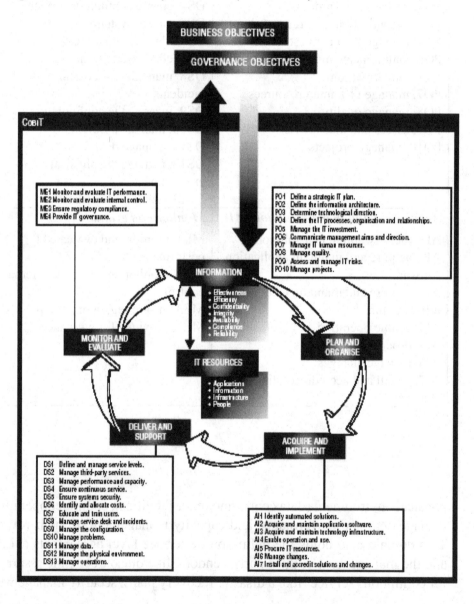

requirements for all previous mentioned processes. It addresses performance management, monitoring of internal control, regulatory compliance, and providing governance.

Figure 5 summarises the overall COBIT framework graphically. The organisation defines the business and governance objectives, directly impacting the quality requirements of the IT information criteria. While managing the IT resources, the 34 generic IT processes, organised in four domains, can deliver the information to the business according the business and governance objectives.

For each of the 34 processes the COBIT framework defines control objectives, management guidelines, and a maturity model. Within the COBIT 4.0 publication each process is typically described over four pages: two pages detailing the (high-level and detailed) control objectives, one page describing the management guidelines and one page for the maturity model. The following sections will further explore these different COBIT components.

COBIT Control Objectives

For each of the 34 processes, COBIT describes control objectives. These control objectives can help the IT process owners to build a proper control system into the IT environment. An IT control objective is a statement of the desired result or purpose to be achieved by implementing control procedures in a particular IT activity. COBIT's control objectives are the minimum requirements for effective control of each IT process. A good control comprises procedures, policies, practices, and organisational structures designed to provide reasonable assurance that business objectives are achieved and undesired events are prevented or detected and corrected.

COBIT defines one high-level control objective and several detailed control objectives for each process. It is important to note that in COBIT 4.0 the control objectives are much better aligned with best practices for IT governance and other industry standards, such as ITIL, ISO17799 and others. For instance processes DS8 *manage service desk and incidents* and DS10—*manage problems* is aligned with ITIL. Furthermore, the control objectives have been written in a more active format and as such they can be seen as more detailed process steps within the global IT process. Finally, the list of detailed control objectives has been rationalised resulting in a shorter, more practical list of

Figure 6. COBIT 4.0 process controls (ITGI, 2005)

PC1 Process Owner
PC2 Repeatability
PC3 Goals and Objectives
PC4 Roles and Responsibilities
PC5 Process Performance
PC6 Policy, Plans and Procedures

215 detailed objectives against 318 in the previous edition. Two remarks are important to note with respect to this rationalisation:

All generic detailed control objectives from COBIT 3.0 have been removed. These generic objectives have been defined in COBIT 4.0 as *process controls (PC)* (see Figure 6) and together with the remaining detailed control objectives they provide a complete view of control requirements. These process controls deal with the importance of having a process owner identified, of making a process repeatable, of describing goals, objectives, roles and responsibilities, of measuring and managing performance, and of defining policies, plans and procedures.

From process DS11—*manage data*, all detailed control objectives that could be categorised as an application control (AC) were removed. These controls are not supposed to fall under IT responsibility and therefore in COBIT 4.0 they are no longer defined on process level (DS11). They are still explained in the introductory chapters of the COBIT 4.0 publication as a set of recommended application controls for integration into the business processes. They typically address data origination and authorization controls, data input controls, data processing controls, data output controls, and boundary controls (see Figure 7).

As a result, COBIT 4.0 defines 34 *high-level* control objectives and 214 detailed control objectives. As an example, Figure 8 presents the high-level control objective of process DS1—*define and manage service levels*.

It gives a one-page summary of the process by describing the IT/business goals it supports (*that satisfies the business requirements for IT of*), its most important goals (*is achieved by*), different important activities (*is managed*

Figure 7. COBIT 4.0 application controls (ITGI, 2005)

Data Origination/Authorisation Controls
>   AC1 Data Preparation Procedures
>   AC2 Source Document Authorisation Procedures
>   AC3 Source Document Data Collection
>   AC4 Source Document Error Handling
>   AC5 Source Document Retention

Data Input Controls
>   AC6 Data Input Authorisation Procedures
>   AC7 Accuracy, Completeness, and Authorisation
>   Checks
>   AC8 Data Input Error Handling

Data Processing Controls
>   AC9 Data Processing Integrity
>   AC10 Data Processing Validation and Editing.
>   AC11 Data Processing Error Handling

Data Output Controls
>   AC12 Output Handling and Retention
>   AC13 Output Distribution
>   AC14 Output Balancing and Reconciliation
>   AC15 Output Review and Error Handling
>   AC16 Security Provision for Output Reports

Boundary Controls
>   AC17 Authenticity and Integrity
>   AC18 Protection of Sensitive Information During
>   Transmission and Transport

by) and some metrics that can be applied for its monitoring (*and is measured by*). These high-level control objectives together with the others are derived from the aforementioned research on generic business and IT goals.

An overview of the detailed control objectives for process DS1 can be found in Figure 9. The control objectives for this process emphasises the importance of the existence of a service level management framework, the definition of services and the SLA. Additionally the SLAs should be further worked

Figure 8. High-level control objective for DS1: Define and manage service levels (ITGI, 2005)

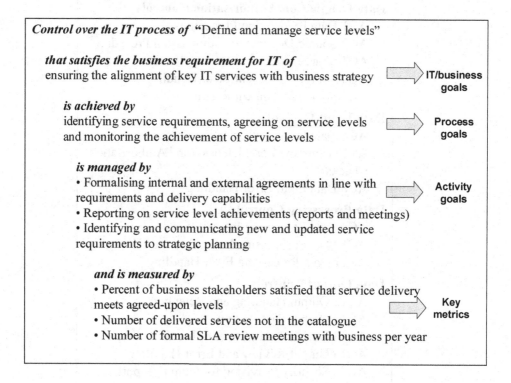

> **Control over the IT process of** "Define and manage service levels"
>
> > **that satisfies the business requirement for IT of**
> > ensuring the alignment of key IT services with business strategy — **IT/business goals**
> >
> > > **is achieved by**
> > > identifying service requirements, agreeing on service levels and monitoring the achievement of service levels — **Process goals**
> > >
> > > > **is managed by**
> > > > • Formalising internal and external agreements in line with requirements and delivery capabilities — **Activity goals**
> > > > • Reporting on service level achievements (reports and meetings)
> > > > • Identifying and communicating new and updated service requirements to strategic planning
> > > >
> > > > > **and is measured by**
> > > > > • Percent of business stakeholders satisfied that service delivery meets agreed-upon levels — **Key metrics**
> > > > > • Number of delivered services not in the catalogue
> > > > > • Number of formal SLA review meetings with business per year

out into operational level agreements containing the more technical aspects. Finally, performance, control and reporting procedures must be integrated and all agreements should be reviewed on regular basis.

COBIT Management Guidelines

The management guidelines in COBIT 4.0 deliver more information for organising, measuring, and controlling a specific process. Compared to the previous edition, some important elements are added:

Figure 9. Detailed control objectives for DS1: Define and manage service levels (ITGI, 2005)

DS1.1 Service Level Management Framework
Define a framework that provides a formalised service level management process between the customer and service provider. The framework maintains continuous alignment with business requirements and priorities and facilitates common understanding between the customer and provider(s). The framework includes processes for creating service requirements, service definitions, SLAs, operating level agreements (OLAs), and funding sources. These attributes are organised in a service catalogue. The framework defines the organisational structure for service level management, covering the roles, tasks, and responsibilities of internal and external service providers and customers.

DS1.2 Definition of Services
Base definitions of IT services on service characteristics and business requirements, organised and stored centrally via the implementation of a service catalogue/portfolio approach.

DS1.3 Service Level Agreements
Define and agree service level agreements for all critical IT services based on customer requirements and IT capabilities. This covers customer commitments, service support requirements, quantitative and qualitative metrics for measuring the service signed off by the stakeholders, funding and commercial arrangements if applicable, and roles and responsibilities, including oversight of the SLA. Items to consider are availability, reliability, performance, capacity for growth, levels of support, continuity planning, security, and demand constraints.

DS1.4 Operating Level Agreements
Ensure that operating level agreements explain how the services will be technically delivered to support the SLA(s) in an optimal manner. The OLAs specify the technical processes in terms meaningful to the provider and may support several SLAs.

DS1.5 Monitoring and Reporting of Service Level Achievements
Continuously monitor specified service level performance criteria. Reports are provided in a format meaningful to the stakeholders on achievement of service levels. The monitoring statistics are analysed and acted upon to identify negative and positive trends for individual services as well as for services overall.

DS1.6 Review of Service Level Agreements and Contracts
Regularly review service level agreements and underpinning contracts with internal and external service providers to ensure that they are effective, up to date, and that changes in requirements have been accounted for.

- The inter-relationship between the different IT processes, by means of *inputs* and *outputs* (in COBIT 3.0 this was a part of the critical success factors)

- An overview of important process tasks, including related roles and responsibilities (in COBIT 3.0 this was also a part of critical success factors)

- Goals and metrics on IT level, IT process level and IT process activity level

The management guidelines are summarized on one page (see Figure 10), comprising for each COBIT process: inputs and outputs, roles and responsibilities in the form of a RACI diagram *(Responsible, Accountable, Consulted, and Informed)* and an overview of metrics defined on different levels. These components are further detailed below.

Figure 10. COBIT 4.0 management guidelines (ITGI, 2005)

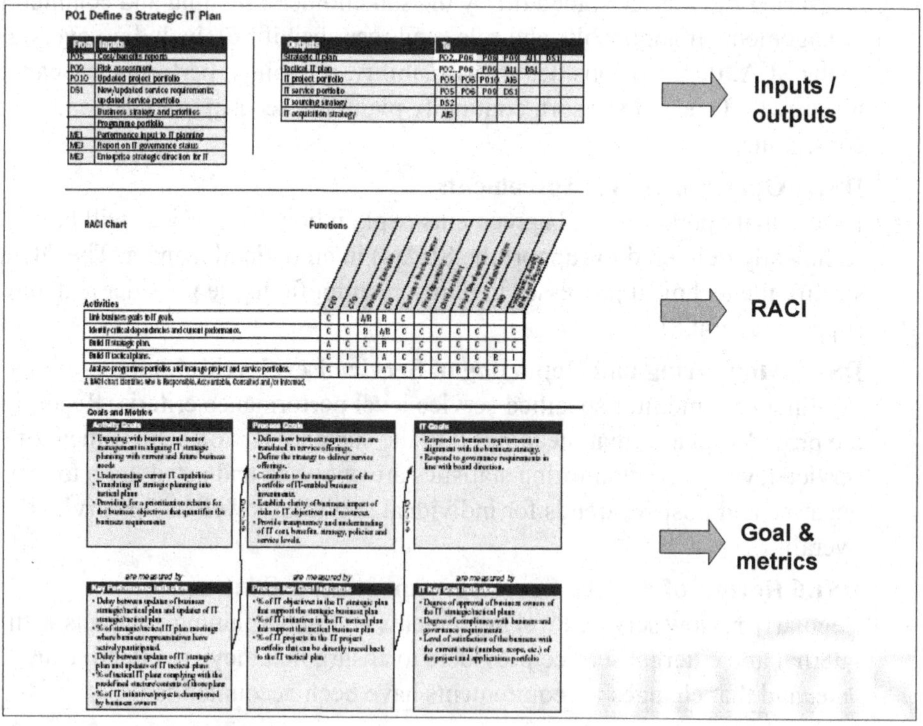

Figure 11. Input/outputs for PO1: Define a strategic IT plan (ITGI, 2005)

PO1 Define a Strategic IT Plan

From	Inputs
PO5	Cost/benefits reports
PO9	Risk assessment
PO10	Updated project portfolio
DS1	New/updated service requirements; updated service portfolio
	Business strategy and priorities
	Programme portfolio
ME1	Performance input to IT planning
ME3	Report on IT governance status
ME3	Enterprise strategic direction for IT

Outputs	To					
Strategic IT plan	PO2...PO6	PO8	PO9	AI1	DS1	
Tactical IT plan	PO2...PO6	PO9	AI1	DS1		
IT project portfolio	PO5	PO6	PO10	AI6		
IT service portfolio	PO5	PO6	PO9	DS1		
IT sourcing strategy	DS2					
IT acquisition strategy	AI5					

Inputs/Outputs

For each process, COBIT defines a list of inputs the process should receive from other processes and a list of possible outputs to send to other processes. For example process PO1—*define a strategic IT plan* (Figure 11), should receive a cost/benefits report from process PO5—*manage the IT investment*. The process PO1 itself should send strategic and tactical IT plans to several other processes.

RACI Diagram

COBIT defines for each process a RACI diagram, where the role and responsibilities related to important process activities are identified. RACI stands for:

- *Responsible*: Who is responsible for the activity
- *Accountable*: Who is accountable for the activity, meaning who provides direction and authorises the activity (is typically hierarchically higher than *responsible)*
- *Consulted*: Who should be consulted for the activity
- *Informed*: Who must be informed about the activity

Figure 12. Roles and responsibilities (RACI diagram) for PO1: Define a strategic IT plan (ITGI, 2005)

RACI Chart Activities	CEO	CFO	Business Executive	CIO	Business Process Owner	Head Operations	Chief Architect	Head Development	Head IT Administration	PMO	Compliance, Audit, Risk and Security
Link business goals to IT goals.	C	I	A/R	R	C						
Identify critical dependencies and current performance.	C	C	R	A/R	C	C	C	C	C		C
Build IT strategic plan.	A	C	C	R	I	C	C	C	C	I	C
Build IT tactical plans.	C	I		A	C	C	C	C	C	R	I
Analyse programme portfolios and manage project and service portfolios.	C	I	I	A	R	R	C	R	C	C	I

A RACI chart identifies who is Responsible, Accountable, Consulted and/or Informed.

For the example process PO1—*define a strategic IT plan*, it seems that especially the business executives together with the CIO are responsible for linking business goals to IT goals (Figure 12).

Goals and Metrics

For each of the 34 IT processes, COBIT defines goals on three levels (see Figure 13). IT goals are located at the level of the IT department, the highest level within COBIT for defining goals (the business goals are not retained because they are often very similar to the IT goals). On a second level, process goals are defined for the IT process itself and fall under the responsibilities of the process owner. And finally activity goals are identified on the level of activities defined within the process. Clearly, achieving activity goals must support the achievement of process goals, which in turn must support the achievement of IT goals.

In order to monitor all these goals, metrics are defined for each of them. It is important to note there are two distinct metrics: key goal indicators and key performance indicators.

Key goal indicators (outcome measures in balanced scorecard terminology) are known as *lag indicators* and they measure the achievement of the defined goals. Two levels of key goal indicators (KGIs) are known within COBIT:

Figure 13. COBIT 4.0 goals and metrics overview

Activity goals	Process goals	IT goals
Activity KGI	Process KGI	IT KGI

KGIs for measuring the IT goals and KGIs for measuring the IT process goals. As an example, for process DS5—*ensure system security* (see Figure 14) one of the IT process goals is defined as *"permit access to critical and sensitive data only to authorised users"* and a possible KGI to measure this process goal is *"number and type of suspected and actual access violations."*

Figure 14. Goals and metrics for the process DS5: Ensure system security (ITGI, 2005)

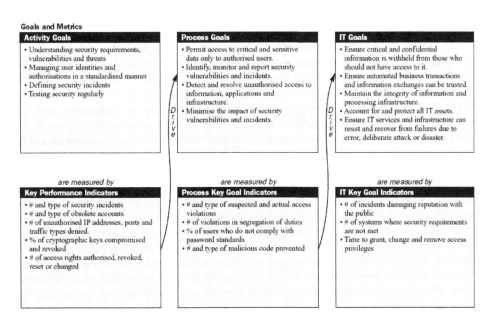

Key performance indicators (key performance drivers in the balanced scorecard terminology) are known as *lead indicators*, and they measure the effectiveness of the process execution. The key performance indictors (KPIs) define measures that determine how well the IT process is performing in enabling the goal to be reached. This means there is an important causal relationship between KGIs and KPIs. In previous example the KGI *"number and type of suspected and actual access violations"* was identified on IT process level for the IT process goal *"permit access to critical and sensitive data only to authorised users."* In order to reach this goal, several activity goals must be executed, such as *"managing user identities and authorisation in a standardised manner"* (Figure 14). This goal can be measured by a KGI on activity level, which also represents a KPI on IT process level, such as *"number and type of obsolete accounts."* It is assumed that a lower score for this metric implicates a better indication for reaching the IT process goal.

Figure 15. Cascade of metrics

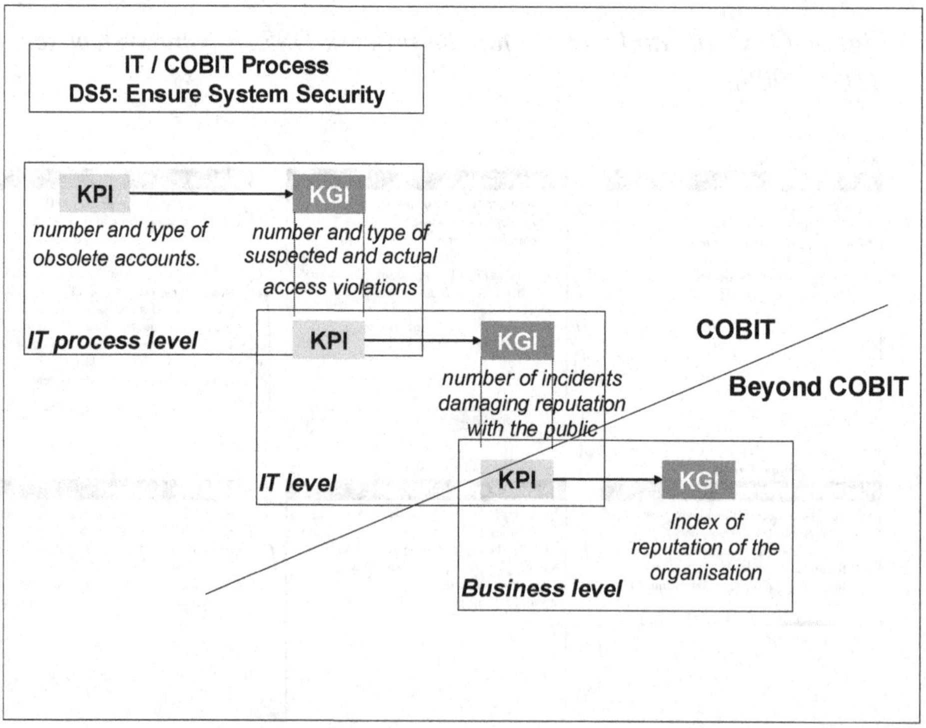

It is important to note that a KGI on one level becomes a KPI on a higher level, as illustrated in Figure 15. For example, on IT process level *number and type of suspected and actual access violations* was defined as KGI for the IT process goal. This is an important activity in supporting the IT goal *ensure critical and confidential information is withheld from those who should not have access to it*, which in turn is measured by the IT level KGI *number of incidents damaging reputation with the public* (Figures 14 and 15). This means, on IT level that the IT process KGI *number and type of suspected and actual access violations* now becomes a KPI, which is operating as a lead indicator for the IT KGI *number of incidents damaging reputation with the public*. Next, this KGI can become a KPI for a business level goal like for example the organisation's reputation, measured *reputation index of the organisation*. In COBIT, metrics on business level are not included. The COBIT management guidelines only deliver IT related goals and metrics, but as mentioned previously, guidance is provided on how IT processes and IT goals can support the business goals (Figures 2 and 3).

COBIT Maturity Models

A maturity model can be seen as a scoring technique for organisations to assess the maturity level of a specific process between 0 (not existent) and 5 (optimised). This instrument offers a comprehensible method for identifying the current (as-is) situation against the desirable (to-be) situation. Additionally, the organisation can compare its situation against industry specific best practices and standards. Gaps between the "as-is" and the "to-be" situation can be identified and specific actions to evolve towards the desirable situation can be set up. Whenever the maturity level of a process is being analysed, it is important to apply the base principles of a maturity measurement: an organisation can only evolve to a next maturity level, whenever all the criteria of that level are fulfilled.

The maturity levels of the process DS1—*define and manage service levels*, are listed in Figure 16. If an organisation reaches level 1 for this process, it is aware of the need to manage service levels, but the process is still informal. When the organisation reaches maturity level 5, all defined service levels are continuously monitored and reviewed in order to guarantee an optimal alignment between business and IT objectives.

Figure 16. Maturity model for the process DS1: Define and manage service levels (ITGI, 2005)

---

0 Non-existent when

Management has not recognised the need for a process for defining service levels. Accountabilities and responsibilities for monitoring them are not assigned.

1 Initial/ Ad Hoc when

There is awareness of the need to manage service levels, but the process is informal and reactive. The responsibility and accountability for defining and managing services are not defined. If performance measurements exist, they are qualitative only with imprecisely defined goals. Reporting is informal, infrequent and inconsistent.

2 Repeatable but Intuitive when

There are agreed-upon service levels, but they are informal and not reviewed. Service level reporting is incomplete and may be irrelevant or misleading for customers. Service level reporting is dependent on the skills and initiative of individual managers. A service level co-ordinator is appointed with defined responsibilities, but limited authority. If a process for compliance to service level agreements exists, it is voluntary and not enforced.

3 Defined Process when

Responsibilities are well defined, but with discretionary authority. The service level agreement development process is in place with checkpoints for reassessing service levels and customer satisfaction. Services and service levels are defined, documented and agreed-upon using a standard process. Service level shortfalls are identified, but procedures on how to resolve shortfalls are informal. There is a clear linkage between expected service level achievement and the funding provided. Service levels are agreed to but they may not address business needs.

4 Managed and Measurable when

Service levels are increasingly defined in the system requirements definition phase and incorporated into the design of the application and operational environments. Customer satisfaction is routinely measured and assessed. Performance measures reflect customer needs, rather than IT goals. The measures for assessing service levels are becoming standardised and reflect industry norms. The criteria for defining service levels are based on business criticality and include availability, reliability, performance, growth capacity, user support, continuity planning and security considerations. Root cause analysis is routinely performed when service levels are not met. The reporting process for monitoring service levels is becoming increasingly automated. Operational and financial risks associated with not meeting agreed-upon service levels are defined and clearly understood. A formal system of measurement of KPIs and KGIs is instituted and maintained.

5 Optimised when

Service levels are continuously re-evaluated to ensure alignment of IT and business objectives, while taking advantage of technology including the cost-benefit ratio. All service level management processes are subject to continuous improvement. Customer satisfaction levels are continuously monitored and managed. Expected service levels reflect strategic goals of business units and are evaluated against industry norms. IT management has the resources and accountability needed to meet service level targets and compensation is structured to provide incentives for meeting these targets. Senior management monitors KPIs and KGIs as part of a continuous improvement process.

The results of a survey, conducted by ISACA in 2003, show that for a majority of the organisations the maturity level of the process DS1—*define and manage service levels* hovers between 2 and 2.5. When further analysing these results, multinationals, organisations in the finance sector and IT service companies reached on average a higher score (between 2.5 and 3). These average numbers can help organisations in analysing their maturity level against industry best practices.

Within COBIT 4.0 the maturity models have been improved, starting from a new generic qualitative model based on following attributes:

- Awareness and communication
- Policies, standards and procedures
- Tools and automation
- Skills and expertise
- Responsibility and accountability
- Goal setting and measurement

The characteristics for these attributes, already partially available in COBIT 3.0, are more systematically and consistently applied for each IT process in this edition.

Adapting COBIT to Your Organisation

COBIT developed a generic framework, suitable for 'any' organisation. It does contain a lot of valuable information, but by first reading the documentation it may be difficult to grasp the essence and/or the practical elements. For a practical approach it is important for an organisation to rework and extract the necessary information and transform it to an organisation-specific template. Some processes may be more important for one organisation than another. The process DS 4—*ensure continuous service* for example will be of high importance in a financial organisation. Indeed, if the IT systems of a commercial bank are not available for a certain time, this may have a negative impact on the financial results of the bank. On the contrary the same process will most probably have a lower priority for a concrete factory, resulting in lower maturity level requirement. It is important that a clear set of business goals and IT goals exisits before starting with a COBIT implementation.

ISACA developed some guidance that can support organisations in implementing COBIT: *IT governance Implementation Guide using COBIT*. This publication explains how COBIT can be practically applied within an organisation. ISACA did use this guidance for a COBIT implementation within a SMB (Small and Medium Businesses), which resulted into *COBIT Quickstart*, which includes a SME specific subset of the COBIT material. More information about these publications can be found on www.isaca.org.

COBIT and Compliancy for Sarbanes-Oxley

In response to well-known financial scandals, the US introduced the Sarbanes-Oxley (SOX) law in 2002. This act intends to regain public trust into the capital markets by enhancing the accountability of executive management to their shareholders. With the higher attention for compliancy, IT governance and its frameworks has gained adoption into IT and business departments. The SOX law requires senior managers to take personal responsibility for the accuracy of the company's financial reports. It applies to all companies listed on the American stock exchange, but also impacts those companies that deliver services to them.

Although the SOX-Act is defined with a strong financial perspective, the role of IT and the impact on the IT processes is fundamental. Financial reporting processes are heavily dependent upon reliable IT systems, which are in charge of the, storage, processing, transfer, and reporting of the financial data. Only a good working and controlled IT environment can sustain the integrity of the data and provide the basis for reliable reports.

With the SOX-law the need arose for good and practical control frameworks. Where previously, internal control may have been organized ad-hoc with no strict guidelines, the SOX-act now specifically mentions the international control framework of the Committee of Sponsoring Organisations of the Treadway Commission (COSO). COSO defines internal controls as processes that are designed to offer a reasonable assurance regarding the achievement of those objectives related to the reliability of financial reporting, the effectiveness and efficiency of operations, and compliancy with laws and regulations (COSO, 1992). The COSO framework is a broadly accepted framework for internal control of financial reporting, but it does not cover the control for the supporting IT processes. COBIT does fill in this gap and a good implementation of its framework offers management with the information to provide reasonable assurance that the necessary IT control mechanisms are in place for complete and correct reporting, as prescribed by SOX. Like recognized by PCAOB and ITGI, there is not a ready-made solution and each organization should carefully consider their company-relevant IT control objectives, in line with the business requirements for SOX compliancy.

Companies that want to make use of COBIT for their compliancy work may find guidance in the published ITGI document *Control Objectives for Sarbanes-Oxley* (ITGI, 2006). This report is based on best practices and helps making a company specific SOX-compliancy plan for IT control objectives. It presents a selected list of 12 IT Control Objectives that play a crucial role in SOX compliancy (Figure 17) and maps them to 14 COBIT processes and four IT general control domains, defined by PCAOB (US Public Company Accounting Oversight Board): *Program development, Program changes, Computer Operations,* and *Access to Programs and Data.*

These IT control objectives and their supporting IT processes do play an important role in the path towards compliancy. The first four processes in

Figure 17. COBIT control objectives mapped to PCAOB IT general controls (ITGI, 2006)

IT Control Objectives for Sarbanes-Oxley	CobiT Mapping to CobiT 4.0 Processes	PCAOB IT General Controls			
		Program Development	Program Changes	Computer Operations	Access to Programs and Data
1. Acquire and maintain application software.	AI2	•	•	•	•
2. Acquire and maintain technology infrastructure.	AI3	•	•	•	
3. Enable operations.	AI4	•	•	•	•
4. Install and accredit solutions and changes.	AI7	•	•	•	•
5. Manage changes.	AI6		•		•
6. Define and manage service levels.	DS1	•	•	•	•
7. Manage third-party services.	DS2	•	•	•	•
8. Ensure systems security.	DS5			•	•
9. Manage the configuration.	DS9			•	•
10. Manage problems and incidents.	DS8, DS10			•	
11. Manage data.	DS11			•	•
12. Manage the physical environment and operations.	DS12, DS13			•	•

the list (Figure 17) are important because wrongful or fraudulent procedures could already be introduced during the implementation or set up phase of financial systems. Afterwards it is important that changes to an existing system are well controlled; especially during the emergency change process, non-controlled malfunctions may be introduced. Therefore, the fifth process in the list, *Manage changes,* ensures that every modification to a financial system is correctly authorized and logged and that the necessary impact-analyses and test procedures take place. Other SOX-dependent IT processes apply to being 'in control' over service levels and third-party services (*Is outsourced development under control?*), system security (*Are the financial reporting systems secured to prevent unauthorized use, modification, damage or loss of data?*), problem and incident management (*What is the process for reporting, logging and solving problems?*), data management (*Is data integrity assured?*), and operations management (*What are the controls over job scheduling, processing and error monitoring?*)

Other standards and frameworks such as ITIL, ISO 27000 and Six Sigma may provide complementary elements for organizing internal control. For example, the ITIL processes, *Change management, Service Level management, Problem Management,* and *Incident Management* will provide more detailed information in the area of service management, while the ISO2700 series will complement the COBIT process *Ensure Systems security.*

Other COBIT Products

ISACA publishes on a regular basis, new and updated publications and products, based on COBIT. Besides *COBIT Quickstart* and *IT Governance Implementation Guide using COBIT,* following publications may be of interest.

In 2002, ISACA started with the development of *IT Control Practices.* Where the COBIT IT processes and control objectives define the "what's" when setting up a control structure, the IT control practices deliver a more detailed approach by focusing on the "how" when implementing these controls. For each of the existing detailed control objectives, IT control practices have been developed.

In 2004, *COBIT Online* was launched. This is an online platform, designed as a Web-based service containing all available COBIT material.

In the information security domain related to COBIT, there is an interesting publication available: *"Security Baseline."* For this domain, this publication helps an organisation focus on the essential steps to take by extracting the most important security-related objectives from the COBIT framework.

Similarly, the publication *IT Control Objectives for Sarbanes-Oxley* provides a practical guide using the COBIT framework for organisations that seek Sarbanes Oxley compliancy or more broadly a robust, secure financial reporting system.

In addition, a series of publications is available about how COBIT relates to other standards, like ITIL, ISO17799, and so forth.

Conclusion

Today, COBIT is seen more and more as a generally accepted framework for IT governance. This chapter places the COBIT framework and its components within the overall IT governance frame and discuses their most important concepts.

The essence of COBIT lies in the fact that IT processes must support IT and business goals. This implicates that COBIT is not a cookbook with very precise recipes. The organisation-specific environment is the starting point for implementing good IT governance and it is important to take out those processes, components and elements from COBIT that could help in achieving the organisation's own business an IT objectives.

Another advantage of COBIT is its continuous development and refinement by gathering best practices based on the experiences of different managers in the field. As a consequence it may be a challenge to extract and interpret only these components that are relevant for the organisation.

Finally, while building upon its previous editions, COBIT 4.0 went through a substantial review, making the framework more practical in its usage. It is important though to note that implementations based on previous editions should not be redone; in this context COBIT 4.0 can be considered as an extension upon the "old" model.

References

Committee of Sponsoring Organizations of the Treadway Commission (COSO). (1992) Internal control: Integrated framework. Retrieved from www.coso.org

ITGI (2005). *COBIT 4.0*. Retrieved from www.itgi.org

ITGI (2006). IT control objectives for Sarbanes-Oxley (2nd ed.). Retrieved from www.itgi.org

Van Grembergen, W., De Haes, S., & Moons, J. (2005). IT governance: Linking business goals to IT goals and COBIT processes. *Information Systems Control Journal, 4*.

Chapter III

Leveraging the IT Balanced Scorecard as Alignment Instrument

In Chapter I, the IT balanced scorecard was introduced as a possible measurement and management tool to support the achievement of strategic alignment. In this chapter, the application of the balanced scorecard is illustrated in more detail through a case study of a major Canadian financial group, where the balanced scorecard was adopted in its full scope. This chapter is based on the publication "Linking the IT balanced scorecard to the business objectives at a major Canadian Financial Group" (Van Grembergen, Saull, & De Haes, 2003).

Case Company Introduction: A Tri-Company

The Great-West Life Assurance Company, London Life, and Investors Group are members of the Power Financial Corporation group of companies, with

London Life as a wholly owned subsidiary of The Great-West Life Assurance Company. In 2001, MacKenzie financial was also acquired by the Power Financial Corporation Group, but as the IT balanced scorecard project does not cover this company, MacKenzie's organization and IT division will not be taken into account in this chapter.

The Great-West Life Assurance Company is an international corporation offering life insurance, health insurance, retirement savings, specialty rein-surance, and general insurance, primarily in Canada and the United States. Great-West serves the financial security needs of more than 13 million people in Canada and the United States. Great-West has more than $86.9 billion (all figures presented in the case study are in Canadian dollars) in assets under administration and $477 billion of life insurance in force. Founded in Winnipeg in 1891, Great-West is now a leading life and health insurer in the Canadian market in terms of market share.

London Life was founded in Ontario in 1874, and has the leading market share of individual life insurance in Canada. London Life markets life insur-ance, disability insurance, and retirement savings and investment products through its exclusive sales force. The company is a supplier of reinsurance primarily in the U.S. and Europe, and is a 39 precent participant in a joint venture with life insurance company Shin Fu in Taiwan. London Life has more than $30 billion assets under administration and $142.6 billion of life insurance in force.

Investors Group, with its corporate headquarters in Winnipeg, was founded more than 70 years ago. Investors Group is Canada's leading provider of mutual funds, offering a wide spectrum of funds, including those created through strategic partnerships with some of the best known Canadian and international investment management firms. It also offers a wide range of insurance and mortgage options, and currently has $17.1 billion of life insur-ance coverage in force through three different carriers, and administers with more than $7.6 billion of primarily residential mortgages. Investors Group manages assets of $40.5 billion.

The Tri-Company IT Merger

The trend in financial services industry consolidation was a motivating factor behind the acquisition of London Life by Great-West Life and the merger of the IT divisions of the three companies in November, 1997. At that time, the tri-company IT expenditures had exceeded $200 million. The ability to reduce these costs and to achieve true synergies and economies of scale within the IT operations was clearly a driver and opportunity for the companies to realize. The merger enabled single systems solutions across all three companies to be explored and implemented as well as single operational processes. Forming a tri-company shared services organization positioned management to:

- Achieve world-class status as an information services group
- Maximize purchasing power and operating efficiency
- Leverage technology investments
- Optimize technical infrastructure and application support costs

Figure 1. Organization chart of the merged IT division

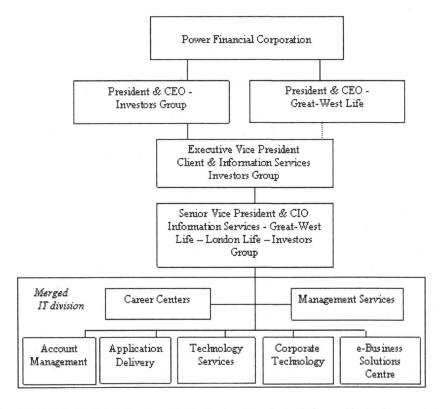

Figure 1 depicts the current IT organizational structure of the merged IT division, which employed 812 full-time/part-time employees at the time of the second research period. The position of the IT division relative to the higher reporting levels is also indicated. *Application Delivery* and *Technology Services* are respectively the traditional IT department's systems development and operations of the combined organizations. Application delivery is separated from account management and people management in order to focus on continuous improvement of delivery performance. *Account Management* is the linkage with the clients/users. This component ensures effective communication and translation of business needs into IT processes and educates users on the IT corporate agendas. Account Management employs IT generalists who provide IT insights into business strategy and decision making. *Career Centres* are focused on the professional development of IT people and ensure attention to people issues in order to reduce turnover of talented IT employees. *Corporate Technology* enables the development of a common architecture and provides technology directions. The *eBusiness Solution Centre* works on the introduction of new technologies that enable eBusiness solutions for The Group. *Management Services* focuses on running IT as a business and ensures effective financial management and management reporting including IT scorecard reporting.

IT BSC Project and Its Organization

Before the merger, the CIO of Great-West Life (who is the present CIO of the merged IT division), began focusing on the scorecard as a (potentially) effective measurement tool. His objective was to ensure that IT was fairly evaluated. In his own words: *"Through the balanced scorecard I would know what was important to the business and I would not fall victim to the early termination syndrome. Or at least I would have a better chance of survival."*

However, once the three companies came together through the acquisition and merger of the IT groups, the stakes were raised considerably. Now, the IT division had exposures on multiple fronts with stakeholders who were concerned about the perceived loss of control over their vital IT services. This prompted an executive request for a formal measure of factors to measure IT success. The response of the merged IT division was to formalize the criteria into a new and extended IT scorecard based on the experiences gained within Great-West Life.

Senior management of all the three companies questioned the benefits of huge investments in IT and how more value might be achieved through better alignment of business strategy and IT strategy. Figure 2 shows the specific concerns for the different stakeholders within the group.

Figure 2. IT concerns of the different stakeholders

Stakeholders	Key questions
Board of Directors	Does IT support the achievement of business objectives?
Executive Management Committee	What value does the expenditure on IT deliver? Are IT costs being managed effectively? Are IT risks being identified and managed? Are targeted inter-company IT synergies being achieved?
Business Unit Executives	Are IT's services delivered at a competitive cost? Does IT deliver on its service level commitments? Do IT investments positively affect business productivity or the customer experience? Does IT contribute to the achievement of our business strategies?
Corporate Compliance Internal Audit	Are the organization's assets and operations protected? Are the key business and technology risks being managed? Are proper processes, practices and controls in place?
IT Organization	Are we developing the professional competencies needed for successful service delivery? Are we creating a positive workplace environment? Do we effectively measure and reward individual and team performance? Do we capture organizational knowledge to continuously improve performance? Can we attract/retain the talent we need to support the business?

The concepts of the balanced scorecard and its application to information technology were discovered through an Internet search primarily through the web site of the IT Governance Institute (www.itgi.org). Departing from this Website, relevant publications on the IT balanced scorecard from academics and practitioners were identified and consulted. It was believed that the scorecard could provide an answer to the key questions of the different stakeholders.

The formal development of the IT balanced scorecard began in 1998 and from the start the objectives were clearly stated:

- Align IT plans and activities with business goals and needs
- Align employees' efforts toward IT objectives
- Establish measures for evaluating the effectiveness of the IT organization
- Stimulate and sustain improved IT performance
- Achieve balanced results across stakeholder groups

At the beginning of the initial research period (December, 1999), the situation was that the scorecard effort was not yet approached as a formal project and as a result, progress had been somewhat limited. In 2000, the formality of the project was increased and the CIO (Information Services Executive) was appointed as sponsor. In 2001, a project manager/analyst was formally assigned to the IT balanced scorecard project. Status to-date (end 2002) is that the case company is still completing the scorecard: 66% of the measures are completed, 29 percent are in progress and 5% are not yet started.

Building the IT BSC

It was recognized by the CIO that building an IT BSC was meaningful under two conditions which required (a) a clearly articulated business strategy, and (b) the new information services division (ISD) moving from a commodity service provider to a strategic partner as illustrated by Venkatraman (1999) (Figure 3).

Figure 3. IT division as a service provider or strategic partner

Service Provider	Strategic Partner
IT is for efficiency	IT for business growth
Budgets are driven by external benchmarks	Budgets are driven by business strategy
IT is separable from the business	IT is inseparable from the business
IT is seen as an expense to control	IT is seen as an investment to manage
IT managers are technical experts	IT managers are business problem solvers

The newly constructed ISD is viewed as a strategic partner. During several meetings between IT and executive management, the vision, strategy, measures of success and value of IT were jointly created. Typically, pure business objectives were used as the standard to assess IT. The vision and strategy of ISD were defined as:

- ISD is a single IT organization focused on developing world-class capabilities to serve the distinct customer needs of its three sponsoring companies

- ISD operates as a separate professional services business on a full recovery, non profit basis

- ISD supports the achievement of company strategies and goals through the industry consolidation period

- ISD becomes the "supplier of choice" of information services

- ISD establishes a forward looking enterprise architecture strategy which enables the use of technology as a competitive edge in the financial service market place

- ISD becomes the "employer of choice" for career-oriented IT professionals in the markets in which ISD and the group operate

These issues go to the heart of the relationship between IT and the business and will be reflected in the IT strategic balanced scorecard as is illustrated in

Figure 4. Perspective questions and mission statements of the IT strategic scorecard

CUSTOMER ORIENTATION	CORPORATE CONTRIBUTION
Perspective question How should IT appear to business unit executives to be considered effective in delivering its services? Mission To be the supplier of choice for all information services, either directly or indirectly through supplier relationships.	Perspective question How should IT appear to the company executive and its corporate functions to be considered a significant contributor to company success? Mission To enable and contribute to the achievement of business objectives through effective delivery of value added information services.
OPERATIONAL EXCELLENCE	FUTURE ORIENTATION
Perspective question At which services and processes must IT excel to satisfy the stakeholders and customers? Mission To deliver timely and effective IT services at targeted service levels and costs.	Perspective question How will IT develop the ability to deliver effectively and to continuously learn and improve its performance? Mission To develop the internal capabilities to continuously improve performance through innovation, learning and personal organizational growth.

Figures 4 and 5. Figure 4 shows the perspective questions and mission statements for the four quadrants: corporate contribution, customer orientation, operational excellence and future orientation. Figure 5 displays the measures for each perspective. The details regarding the individual perspectives and their measures can be found at the end of this chapter.

Maturity of the Developed IT BSC

At the beginning of the project, the IT BSC was primarily focused on the operational level of the IT department. It was acknowledged from the begin-

Figure 5. IT strategic scorecard framework

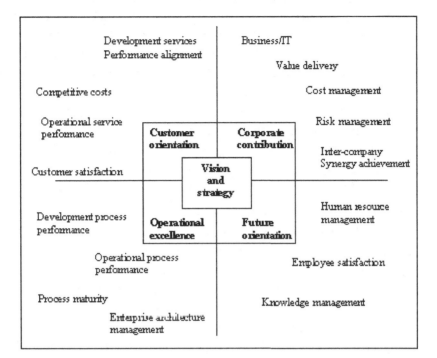

ning that this could not be the end result. Therefore, actions were started to go beyond the operational IT BSC and to measure the true value of IT at the business level. The vice president of information services emphasized: "*The balanced scorecard gives a balanced view of the total value delivery of IT to the business. It provides a snapshot of where your IS organization is at a certain point in time. Most executives, like me, do not have the time to drill down into the large amount of information.*"

The organization established two ways to demonstrate the business value, one at service delivery level and one at the IT strategy level. As will be illustrated hereafter, the goal is to evolve to an IT strategic BSC that shows how the business objectives are enabled by IT.

A cascade of balanced scorecards has been established to create a link between the scorecards at the unit level and the overall business objectives (see Figure 6). A link between the IT BSC and the business BSC is not yet implemented as there is currently no formal business BSC for the group. The scorecards at the unit level are classified into three groups: operational services scorecards (e.g., IT service desk scorecard), governance services scorecards (e.g., career centre scorecard), and development services scorecards (e.g., application development scorecard). The measures of these unit scorecards are *rolled-up* or *aggregated* in the IT strategic balanced scorecard. This, in turn is fed into and evaluated against the business objectives. In this way, the service (and value) delivered by IT is directly measured against the objectives of the overall business. Further, on an annual basis, the IT strategic BSC is reviewed by business and IT management and the result is fed back into the next annual planning cycle. This planning cycle defines what the business needs are and what IT must do to accomplish those needs.

For example, from the IT service desk scorecard (i.e., a unit scorecard, which is situated in the operational services scorecard group), metrics such as average speed of answer, overall resolution rate at initial call and call abandonment rate (all three customer orientation metrics) are *rolled-up* to service level performance metrics in the IT strategic balanced scorecard. Other metrics of this unit scorecard such as expense management (corporate contribution perspective), client satisfaction (customer orientation perspective), process maturity of incident management (operational excellence perspective) and staff turnover (future orientation perspective), will *aggregate* as part of the IT strategic scorecard. The overall view of the IT strategic balanced scorecard is then fed into and evaluated against the defined business objectives.

Figure 6. Cascade of scorecards

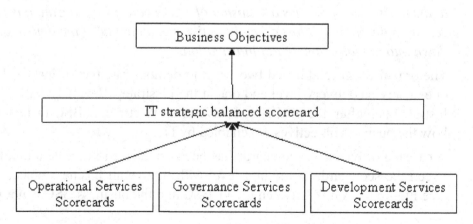

The second way to demonstrate business value is situated within the IT strategic balanced scorecard. The cause-and-effect relationships between performance drivers and outcome measures of the four quadrants are established as indicated in Figure 7. These connections help to understand how the contribution of IT towards the business will be realized: building the foundation for delivery and continuous learning and growth (future orientation perspective) is an enabler for carrying out the roles of the IT division's mission (operational excellence perspective) that is in turn an enabler for measuring up to business expectations (customer expectations perspective) that eventually must lead to ensuring effective IT governance (corporate contribution perspective). The construction of cause-and-effect relationships is a critical issue in the further development of the IT strategic BSC. These relationships are not yet been explicitly defined although they are implicit in the existing scorecard. For example, the *professional development days per*

Figure 7. IT strategic scorecard objectives and cause-and-effect

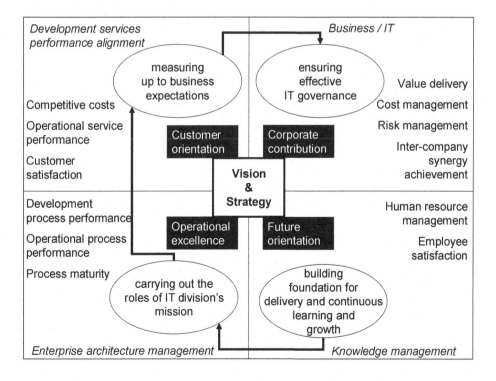

staff member measure (Figure 12) can be identified as a performance driver for the outcome measures *development process performance* (Figure 15).

The corporate contribution perspective of Figure 9 is an enabler (performance driver) of the (generic) business objectives of the financial group with its specific measures, such as *business/IT alignment, value delivery, cost management, risk management,* and *inter-company synergy achievement.* The CIO and its executive management are aware that an explicit articulation of these relationships has to be done and that it may help to improve the IT strategic BSC and its link with the business objectives, later on with the implementation of a business BSC. Figure 8 displays the concrete improvements plans for the further development of the scorecard as articulated by IT management.

The improvement in unit cost measurements should enable the organization to break down the IT activities' costs in a more detailed level. The second improvement in progress refers to the approval processes of both the overall enterprise architecture and the systems level architectures delivered through major projects. The enterprise architecture dictates certain architectural and technical standards for application and technical systems and is reviewed and re-approved on a regular basis. Operational services baselines and targets, and unit scorecards will be developed and a measurement process for personal development will be implemented. Further improvements include the establishment of a risk management measure. The goal is to develop an

Figure 8. Improvement plans for the IT BSC

Improvements (in progress)
Improvement in unit cost measurements
Target state and project architecture approval process
Development of operational service baselines and targets, and unit scorecards
Implementation of personal development days measurement process
Further improvements (in order of priority)
Risk management measure
Customer satisfaction
'State of the infrastructure' assessment
'Lessons learned' sharing process
Explicit articulation of cause-and-effect relationships

overall risk management strategy and measure the attainment of the defined target state risk level. Next, a regular survey process using generic questions needs to be developed to measure customer satisfaction and a process for assessing the "state of the infrastructure" will be implemented. This assessment compares the status-to-date of the existing infrastructure against the "to-be" position. Lowest priority but scheduled on the short and mid-term improvements plan is the sharing process of "lessons learned" on development projects.

The most important aspect is that all stakeholders in the process were engaged and that progress is made each subsequent year. At this moment, most metrics are manually captured, which is a labour-intensive task. However, the mainframe technical support manager states: "*It is important to first identity the correct metrics that need to be captured before implementing tools that automate the data collection.*"

Lessons Learned

The following lessons can be attributed to this IT BSC case:

1. **Start simultaneously constructing a business and IT scorecard**

   The IT BSC within the case company was started within the IT organization primarily with the objective to ensure that IT is fairly evaluated by the business. This is a rather defensive approach and focuses merely on the internal IT processes. Although it is clearly recognized within the case company, that a more explicit linkage with the business (with a business balanced scorecard) has to be developed and supported, the question still remains whether it is more appropriate (a) to start with a business balanced scorecard followed by the subsequent creation of the corresponding IT scorecards or (b) to develop both scorecards simultaneously? It is probably more ideal to start simultaneously with both scorecards which require both IT and senior management to discuss the opportunities of information technologies which supports the IT/business alignment and IT governance process.

2. **Consider the scorecard technique as a supportive mechanism for IT/business alignment and IT governance**

Recurring issues in IT practice and IT academic publications focus on how to align IT and business and how to control IT. A cascade of business and IT balanced scorecards may support both processes. However, as is shown in this case study, the balanced scorecard is just a technique that can only be successful if the business and IT work together and act upon the measurements of the scorecards. The balanced scorecard approach will only have results when other mechanisms such as a well functioning board and IT steering committee are in place.

3.   **Consider the construction and implementation of an IT balanced scorecard as an evolutionary project**

Constructing an IT balanced scorecard is not a one-week project. It requires considerable time and other major resources. Moreover, it is a project that is to be matured over time and that is characterized by different stages as is illustrated by the IT BSC maturity model introduced in this paper. This iterative approach is confirmed by this case. The described IT BSC began at a lower level with actions currently in place to reach a higher level where a more explicit connection exists between outcome measures and performance drivers, and where an explicit linkage is established with business requirements.

4.   **Provide a formal project organization**

Good project management is a critical success factor for effective construction and implementation of an IT balanced scorecard. IT management of the case company confronted with the question of how the IT BSC project was organized, had to admit that in the beginning, there was no real formal organization in place and that this delayed the progress of its implementation. Currently, the sponsor of the IT BSC is the CIO, and one full-time project manager is assigned to the project. A group of 15 individuals have key roles and accountabilities for scorecard deliverables.

5.   **Provide best IT practices**

Introducing an IT balanced scorecard in an IT environment with poor management and IT practices is too large a challenge. The implementation of the IT BSC within the case company was certainly supported by practices already in place such as ROI-evaluation of IT projects, the existence of IT steering committees, service level sgreement practices, and so forth. If it is decided to implement, for example, the information economics approach to score and evaluate projects and to integrate this method within the IT BSC, this will take considerable time and is to be seen as a separate project.

6.   **Revisit the dynamic measures**

The implementation of the IT balanced scorecard requires the establishment and definition of a large number of metrics. The appropriateness of these metrics should be regularly evaluated. In the words of the mainframe technical support manager: *"As business requirements change, the metrics are dynamic and should be re-evaluated on a regular basis. Most important in this regard is that it should always remain very clear why a certain issue is measured, i.e., what the value is of measuring it. When this value can not be demonstrated any more, a measure should be challenged and changed or replaced by another one."*

Details on the Measures of the IT Strategic Scorecard

In this section, the IT strategic balanced scorecard is discussed in more detail (see also Saull, 2000). In each of the four quadrants, the objectives, measures and benchmarks will be elaborated. Many of the measures are rolled-up or aggregated from the unit scorecards (e.g., data centre scorecard) to metrics in the IT strategic scorecard. Some of the measures defined in the IT strategic scorecard are high-level but cover specific concrete metrics. At this moment, the collecting process of the data is often very labour intensive, but it is the belief of management that first the correct measures have to be defined before implementing tools that can automate the data collecting process.

Corporate Contribution Scorecard

The corporate contribution perspective evaluates the performance of the IT organization from the viewpoint of executive management, the board of directors and the shareholders, and provides answers to the key questions of these stakeholders concerning IT governance (cf. Figure 2). The key issues, as depicted by Figure 9, are business/IT alignment, value delivery, cost management, risk management, and inter-company synergy achievement.

Benchmarks have been used where an objective standard was available or could be determined in most cases from external sources.

The main measurement challenges are with the areas of business/IT alignment and the value delivery.

Currently, *business/IT alignment* is measured by the approval of the IT operational plan and budget. Although not a discrete measure of alignment, the approval process within the group is particularly thorough and as a result is accepted by business executives as a good indicator. All aspects of development, operations and governance/support services are examined and challenged to ensure they are essential to achieving business objectives or supporting the enabling IT strategy.

In the *value delivery* area, the performance of a specific IT services group delivering to a specific business unit (e.g., 'group insurance' services) is measured. For each business unit, specific metrics are and/or will be defined. The ultimate responsibility for achieving and measuring the business value of IT rests with the business and is reflected in the business results of the individual lines of business in different ways, depending on the nature of value being sought.

Cost management is a traditional financial objective and is in the first place measured through the attainment of expense and recovery targets. The expenses refer to the costs that the IT organization has made for the business, and the recovery refers to the allocation of costs to IT services and the internal charge back to the business. All IT costs are fully loaded (no profit margin) and recovered from the lines of business on a fair and equitable basis as agreed to by the companies' CFOs. Comparisons with similar industries will be drawn to benchmark these metrics. Next to this, IT unit costs (e.g., application development) will be measured and compared to the 'top performing levels' benchmark provided by Compass.

The development of the *risk management* metrics are the priority for the upcoming year. At this moment, the results of the internal audits are used and benchmarked against criteria provided by OSFI, the Canadian federal regulator in the financial services sector. The execution of the security initiative and the delivery of a disaster recovery assessment need to be accomplished in the upcoming year. This will enable the business to get an insight on how well they are prepared to respond to different disaster scenarios.

Synergy achievement is measured through the achievement of single system solutions, targeted cost reductions and the integration of the IT organiza-

Figure 9. Corporate contribution scorecard

Objective	Measures	Benchmarks
Business/IT alignment	• Operational plan/budget approval	• Not applicable
Value delivery	• Measured in business unit performance	• Not applicable
Cost management	• Attainment of expense and recovery targets • Attainment of unit cost targets	• Industry expenditure comparisons • Compass operational 'top performance' levels
Risk management	• Results of internal audits • Execution of security initiative • Delivery of disaster recovery assessment	• OSFI sound business practices • Not applicable • Not applicable
Inter-company synergy achievement	• Single system solutions • Target state architecture approval • Attainment of targeted integration cost reductions • IT organization integration	• Merger & acquisition guidelines • Not applicable • Not applicable • Not applicable

tions. This measure is very crucial in the context of the merger of the three IT organizations in the sense that it enables a post evaluation of this merger and demonstrates to management whether the new IT organization is effective and efficient. The selection of single system solutions was a cooperative effort between business leaders and IT staff, resulting in a *"target state architecture"* depicting the target applications architecture. The synergy targets were heavily influenced by the consulting firm (Bain & Co.) that was used to assist in evaluating the London Life acquisition and the tri-company IT merger potential. The consultants suggested specific dollar reduction targets for technology services (IT operations) and application delivery services (IT development) largely based on norms they had developed from their previous merger and acquisition work. The approval of the target state architecture plan and the attainment of the targeted integration cost reductions will be measured. The IT organization integration metric refers to the synergies within the IT organization, e.g., is there one single service desk for the three companies or are there three different ones?

Customer Orientation Scorecard

The customer orientation perspective evaluates the performance of IT from the viewpoint of internal business users (customers of IT) and, by extension the customers of the business units. It provides answers to the key questions of these stakeholders concerning IT service quality (cf. Figure 2). As shown in Figure 10, the issues this perspective focuses on are competitive costs, development services performance, operational services performance, and customer satisfaction.

In the *customer satisfaction* area, the IT BSC of the merged IT organization is relying on annual interviews with key business managers. It is the intent to set up one generic survey, which can be re-used, with relevant questions that cover the topics mentioned in Figure 10.

Insight into the *competitive costs* area can demonstrate to the business how cost competitive the IT organization is compared to other (e.g., external) parties. This insight is realized by measuring the attainment of IT unit cost targets and the blended labour rate. This rate model provides an overall single rate for any IT professional who is appointed to the business. The competitive costs measures are benchmarked against Compass's operational 'Top Performing level' and against the offerings of commercial IT service vendors (market comparisons).

Development services performance measures are project oriented using attributes such as goal attainment, sponsor satisfaction and project governance (i.e., the way the project is managed). These data are mostly captured by interviews with key managers. The most effective time to establish the basis for these (project) development measures is at the point where business cases are being prepared and projects are evaluated. Each IT project initiative will be evaluated by the IS Executive Committee in which IT and business managers determine—based on the business drivers, budget and state architecture compliance—which projects need to be executed. When a project is approved, the project manager defines clear targets for cost, schedule, quality, scope, and governance. The quantitative data (e.g., budget) are reported throughout the lifecycle of the project. After completion of the project, the quantitative and

Figure 10. Customer orientation scorecard

Objective	Measures	Benchmarks
Customer satisfaction	• Business unit survey ratings: • Cost transparency and levels • Service quality and responsiveness • Value of IT advise and support • Contribution to business objectives	• Not applicable
Competitive costs	• Attainment of unit cost targets • Blended labour rates	• Compass operational 'Top Level Performing' levels • Market comparisons
Development services performance	• Major project success scores: • Recorded goal attainment • Sponsor satisfaction ratings • Project governance rating	• Not applicable
Operational services performance	• Attainment of targeted service levels	• Competitor comparisons

qualitative data are evaluated during the major project review and the main success drivers, delivery issues and lessons learned are documented.

In terms of *operational service performance,* IT management measures achievement against targeted service levels. For each operational unit (e.g., data centre), average response time, service availability and resolution time for incidents are rolled-up to these service performance metrics in the strategic balanced scorecard. The results are benchmarked against the performance of competitors.

Operational Excellence Scorecard

The operational excellence scorecard provides the performance of IT from the viewpoint of IT management (process owners and service delivery managers) and the audit and regulatory bodies. The operational excellence perspective copes with the key questions of these stakeholders and provides answers to questions of maturity, productivity and reliability of IT processes (cf. Figure 2). The issues that are of focus here, as displayed in Figure 11, are development process performance, operational process performance, process maturity and enterprise architecture management.

Figure 11. Operational excellence scorecard

Objective	Measures	Benchmarks

Development process performance	• Function point measures of:
	   • Productivity
	   • Quality
	   • Delivery rate
		• To be determined

Operational process performance	• Benchmark based measures of:
	   • Productivity
	   • Responsiveness
	   • Change management effectiveness
	   • Incident occurrence levels
		• Selected Compass benchmark studies

Process maturity	• Assessed level of maturity and compliance in priority processes within:
	   • Planning and organization
	   • Acquisition and implementation
	   • Delivery and support
	   • Monitoring
		• To be defined

Enterprise architecture management	• Major project architecture approval • Product acquisition compliance to technology standards • "State of the infrastructure" assessment	• Not applicable

In relation to *development process performance*, function point based measures of productivity, quality, and delivery rate, such as number of faults per 100 installed, function points and delivery rate of function points per month, are defined. Benchmark data on industry performance will be gathered from a third party (e.g., Compass). In the *operational process performance* area, measures of productivity, responsiveness, change management effectiveness and incident occurrence level are benchmarked against selected Compass studies (e.g., on data centres, client server, etc.).

The *process maturity* is assessed using the COBIT (control objectives for IT and related technology) framework and maturity models (ITGI, 2000). The group has identified 15 out the 34 priority processes that should have a maturity assessment in 2003 and the other processes will be measured later.

Enterprise architecture management deals with the IT responsibility to define an enterprise architecture which supports long term business strategy and objectives and to act as a steward on behalf of business executives to protect the integrity of that architecture. Major project architecture approval measures the compliance of net new systems as they are proposed, developed and implemented. Product acquisition compliance technology standards measure the adherence to detailed technology standards which are at the heart of minimizing technology diversity and maximizing inter-company technology synergies. The "State of the Infrastructure" assessment measures the degree to which IT has been able to maintain a robust and reliable infrastructure as required to deliver effectively to business needs. It does so by comparing each platform area against risk based criteria for potential impact to business continuity, security and/or compliance.

Future Orientation Perspective

The future orientation perspective shows the performance of IT from the viewpoint of the IT organization itself: process owners, practitioners and support professionals. The future orientation perspective provides answers to stakeholder questions regarding IT's readiness for future challenges (cf. Figure 2). The issues focused on, as depicted in Figure 12, are human resources management, employee satisfaction and knowledge management. The metrics that will appear in the future orientation quadrant of the IT strategic balanced scorecard are in many cases the aggregated results of measures used in the unit scorecards (e.g., career centre).

Human resource management is an objective that is tracked by comparing measures as described in Figure 12 against predefined targets: the staff complement by skill type (number of people with a certain profile, e.g., systems analyst), staff turnover, staff 'billable' ratio (i.e., hours billed/total hours salary paid; if this ratio can be increased, the IT organization can charge lower rates to the business for the IT assigned people), and professional development days per staff member.

Employee satisfaction is measured by using surveys with questions relating to compensation, work climate, feedback, personal growth, and vision and purpose. Benchmark data of North American technology dependent companies are provided by a third party.

In the *knowledge management* area, the delivery of internal process improvements to the 'Cybrary' is very important. The 'Cybrary' refers to the intranet that all employees can assess for seeking and sharing knowledge. To measure

Figure 12. Future orientation scorecard

Objective	Measures	Benchmarks

Human resource management	• Results against targets:
	  • Staff complement by skill type
	  • Staff turnover
	  • Staff 'billable' ratio
	  • Professional development days per staff member
		• Not applicable
		
		• Market comparison
		• Industry standard
		• Industry standard

Employee satisfaction	• Employee satisfaction survey scores in:
	  • Compensation
	  • Work climate
	  • Feedback
	  • Personal growth
	  • Vision and purpose
		• North American technology dependent companies

Knowledge management	• Delivery of internal process improvements to 'Cybrary' • Implementation of 'lessons learned' sharing process	• Not applicable • Not applicable

Copyright © 2008, IGI Global. Copying or distributing in print or electronic forms without written permission of IGI Global is prohibited.

improvements, metrics (e.g., number of hits per day on the Cybrary) still need to be developed. Closely linked to this, knowledge management is also measured by the implementation of the 'lessons learned' sharing process. Here too, specific metrics still need to be developed.

Conclusion

In this chapter, the development and implementation of an IT balanced scorecard within a large Canadian insurance group is described and discussed. It was shown that building and implementing such a scorecard is a project that needs substantial human and financial resources. Furthermore, setting up an IT BSC is a project that is characterized by different phases in time. The current status of the case scorecard is Level 2 of the IT BSC maturity model. This implies that the case IT scorecard to-date has to be linked with the business scorecard or at least the business objectives to support the IT/business alignment process and the IT governance process. Currently, a plan for the next two years has been developed with the objective to build a mature IT BSC explicitly linked to the business. It is recognized within the case company that this will be a great challenge for both IT and business people.

The case under review illustrated one of the most crucial issues in building and implementing an IT strategic balanced scorecard: its required linkage with the business objectives. To create this link a cascade of balanced scorecards has been established with at the lower level unit scorecards for the operational and development services. The measures of these unit scorecards are rolled-up or aggregated in the IT strategic scorecard that ultimately realizes the link with the business objectives through its corporate contribution perspective. The precise articulation of the cause-and-effect relationships through the identification of outcome measures and their corresponding performance drivers seemed to be a critical success factor. These relationships are implicit in the current IT strategic balanced scorecard but are to be defined more explicitly.

References

Van Grembergen, W., Saull, R., & De Haes, S. (2003). Linking the IT balanced scorecard to the business objectives at a major Canadian financial group. *Journal for Information Technology Cases and Applications (JITCA)*, 5(1).

Venkatraman, N. (1999). *Valuing the IS contribution to the business*. Computer Sciences Corporation.

Chapter IV

IT Governance in Practice:
Six Case Studies

Introduction

In order to obtain an understanding on how large organizations implement IT governance in a pragmatic way, six pilot cases were selected from different sectors. Case research is particularly appropriate for research within the IT area because researchers in this field often lag behind practitioners in discovering and explaining new methods and techniques (Benbasat, Goldstein, & Mead, 1987). This is certainly true for the concept of IT governance. The purpose of this case study research is to look for different IT governance elements in use and how they contribute to better IT governance within the organisation. In Figure 1, a schematic representation of necessary elements for IT governance is summarized.

For this case research, data was gathered by conducting several face-to-face, in-depth interviews with both IT and business representatives of the case study

Figure 1. Necessary elements of an IT governance framework

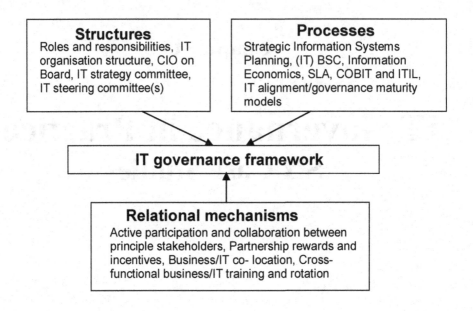

organisations. IT representatives included, amongst others (global), IT and ICT directors, while business representatives included controllers, directors finance, executive vice presidents, and others. Starting from the IT governance framework, two different interview questionnaires were developed, one for the IT people and one for the business people. The pilot in-depth case of KBC is based on six extensive interviews with both business and IT representatives. Five additional pilot mini cases are based on two to three interviews with business and IT people. After-interview consultation of the interviewees or people in the particular organisation took place in order to better grasp the situation and the IT governance context. Figure 2 gives an overview of the six case studies.

For the sake of meticulous case study writing, the interviews were tape-recorded. This allowed for a better understanding of the interviewees' insights and perceptions on their organisation's IT governance mission, as well as the use of accurate citation. Other data collected for the case study writing included case study organisations' websites, company brochures, internal reports, internal presentations, and so forth. Obviously, all prepared materi-

Figure 2. Overview of the pilot case studies

Company name	Industry	Interviewees
KBC (in-depth case)	Finance	• CIO • IT governance project managers—member of board of directors and executive committee • Director of 'organisation' (a staff function within KBC which facilitates the optimisation of the organisational processes)—IT auditor
Vanbreda (mini case)	Insurance	• CIO • Director IT operations—director of finance
Sidmar (mini case)	Steel	• CIO • Director controlling
CM (mini case)	Insurance	• CIO • General director CM Antwerp—IT director CM Antwerp
AGF Belgium (mini case)	Insurance	• CIO • Director fire, accidents and other risks
Huntsman (mini case)	Chemicals	• Director global IT enterprise business systems • Vice president

als were sent back to the case study organisations for formal approval and validation before issuing a final version.

Case Study: KBC

Company Introduction

KBC is a major Belgian financial services organisation that was founded in 1998 after the merger of Kredietbank, Cera Bank, and ABB Insurance. These former companies already had a history before the merger of more

than 100 years. KBC, as a merged company, is now the third largest banking and insurance organisation in its home market of Belgium. Comparing
market capitalisation of other banks in Europe, KBC is ranked number 12
in the Euroland Bank Ranking (Dow Jones Euro Stoxx). The company has
focused its international expansion on growth countries in Central Europe
(Czech Republic, Hungary, Poland, and Slovenia). By the end of 2003, KBC
achieved a consolidated net profit of 1,119 million Euro on a gross operating
income of 6,498 million Euros. In the same year, KBC employed 49,725 FTE
professionals worldwide, of which 2,403 (internal and external) worked in the
central IT department. Total IT budget for 2003 was 430 million Euros. As
mentioned in the introduction of this book, this case study was described in
the period 2003-2005. It should therefore be noted that this case description
only describes the IT governance status at that time in the organisation.

The decision-making structures of KBC are organised in function of five
core activity domains of the business as shown in Figure 3.

Retail and private bancassurance encompasses the activities of the bank
branches, agents, and brokers, as well as those conducted via electronic
channels, that cater for private persons, the self-employed and local businesses (retail bancassurance), and for high-net-worth individuals (private

Figure 3. Activity domains of KBC

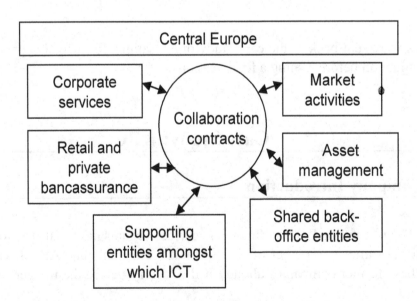

bancassurance). *Corporate services* contain all the banking and assurance activities towards companies. *Asset management* is the business of managing the assets of private persons and institutional investors, as well as the assets of investment funds that are sold primarily via the retail network. *Market activities* refer to activities of the bank's dealing rooms in Belgium and abroad, the market activities of KBC Securities, and all the activities engaged in KBC Financial Products, KBC Clearing, and KBC Peel Hunt. KBC's businesses on its second home market are grouped under the separate area of activity referred to as *Central Europe*. This encompasses all retail banking and insurance services, corporate services, asset management, and market activities in the Czech Republic, Slovakia, Hungary, Poland, and Slovenia. These activity domains are supported by shared back-office entities, such as the logistic back-office for payments and securities, and supporting entities, such as bookkeeping and IT. Each of the activity domains has its own management committee. The supporting entities are regarded as being a separate organisation that will charge-back costs in a non-profit manner. That is why collaboration contracts needed to be established between the activity domains and the supporting entities.

IT Governance Context

To be able to attract new clients and to retain existing clients in the competitive financial market, the business units of KBC are continuously looking for ways to increase the internal and external process efficiency. To be able to meet these business requirements, a flexible IT department is needed offering high-quality services. But as one of the IT governance project managers stated: *"Previous years, the management of IT was organised around major projects such as Y2K and the Euro conversion. While working on these projects, however, an enormous backlog grew of other projects to be accomplished. And the questions rose: How to tackle new requests of the business when the current major projects are completed? What if an enormous amount of new projects is initiated? How to give priorities?"*

Moreover, the business units of KBC were becoming more aware of what the IT market in general had to offer, which resulted sometimes in the belief that IT services should be best delivered by a third party. The IT governance project manager continues: *"IT becomes bigger and bigger, which is reflected in the outline of IT costs for the business. From that, the feeling emerges within the business that there is not much synergy and control achieved within IT. The*

*business requests more and more projects that the IT department cannot im-
mediately respond to and as a result business starts looking for third parties.
This way of working can be beneficial in the short-term, but it endangers the
coherence and synergies of IT systems on the long-term."*

Finally, one of the drivers for the merger in 1998 between Kredietbank,
Cera Bank, and ABB Assurance was achieving economies of scale in the IT
department. According to the member of the Board of Directors: *"When the
merger was officially completed, one of the first missions for the IT department was to set up a model that would enable the achievement of economies
of scale, the set up of a solid IT architecture and the alignment between
business and IT."*

This context of high business expectations and the awareness that IT is
needed to respond to it, together with the need to achieve economies of scale
within IT after the merger, prompted the IT governance project in 2000.
The IT governance project started at a moment that a lot of other important
KBC projects were initiated, as the board of director's member points out:
*"An important challenge was that this project was executed in parallel with
other major projects such as the fusion of all other KBC departments and
the introduction of the Euro. In a way, we were changing tires and axes of
the car, while riding."*

It was the executive committee that initiated the project in 2000 by asking
the CIO to develop a business-IT governance model. After this request, the
CIO developed an 'IT charter' (see infra) clarifying how IT and the business
should collaborate in the future. This first proposal from IT created some
resistance in the business as they felt that a model was being imposed on
them by IT which inhibited flexibility. The former chairman of the executive
committee therefore requested an audit to evaluate the model. This audit
was however never performed, as very quickly, the model was fine-tuned
and the department 'organisation' got involved to assist in implementing the
processes behind the IT charter and to act as gatekeeper in certain decisions
points (see infra).

From the start on, the goal of the IT governance project was clearly defined:
*"set up a governance model for business-IT for the KBC Group for the
coming 4-5 years, in a way that the model is resistant to and anticipates
organisational changes."* It was believed that this governance model would
result in: (1) high flexibility for the organisation, (2) effective allocation of
the IT resources, and (3) economies of scale and specialisation through the
centralisation of IT knowledge.

The goals of the IT governance project were widely communicated and explained. An internal KBC magazine explaining the project stated: "*The business units need to learn to manage IT in a well-thought out manner. They need to make choices and accept the consequences of these choices. The IT department from its side needs to create an environment which enables business to make these well-considered decisions. IT needs to create an insight into the needs of the business, and needs to establish clear agreements and engagements. IT has to define what it can deliver, by when and at which price, in a way that the internal customer knows what his return is for the money spent.*"

In order to achieve these goals, KBC established structures, processes, and relational mechanisms, which are described in the following sections. In the very beginning, a project manager was assigned to install the basic processes and structures. Later on, a committee composed of the general directors of the business units, the CIO and the director of 'organisation' regularly initiated improvement projects, and also now, the model is still growing. For example, in 2004, the IT audit department finalised an IT governance audit, which they initiated themselves, and resulted in some improvement recommendations, which were under review at the time that this paper was finalised (spring, 2004).

IT Governance Structures

Organisational Structures

Effective IT governance is of course determined by the way the IT function is organised and where the IT decision-making authority is located within the organisation. Figure 4 shows how the IT department is structured and its relation to higher reporting levels and other business departments.

The IT department is headed by the CIO, who reports directly to the executive committee. In this way, the CIO has the same direct reporting line to the executive committee as the general directors of the business lines of KBC Bank and KBC Assurance (for example general director corporate services) and staff functions (for example marketing, 'organisation'). The CIO manages a number of IT divisions. The division *Strategic Processes* is responsible for management reporting, charge back models, education, communication, knowledge management, and so forth. The division *Process Management* is responsible for the management of IT projects with an impact over several IT divisions, such as Y2K and the Euro conversion. This division also provides advice on architecture, design, testing, tools, and so forth. There are three product factory divisions, each one responsible for the development in one or more lines of business (for example, product factory 3 in the assurance domain). Finally, there is a division responsible for distribution channels and markets (e.g., bank cards and cash dispensers, and B2B-B2C e-commerce) and two divisions, grouped per technology domain (open systems and mainframe) responsible for maintenance and development of the technical infrastructure (databases, networks, operation systems, etc.).

The board of directors, the top-level in Figure 4, was composed of 23 members in 2003. This group is constituted of eight managing directors forming together the executive committee, 11 representatives of the principle shareholders and four independent directors. In order to permit the board to fulfil its supervisory task, the executive committee reports to it each month on the trend of results and on the progress of major events and projects. Each member of the executive committee is responsible for supervising the activities of a number of business units and/or supporting entities such as IT. They meet once a week and address IT issues on a regular basis in terms of decisions on IT budgets and decisions on investment projects (see infra). The CIO, although not part of the executive committee, reports directly to one of its members and is frequently invited to the executive committee

Figure 4. IT organisation structure

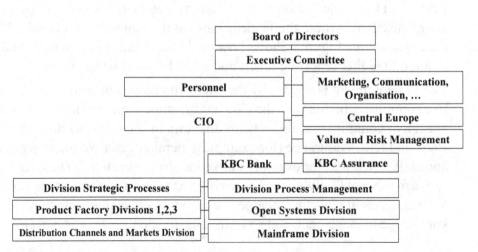

meetings. In this way, a close link between business and IT at a high level in the organisation is established.

KBC documents roles and responsibilities for all hierarchical levels involved in the governance framework. An intranet site was developed were all roles and responsibilities are explained and can be consulted by both business and IT.

Committees Supporting IT Governance

As argued before, IT governance should be the prime responsibility of the board of directors, and IT therefore should be regularly addressed in the board meetings. A supportive mechanism to obtain this is establishing an IT strategy committee of which the role is defined by ITGI (2003) as follows: "an IT strategy committee has to consider how the board should become involved in IT governance, how to integrate the board's role in IT and business strategy, and the extent to which the committee has an ongoing role in IT governance." KBC established such a committee composed of three board members (who are also member of the executive committee), the CIO and directors of the strategic processes and process management IT divisions. This committee focuses on establishing and reviewing the IT strategy, but does not enable a more thorough and ongoing involvement of the board in IT governance. KBC's board works at a very high, strategic level and they are consequently not the 'steering power' for IT or IT governance. Nevertheless, it could be argued that the board is maybe not involved as a whole, but still via its members of the executive committee who also have a seat in the board.

KBC also established a number of other committees that enable the involvement of both business and IT in the preparation of new projects, in the development of projects and the maintenance of systems. There is one IT/business steering committee (IBSC) per activity domain (Figure 3) that can set up one or more domain consultative body's (DCB) for specific functional business domains such as credit loans or securities. These two committees play an important role in the preparation and decisions of new investment projects (large development projects with a major architectural impact, like for example the implementation of SAP) and continuity projects (development projects mostly driven by evolutions in the market or legislation, for example the implementation of specific reporting due to legal requirements) (see Figure 5).

Figure 5. IT budget composition

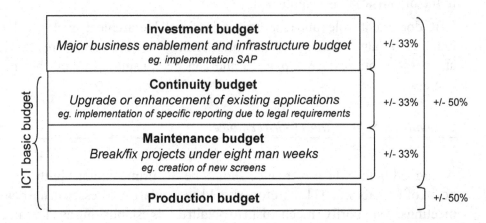

Figure 6. Committees representing business and IT

Committee	Authority	Composition	
		IT Representatives	**Business Representatives**
IT business steering committee (IBSC)	Project prioritisation Defines the needed budgets	Members of product factory, open systems and mainframe division	Member of executive committee; members of management committee of corresponding activity domain; 'organisation'
Domain consultative body (DCB)	Evaluate the business value of new ideas	IT architect; business analyst	Director of involved domain; business architect; process manager
Program Man. Steer. Group (PMSG)	Project management	Involved IT director(s); program manager	Sponsor of the project; involved business director(s)
Man. Operational Systems Committee (MOSC)	Decide on maintenance projects	Business analyst; system manager	Director of involved domain; process manager; application manager

The Program Management Steering Group (PMSG) is responsible for the project management of investment projects and clusters of continuity projects as soon as they are approved. During the lifetime of a system, the Management Operational Systems Committee (MOSC) decides on maintenance projects (small projects under eight man weeks, for example the enhancement of a specific screen) within the strategy and budget approved by the IBSC.

The roles and responsibilities of these committees are described in more detail in next chapter, which focuses on processes. In each committee, business and IT people are represented as shown in Figure 6, which enables alignment throughout the different stages of an IT project. Some of the roles mentioned (IT architect, business architect and analyst, process manager, system manager and application manager) are explained in detail in the chapter on relational mechanisms.

IT Governance Processes

Figure 7 illustrates how the committees are involved in the initiation, development, and maintenance process. The process described in the following paragraph does not cover the management of the production budget (bottom block of Figure 5), as this is still managed as one separate budget for all

Figure 7. IT project life cycle

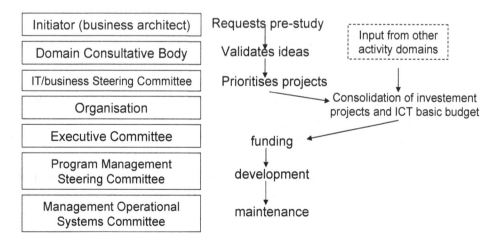

activity domains. It is the intention to also redistribute this production over the activity domains in the future.

New projects are always initiated by the business, for example by a business architect. This is a role assigned to a business representative, who needs to collect and manage business information that is essential for making business cases of IT projects (see infra). The business architect can initiate continuity or investment projects by developing a first idea, and these requests go to the DCB, who will evaluate the business value of the new ideas based on the results of a pre-study, that includes the business case, planning, sourcing, identification of synergies and risks, and infrastructure review. To obtain sufficient accuracy, 10-20 percent of the total cost of a development project is dedicated to this pre-study in which business and IT are involved. The business defines targeted goals, benefits, and costs, while IT more focuses on development costs, architecture, and so forth. The pre-study results in a kind of service level agreement, offering a fixed-time/fixed-price development project. For every project, a buffer of 10 percent of development costs is retained in the total price to pay for any cost over-runs.

When the DCB finds the project value-adding, it goes to the IBSC of the corresponding activity domain. Every year, this IBSC prioritises the continuity and investment projects needed for year x+1 and sets the needed maintenance budget, all within the overall target budget, which is set in advance by the executive committee. This target defines one overall budget for both maintenance and continuity projects. The IBSC itself has no investment budget. Funding for investment projects always needs to be requested at the executive committee, but the IBSC can decide to co-fund an investment project with a part of its continuity budget. When all the IBSCs defined what they need in year x+1, 'organisation' will aggregate the data before sending it to the executive committee.

The executive committee then approves or amends the IT basic capacity for year x+1 per activity domain and will decide which investment projects will receive budget. It was noted by one of the interviewees that, when the business case is developed, the decision at IBSC, or executive committee level, is mostly based on budget considerations and less on the content of the complete business case. This situation can be frustrating for business and IT people spending a lot of time in preparing the detailed business cases which go much beyond only financial estimations. On the other hand, by using this process, *"barriers are embedded that inhibit—partially—the initiation of irrelevant projects, create a natural filter and diminishes the possibility of*

Figure 8. Information economics at KBC

Return on investment	Alignment with strategy	Competitive advantage/need	Necessity (legal, organ.)	Reduces operat. risks
Support management	Project and organis. risks	Support future informat. architecture	Functional uncertainty	Technical uncertainty

people asking directly to the executive committee for specific funding without a thorough preparation." It could be argued that the model is rather heavy, which possibly endangers the ability of the organisation to quickly jump on new opportunities. However, a member of the board of directors, who is also part of the executive committee, challenges this argument: *"There will always be people who experience the model as being too complex and over-bureaucratic. But we now at least have a model which clearly shows how projects are initiated and decided upon. It is obvious that the business people prefer a very quick time-to-market, but they have to take the impact on the back office into account. If we take unprepared decisions, the danger exists of creating a mess in the back-office, and the cost of cleaning up this mess is much higher then doing a well-considered pre-study in advance."*

The executive committee prioritises between the investment projects based on the business case which is complemented with an 'information economics' assessment. In essence, information economics is a scoring technique resulting in a weighted total score based on the scores for the ROI and some qualitative criteria (Parker, 1995). The generic information economics method as developed by Benson and Parker is adapted to the own needs of KBC, retaining 10 criteria that are relevant (Figure 8).

Besides the financial criterion of return on investment, non-financial criteria, such as 'alignment with strategy,' are covered. For each criterion, a number of questions are developed. The questions for 'competitive advantage and need' for example are: "Does the program deliver competitive advantage?" and "Is the program a necessity to remain competitive?" The criterion gets a red colour if the average of the underlying questions is lower then 2.4, yellow if the average is between 2.4 and 3.8, and green if the average is above 3.8. There is no overall average calculated over all criteria, so in this way, a kind of traffic light report is generated for each investment project, as visualised in Figure 9.

Figure 9. Traffic light report for all investment projects

Scoring Investment files				Category							Risks		
ATS	Trekk. ATS	Pnr	Name	Return	Alignment to strategy	Competitive benefit	Necessity	Legal necessity	Information architecture	Reduction operational risk	Project & organisational risks	Functional uncertainties	Technical uncertainties
Projects													
RET	MKT	0020	Intrest and liquidity risk (ALM_TDI)	1	5	4	5	5	5	5	2	5	5
OND	OND	0021	Quantitative Credit Risk Management (QCR)	4	5	5	5	5	5	1	4	5	5
RET	RET	0119	KBD : Multichannel credit app.	4	5	4	3	3	5	5	2	1	1
RET	RET	0202	KIT	4	5	4	4	3	3	5	3	1	3
RET	RET	0232	Oleander	1	5	5	1	3	5	3	3	1	2
NAV	NAV	0245	Collateral Management Fase 2	5	3	3	1	3	5	5	3	3	4
BED	BED	0292	Web-enabling of ICM application	4	5	5	1	3	1	1	4	1	3
NAV	NAV	0397	IPE / EBOBA	1	5	4	1	3	5	3	4	5	4
NAV	NAV	0399	Processing OTC Derivates	4	5	4	4	3		5	4	1	
RET	RET	0403	VA Front-end Life										
RET	RET	0408	Product factory insurance	2	5	4	1		5	3	4	1	3
OND	OND	0442	Operational Risk management	5	5	5	5	5	3	5	3	3	3
RET	RET	0449	Rework client output	5	5	4	5		5	5	3	5	2
OND	OND	0456	IAS Insurances	4	5	4	5	5	3	3	4	5	3
OND	OND	0479	Limit volatility for IAS	1	5	3	5	5	3	1	4	5	2
OND	OND	0501	ERP for supporting services B+V										
RET	RET	0518	OFS (Development Financial Services)	4	5	4	1	3	5	5	3	1	3
Nieuwe													
RET	RET	0308	Migration Centea	1	5	3	1	5	5	3	3	1	3
OND	OND	0480	Reconciliationtool	1	5	1	3		3	5	1	3	3
RET	RET	0894	Pleander Pre-study private Life others	1	5	5	2	3	5	3	2	5	2
OND	OND	0887	European taxation savings	1	5	4	3		3	5	4	5	1
OND	OND	0899	ERP - phase 2	1	5	5	5	5	3	5	4	5	3

Yellow | Green | Red

This scoring is performed by the initiator of the investment project, mostly the business architect. To obtain an objective measurement and a consistent scoring, representatives of 'organisation' always challenge and overview the scores when they consolidate all investment projects prior to going to the executive committee.

For each new agreed investment project or cluster of continuity projects within an activity domain, a PMSG is assigned by the IBSC, again composed of business and IT people to ensure alignment throughout the development process. When a newly developed system goes into production, the further management is transferred to MOSC, also composed of business and IT people. The goal of the MOSC is to decide on maintenance projects within the strategy and budget approved by the IBSC.

Another process that can be leveraged for achieving more alignment is the use of the balanced scorecard (BSC). In KBC, a detailed scorecard is developed for the complete IT department, containing five perspectives: financial and corporate perspective, customer perspective, efficiency perspective, innovativeness and entrepreneurship perspective, and staff perspective. The latter proves that KBC pays a lot of attention to the development of its own IT staff. Some example objectives in each of these domains are shown in Figure 10. The CIO describes the major advantage of this IT BSC as *"a systematic translation of the strategy into critical success factors and metrics, which materialises the strategy."* As demonstrated in Van Grembergen, Saull and

Figure 10. IT balanced scorecard at KBC

User Orientation	Operational Execellence	Future Orientation	Staff	Corporate Contribution
• Establish (long-term) contractual relationship with all lines of business • Realize the goals together with the business • Make clear agreements and deliver against them regarding timing, content, quality, cost, availability, performance, reliability, safety, stability and continuity of the operational infrastructure and applications	• Synergies within KBC Group • Offer good quality/cost ratio (better than the market) • Optimize re-use and use of packages, establish joint ventures • Organise internally to be able to quickly react on opportunities and questions of the business • Achieve a Capability Maturity Level (CMM) that is 'Best in Class' in the financial industry	• Leverage innovativeness and entrepreneurship of IT towards to realisation of the Group's strategy • Translate new technologies and processes into new opportunities for lines of business • Translate entrepreneurship to the engagement of operational service delivery • Be a learning organisation	• Be an attractive employer • Promote roles with added value and assign most appropriate (preferably internal) people to them • Employ staff who is strongly involved in the IT strategy and work for client friendliness, efficiency, entrepreneurship and innovativeness of IT.	• Offer every line of business optimal solutions, with an efficient use of IT • determine market-conform price of service delivered based on full-cost charging, including risk- and investment margins • Be responsible high-quality risk management and security • Create insight into IT costs

De Haes (2003), the IT BSC only becomes a real alignment mechanism when causal relationship between metrics, and if possible between scorecards, are defined. There are, however, no formal causal relationships defined between metrics, nor are there scorecards defined at lower levels in the IT department (e.g., development department) or links developed with a business scorecard. The BSC within KBC is implemented as a measurement tool, but not as a strong alignment or management tool.

Operational costs, such as maintenance and user administration, are charged back to the business according to activity-based costing (ABC) principles, which provides a methodology to assign direct and indirect costs to real cost drivers (Romano, 1994). KBC's management found that for operational costs, the real cost drivers were not enough taken into account and that indirect costs were only assigned using arbitrary criteria. For example, in the previous cost-model, there was a cost object 'workstation,' without making any differentiation between PCs or laptops, standard or non-standard. The defined cost also included software and hardware. The only steering factors for the business to reduce its workstation costs were therefore reducing the number of workstations. Identifying more clearly the real cost drivers would enable the business to intelligently manage their workstation. The ABC implementation project started at the end of 2002 with four major goals: (1) achieve more cost awareness by end-users, as well as by the IT department; (2) achieve an optimal allocation of IT costs; (3) set up a mechanism that justifies costs charged back to the business; (4) achieve more market conformity through benchmarking. During the ABC project, all the direct and indirect costs were identified, activities were defined based on ITIL (Information Technology Infrastructure Library) and the consumption of products and services of activities was described. All standard services and products are consolidated in the service catalogue, which creates more cost-transparency for the end-users and enables them to make well-considered decisions.

Relational Mechanisms

Relational mechanisms are very important. It is possible that an organisation has all IT governance structures and processes in place, but that it does not work out because business and IT do not understand each other and/or are not working together. It may be that there is little business awareness on the part of IT or little IT appreciation from the business. So, as explained in chapter 1, to reach effective IT governance, a two-way communication and a good participation/collaboration relationship between business and IT people is needed.

One of the important steps KBC took to implement relational mechanisms is the definition of—in their terminology—the IT charter (Figure 11). This IT charter defines mirror roles between business and IT people, and these people need to interact directly. A person can have different roles but some roles are on the other hand divided over several persons. The *business architect* collects and manages information from the business, essential for making the business case of IT projects. He/she is also responsible for managing the business architecture (business functions, processes, etc. and for analysing the gap between 'as-is' and 'to-be' situation of this architecture. The business architect needs to collaborate with the IT architect, who will use all this information to align the IT strategy with business priorities and to analyse were IT can play an enabling role for the business strategy. The *IT architect* is also responsible for ensuring that IT infrastructure responds to the needs of the business infrastructure and for analysing the as-is and to-be situation of the IT infrastructure. The *process manager* oversees the process of handling products and services in a specific line of business. This person collaborates with the *business analyst*, a person on IT site who knows the business very well, and who prepares input for pre-studies and need's analysis. The *product manager* is the developer of new products, and reviews all products and services from a commercial and marketing point of view. The *application manager* is responsible for the functional management of IT for a product, service or channel, which includes involvement in development projects and testing of systems before final delivery. He/she is typical a lead user, which

Figure 11. IT charter

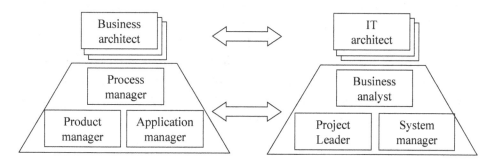

implies that this can not be a full-time role. The applications manager acts as a contact point for the system manager, responsible for delivered systems.

While in this IT charter model, IT and business people need to interact directly in the business lines, KBC also organises account management meetings that establish a bridge between business and IT at the higher level of the different business directions of the bank and assurance activities (Figure 3). As explained before, business and IT people are involved in the project initiation and decision making process via different committees, such as IBSC and MOSC. The account management meeting only focuses on the relational aspects between business and IT; it is not project driven as for example the IBSC and MOSC, discusses general ideas and needs, and the ways specific issues can the handled. Per business direction, these account management meetings are composed of the most involved IT division, the service delivery owner (a function within IT), the general director of the business unit and a business architect.

Finally, KBC also uses other relational mechanisms to manage the 'soft' side of the IT-Business relations, such as co-location, language use (for example 'partnership' instead of 'à-la-carte relationship'), senior IT management giving the good example of collaborating with the business, job rotation (senior IT people moving to key position in the business), training sessions on business activities, and so forth. KBC uses internal magazines to explain the governance model and established a 'business-IT governance' site on their intranet, with explanations of the roles and responsibilities, the committees, templates, and so forth.

In all these ways, KBC tries to achieve an active participation, collaboration, and shared understanding between business and IT people in every stage of the project, from a shared understanding of the objectives to collaborative implementation. Yet, as already mentioned, in the beginning the model was experienced as being imposed by IT, although the initial request came from the business. There was indeed a short communication line between the CIO and the executive committee, but perhaps a stronger communication was needed towards the general directors of the business departments stating that this new model was requested by the executive committee and for the best interest of as well business and IT. Moreover, the model is quite complex, and everyone needs to understand its role in it, so pro-active training and competence management are very important. The provision of the intranet site is of course very good, but it still remains a pull-technology, while it could be very worthwhile that people be introduced to the governance model via some training. For example, when using information economics in business cases, it is important that everyone understands the same things behind the metrics. This is very hard to achieve via a short explanation on the intranet, and could be better realised via a more extensive training. Moreover, when the people better understand the 'why' of making business cases and information economics assessments, this effort will not be regarded as overhead anymore.

Maturity Measurement/Assessment

Finally, the use of maturity models as an IT governance mechanism is investigated within this organisation. The IT governance maturity model as developed by the IT Governance Institute (2003) and described in chapter 1 provides an excellent base. The maturity model offers a methodology to define the as-is and to-be situation of a specific IT governance model, analyse the gaps between it, and extract improvements projects. The scores of the KBC interviewees ranged from 2 to 4, with the member of the board of directors assigning the highest score. The argument for the lowest score was that probably not all involved people in the model completely passed the 'awareness' phase and clearly understand their role. When considering the basic principles of maturity models—which says that one can only move to a higher maturity level when all requirements of the previous level are fulfilled—the researchers argue that at most level 3 is achieved. This level amongst others requires (which can be read in the complete maturity model) goal and performance indicators to be set for the IT governance process. Although these indicators are important to measure the IT governance success, they are not formally set and tracked at KBC. Examples could be the compliance with the overall procedures, the quality of the business cases, the achieved alignment, and so forth. One of the inhibitors identified for moving to a higher maturity level is the difference between business and IT in their history of working in a project or process environment. IT has been working for a longer time in such process and project oriented environments and is more used to analysing problems and challenges in a structured project-oriented way. This difference in approach often causes frictions and lack of respect and consequently inhibits the growth to more mature processes.

Summary of IT Governance Structures, Processes and Relational Mechanisms

Having developed a high-level IT governance model does not imply that governance is actually working in the organisation. Peterson (2003), Van Grembergen, De Haes, and Guldentops (2003), and Weill and Woodham (2002) proposed that IT governance can be deployed using a mixture of various structures, processes, and relational mechanisms. The case demonstrated that KBC did implement a mix of these practices. KBC tries to involve business and IT in the project initiation, development and maintenance process by setting up committees composed of business and IT people. Investment projects are decided by the executive committee using the information economics methodology, measuring financial and non-financial (such as alignment) factors. To enable the business to make well-considered decisions, fixed-time/fixed-price development projects are agreed upon in SLAs and production costs are charged back using ABC. An IT BSC is established as a measurement tool, with a perspective specifically dedicated to IT staff. Finally, a whole set of relational mechanisms is exploited to manage the soft side of IT governance, such as account management roles. Most of the found practices were already mentioned in the first chapters of this book. A newly identified one was ABC, which is certainly an important alignment mechanism as it enables the business to fully understand the cost consequences of the taken decisions.

Although a balanced mix of structures, processes, and relational mechanisms was found, some pathologies were identified. Inconsistent with the IT governance definition, the board is not thoroughly involved and as a consequence, they can not take full responsibility and the leading role in IT governance. Secondly, KBC uses an IT balanced scorecard, but it is used only as a measurement instrument and not leveraged as a real alignment mechanism. Moreover, there are no clear key goal indicators and key performance indicators for the IT/business governance project, to be able to clearly track to process and goal attainment of IT governance. A final observation refers to the perception that the IT governance project was imposed by IT, creating resistance in the business to adopt the model. A better communication by clarifying that the IT governance project was initiated by the business and for the best interest of as well business and IT, could overcome this relational obstacle.

The optimal mix of structures, processes, and relational mechanisms is of course different in every organisation and depends on multiple contingencies (Patel, 2003; Ribbers et al., 2002). For the case of KBC specifically, quite a complex model of processes, structures, and relational mechanisms was established. This complexity was needed to overcome the complex organisational environment with an IT department working as a separate entity for multiple and diverse business activities. However, in a more 'uncomplicated' environment, this model may be overkill and only parts of it would be needed. Determining all the variables that have an impact on the appropriate IT governance model is probably not feasible. It would be an extremely complex endeavour to identify all factors that influence the choice for one specific process, structure or mechanism. Nevertheless, new case studies can provide more insight in specific contingencies which could be very useful for practitioners in defining the optimal mix.

Case Study: AGF Belgium

Company Introduction

AGF Belgium is an organisation active in the insurance market. The company is part of the French AGF Group, which in turn is incorporated in the larger German Allianz Group, since 1998. This Allianz Group is Europe's leader in the insurance market and is ranked within the top three worldwide. AGF Belgium currently executes a strategic acquisition and alliance policy to fortify its position on the Belgian market and to widen its service offerings. The consolidated figures of the Allianz Group, the AGF Group, and AGF Belgium are summarised in Figure 12. It shows that AGF Belgium reached a turnover of approximately € 870 million in 2005 with a headcount of just

Figure 12. AGF key figures

	Allianz	AGF Group	AGF Belgium
Turnover	approx € 75 billion	over € 17 billion	approx € 866 million
Employees	180.000	34.700	1.200

over 1200 employees. As mentioned in the introduction of this book, this case study was described in the period 2003-2005. It should therefore be noted that this case description only describes the IT governance status at that time in the organisation.

Whereas other major Belgian insurance companies choose for multi-distribution, AGF focuses on one unique distribution channel through independent brokers. AGF Belgium's business strategy, named 'growth plan 2006,' clearly distinguishes between two types of agent entities: medium-size professional agents (3-8 staff) and large-size professional agents or supra-regional agents (at least 8 staff). The motivation behind this strategy is that AGF Belgium strongly believes that those two types of professional agents are the most stable and durable in the highly competitive market place. These independent agents have freedom of choice within a diversified set of products and services and can use AGF's supportive tools, such as an extranet, that contribute to

Figure 13. Organisational structure

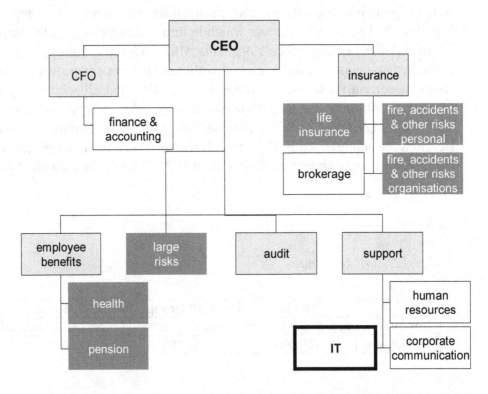

an increased production and to the optimisation of client management and administration. Next to the choice for the unique distribution channel, AGF Belgium aims to focus on its core business, namely *life* and *non-life* (i.e., fire, accidents, and other risks) *insurance* for either private individual, small, and medium enterprises or large businesses.

Figure 13 depicts the organisational structure of AGF Belgium. The business units with a supportive character (e.g., IT) are indicated in the white squares. The core business activities (e.g., life insurance) are visualised in the shaded squares. The business activities *life and non-life insurance* are under the supervision of the director insurance whereas the *employee benefits* and *large risks* components report directly to the CEO.

AGF's organisational structure, standardised by the Allianz Group uses distinct hierarchical levels: L0 is the president or CEO level; level L1 includes all members of the executive committee and L2 is the level of the director IT and all the business unit directors, who are reporting to level L0 or L1. As AGF is part of the Allianz group, it needed to revise its organisational structure to comply with the group's structure. Some functions in this new structure of Figure 13 are not installed yet. This is the case for the support function which means that actually the IT director reports directly to the CEO.

IT Governance Context

There are three important drivers for AGF in order to implement IT governance best practices: straightforward group strategy (including cost reduction and the implementation of best practices), budget pressures, and Sarbanes-Oxley Act compliance.

The insurance industry has experienced a wave of mergers and acquisitions induced by low stock prices. Obviously, the integration of organisations into larger groups also has an impact on the information technology function. After the take-over by the Allianz/AGF group, executive management pushed for the achievement of synergies and economies of scale within IT and AGF Belgium did optimize its organisation and cost structures. But, because it was important for the local entities to keep sufficient flexibility, the execution of the IT strategy is still in the hands of the regional entities.

As in many other industries, cost reduction became an important concern of executives during the last years. This certainly also impacted the pressure on IT budgets. AGF Belgium has faced two consecutive annual IT budget reductions—in 2003 and 2004—forcing IT to carefully establish a project portfolio management process as a governance practice. This effort and focus was clearly planned to be continued in the subsequent years.

Finally, external requirements such as the Sarbanes-Oxley (SOX) Act forces AGF Belgium to adopt more transparent business and IT processes. The SOX Act was shaped in 2002 to "*protect investors by improving the accuracy and reliability of corporate disclosures made pursuant to the securities laws, and for other purposes,*" and is applicable to the Allianz group and its subsidiaries because the group is listed at the New York stock exchange.

Through the aforementioned issues, management of AGF Belgium became aware of the need for a more structured IT governance approach. Initially they were guided by publications of the Gartner Group and the IT Governance Institute *Board Briefing on IT Governance* (ITGI, 2003) was an inspiration for developing the IT governance efforts. In their IT governance effort, AGF Belgium pays a lot of attention to value delivery and strategic alignment. The board is eager to gain an insight into the locus of value creation by IT. As for most other organisations in the sector, up to 85 percent of IT budget resources go to tasks that ensure continuity of the current level of service. Or in the words of the CIO: "*It doesn't take a mathematics genius to observe that only a minor part of the budget is allocated to potentially value adding activities.*" Taken this consideration into account, three important IT governance domains were identified for AGF:

- **Technology:** The director *non-life* argues that "*technology follows strategy, and not the other way around.*" In other words, it should not be the organisation's goal to implement new technology just for the sake of the technology. The business strategy should always be the driver. This is clearly a confirmation of the 'strategy execution perspective,' which is one of the four perspectives identified in Henderson and Venkatraman's strategic alignment model (1993). This perspective is built upon the premise that the business strategy has been articulated and is the driver for both organisational design choices and the design of the IT infrastructure.

- **Change Management:** All organisational changes, including those having an IT-impact, require a good allocation of (scarce) resources. In this context, there is a need for structures and rules that have to be respected.

- **Hardware:** The hardware of the organisation is a critical success factor for ensuring continuity and support of business processes. The quality of these processes largely depends on the underlying hardware infrastructure.

It is important to note that meanwhile, a significant higher percentage of around 40 percent of the development activities is considered to go to added value projects.

IT Governance Structures

Organisational Structures

The organisational structure of the IT department, which counts 166 internal and external employees on a total headcount of 1300, is shown in Figure 14. As already mentioned in the company introduction, there is a direct reporting line between the CEO and the director IT. During a recent reorganisation the director IT was asked what he preferred: reporting directly to the CEO or reporting to the CFO. He chose for the first option because he feared "*a growing distance between IT and executive management and a far too financial approach of the IT function.*" As a result of this, the director IT has good access to the executive committee, although he is not an actual member. He only participates in the executive committee whenever IT is distinctly on the agenda. In addition, the CEO and the IT director have a one-hour meeting once a week. The IT director prepares the very specific agenda for this meeting, which basically covers follow-up and steering.

The four areas of the IT department adhere to the classical model that distinguishes between systems, operations, services and development. Business process management used to be a separate staff-cell that basically worked for top-level management performing strategic studies and optimising processes on a specific business unit's request. Today, the business process managers fulfil a double role for this function: they optimise the organisation to ensure an optimum support for the business strategy and they support the different business units in the process of their organisational optimisation efforts. Additionally they serve as a filter for the business unit's requirements in order to ensure a smooth transition from business needs to project requirements, while at the same time they encourage (and guard) the link between business

Figure 14. Organisation structure of the IT department

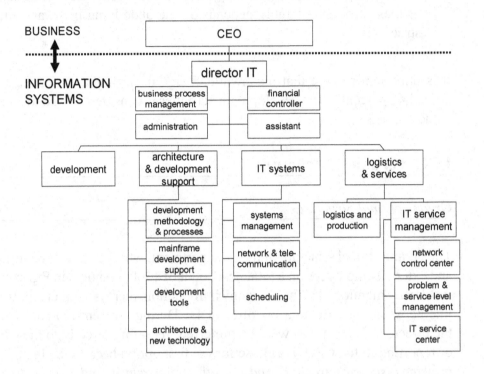

units regarding IT matters. It is important to note that AGF is continuously optimising this organisational structure.

Allianz does allow its subsidiaries a lot of freedom, mainly because they recognise the particularities of regional and national markets. Yet, frequent contact between the Allianz group and its subsidiaries is required. Representatives of the central IT department of Allianz meet twice a year with the regional IT directors. This gives the IT director of AGF Belgium the opportunity to discuss the group standards, policies, and potential synergies with his colleagues from other Western-European subsidiaries.

Roles and Responsibilities

Roles and responsibilities were not formally documented at AGF Belgium. However, "*That does not mean that there were no clear roles and responsibili-*

ties," argues the IT director. The typical company culture at that time implied that strict function descriptions were not used. Meanwhile a major HR-driven project has been initiated, where for each identified company function a complete description is given including the required competencies. The director IT argues that it is important that each function has a clear mission and each individual within the function receives clear objectives each year. However, it is also important that function descriptions do have an order of flexibility built in, so that they do not limit or restrict the individual too much.

Committees Supporting IT Governance

Committees are an excellent way of dealing with IT governance responsibilities on different levels in the organisation. Within AGF, four committees play an important role in the IT governance context: ComDir (executive committee), Comité Stratégique Information Systems (corporate IT steering committee),

Figure 15. Committees supporting IT governance

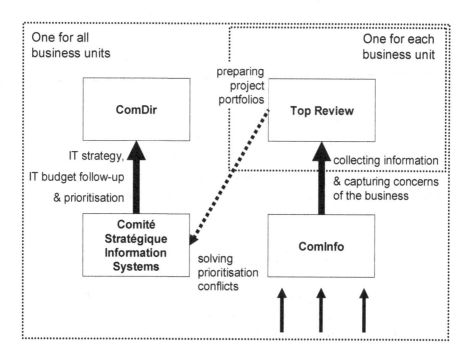

Top Review (business unit IT steering committee), and the ComInfo (operational committee). As can be seen in Figure 15, ComDir, Comité Stratégique Information Systems, and ComInfo are situated at corporate level, while Top Review is situated at business unit level.

ComDir serves as an **executive committee** and is the highest ranked committee within AGF Belgium. It provides the strategic direction of the company and has responsibility over budget decisions for both IT and the business units and over the definition of business projects. In addition, this committee can resolve any conflict that might arise between business units. ComDir is composed of the CEO, the CFO, the director for all broker related activities, and some business unit directors. The CIO is occasionally invited whenever IT is on the agenda.

Within AGF's **Comité Stratégique Information Systems**, the IT strategy is discussed, decisions are taken, and the outcome is communicated to both the IT department and the business units. Furthermore, this committee is responsible for the IT department's budget follow-up and prioritisation conflicts exceeding single business units must be solved here. The committee is composed of the IT director, the IT development manager, the IT systems manager, and the manager of architecture and development support, as well as the business unit directors and ComDir representatives. This committee can be seen as the **corporate IT steering committee** and has four meetings a year, two of which are devoted to the strategic and planning dialogue (see "IT strategy planning process").

AGF also established an **IT steering committee for each individual business unit**. These committees, the so-called **Top Reviews**, are responsible for the management of the business-IT relationship on a tactical level and the preparation of their individual business unit project portfolio and related budgets. The composition of these IT steering committees vary depending on the issues that need to be tackled. Mostly, they are composed of the IT development manager, the IT director, the business unit director, several operational business managers and the tandem account manager (IT)—chief representative for information systems (business unit CIO).

ComInfo is defined by the IT director as *"a transversal committee,"* and can be seen as an **operational committee**. It is a horizontal committee focusing on issues affecting all parts of the organisation, but on an operational level. It serves as a sounding board, capturing all the concerns that live within the business. As such this specific committee has acquired great de facto power although it is a committee that is situated at a relatively low hierarchical level

Figure 16. Typical agenda of ComInfo

1. Report of previous ComInfo
2. Tracking of Projects
Mainframe migration
–   Communication towards the independent professional agents
3. Technological topics
–   Security
–   Identity management
4. Feedback on budgets

within the organisation. ComInfo collects information in various layers of the organisation, and then disseminates it to the appropriate organisational entities, such as the IT steering committees. Figure 16 shows a typical agenda of ComInfo. This committee is composed of the IT director, the IT development manager, the manager of architecture and development support, the IT systems manager, and the chief representative for information systems of the business units (business unit CIO).

Figure 17 shows a summary of the composition of the different committees involved in IT related decisions and their respective authority.

IT Governance Processes

During the last three years there has been a tendency at AGF Belgium to shift from tactical alignment on a business unit level towards strategic alignment of business and IT strategy. Until recently, every single business unit was trying to get as much done as possible from the IT department which often resulted in a disproportionate distribution of IT efforts across the different business units. It was claimed by the IT director that "*those who cry out the loudest, get the most.*" This situation started to change when the definition of organisation-wide priorities took place. Every year, four up to five business priorities are defined. The business priorities are determined during two dialogue rounds in which the executive committee, the directors of the different business units and IT management are involved.

Figure 17. AGF Belgium committees, authorities and composition

Name	Authority	Composition	
		IT	**Business**
ComDir (executive committee)	budget decisions, business project definition and follow-up, conflict resolution across business units	director IT	CEO, CFO, and some business unit directors
Comité Stratégique Information Systems (corporate IT steering committee)	IT strategy definition, IT department budget follow-up, conflict resolution within business units	director IT, IT development manager, IT systems manager, manager architecture and development support	business unit directors, ComDir representatives
Top Review (business unit IT steering committee)	management of the client-supplier relationship (business unit—IT department)	IT manager, IT development manager, account managers	business unit directors, business unit CIOs, operational business managers
ComInfo (i.e., operational committee)	information collection and preparation for the Comité stratégique IS	IT manager, IT development manager, IT systems manager, manager architecture and development support	business unit CIOs

Each year in May, a strategic dialogue takes place during which business goals are determined without carefully taking into consideration the detailed budgetary impact. The outcomes of the first round are product strategies, marketing strategies, market positioning, solvability goals, and so forth, that all the entities within AGF Belgium should strive for and should be focusing on. The strategic dialogue follows a standard template determined by Allianz on group level.

In September/October, a planning dialogue takes place where the outcomes of the strategic dialogue are translated into concrete, mostly IT dependent projects. Budgets are allocated to the different projects, using the zero-based budgeting approach. This means that all expenditures, including those amounts exceeding previous period's funding, are to be justified. The actual budgeting takes place on an enterprise-wide level.

The balanced scorecard technique and the information economics method are not strictly adopted at AGF Belgium, but there is a tendency to move from a pure financial evaluation of proposed projects towards an evaluation in terms of added value for the business taking into consideration the business strategy and its objectives. Project evaluation mostly starts from return-on-investment and/or pay back time considerations. As a complementary input, AGF applies classical and rudimentary cost-benefit analysis, expressed in quantitative and qualitative business terms.

Just recently, a strict and formal business case approach was applied for the new project portfolio, which helped significantly in the budget arbitration exercise.

It should be noted that most other measurements within IT are mainly technical, which is an indication of a fairly low level of IT governance (cf. Luftman's Maturity Model in "*Maturity Measurement/Assessment*"). Yet, a lot of progress has been made. In the past, there was a lack of any operation policy causing servers to be shut down at the operator's best convenience. This of course impacted the work of many people resulting in losses and rework. Today, however, throughput times, quality of service and cost variability, among other things, are carefully measured, resulting in a better planning of operational activities.

AGF uses standards, such as ITIL, CMM and RUP, to organise their IT processes. At the Allianz group, elements of more high-level frameworks that are closer to the business, such as COBIT, are being applied now and it is the intention to further develop these. According to the IT director, "*the Capability Maturity Model, as well as ITIL, is largely contributing to AGF's IT governance methodology. The main reason for this is that both practices are appropriately industry-wide accepted. AGF Belgium—and more generally the entire Allianz group—prefers the use of industry proven methodologies for the sake of their robustness and completeness.*"

ITIL is a widely accepted approach to IT service management, providing a cohesive set of best practices drawn from the public and private sectors internationally (see first chapter of this book). At AGF Belgium, ITIL is specifically used for incident and problem management. The aim is to use ITIL in combination with Microsoft Operations Framework (MOF), which provides answers to many "how-to" questions. Building upon the ITIL framework, MOF further extends it through the inclusion of guidance and best practices derived from the experience of Microsoft operations groups, partners, and customers, and very specifically, provides guidelines for the use of Microsoft products and technologies. AGF chose to use both ITIL and MOF as a basis for all service-providing processes. They started the effort with incident and problem management and will gradually cover other processes as well.

AGF also uses IBM's rational unified process (RUP). RUP is an object-oriented and web-enabled program development methodology. It is a software engineering tool that combines the procedural aspects of development (such as defined stages, techniques and practices) with other components of development (such as documents, models, manuals, and code) within a unifying network. RUP unifies the entire software development team and optimises the productivity of each team member by bringing them the experience of industry leaders and lessons learned from thousands of projects. It provides detailed and practical guidance through all phases of the software development life cycle and is intended to be tailored, meaning an appropriate development process can be selected for a particular software project or development organisation. RUP is particularly interesting for large development teams. At AGF, RUP is used as a basis for the entire development process.

In addition, AGF Belgium uses the capability maturity model (CMM) developed by the software community with stewardship by Carnegie Mellon University's Software Engineering Institute. It is a model for evaluating and measuring the maturity of the software (development) processes of an organisation on a scale of 1 to 5. The CMM describes the principles and practices underlying software process maturity. It is intended to help organisations improve the maturity of their software processes in terms of an evolutionary path from ad hoc, chaotic processes to mature, disciplined software processes. This model makes it possible for organisations to identify the key practices required to help them increase the maturity of these processes.

Relational Mechanisms

A relational mechanism that contributes to a mutual understanding between IT and business issues, is the tandem account manager (IT)—chief representative for information systems (business unit CIO). Both of them are a member of their business unit's IT steering committee (see also "Committees supporting IT Governance") and thus meet on a regular basis. The main objective for this tandem is the attainment of a good communication between IT and the individual business units. On the strategic level, there is still place for improvement. One major cause for the sometimes difficult communication between the business and IT is the fact that the IT department has a technical and specialised history. The challenge that the IT department thus faces, is trying to translate its procedures and practices in non-technical terms that can be understood by the business.

When asked explicitly, the relationship between the business and the IT department is evaluated as being good. Assessing the relationship on a 5-point Likert scale, the IT director gives a score of four, emphasising that *"the operational cooperation has attained a high level of satisfaction."* The director *non-life* agrees to a large extent with the IT director, but he doubts between a score of three and four. The cooperation between the business and IT is good, efficient and effective which could be a motivation for a score close to four. Yet, some of the applications are out-dated and although this is not a factor influencing the IT-business relationship directly, it causes frustration in the business. More flexibility and agility would be desirable, but the aforementioned director does recognise that the available relative low IT budgets—less than 3 percent of the total turnover—do not enable the desired changes within the organisation.

AGF is aware of the importance of IT governance related communication towards all levels in the organisation. An important mechanism here is the existence of team sessions during which important decisions are communicated in understandable, down-to-earth terms. These team sessions repeat information that has already been spread, but may not have been fully captured throughout all levels of the organisation. They are not really sessions with an instructor and an audience; *"it is more a discussion, an 'exchange of ideas' which is organised once a year for all the different teams (one team at a time),"* says the IT director.

IT governance at AGF Belgium is a phenomenon that is initiated by the IT department, and as such still has not yet recieved the attention it deserves

158 Van Grembergen & De Haes

from all other parts of the organisation. This conclusion was confirmed during the interview with the director *non-life*. Apart from the strategic dialogue, the planning dialogue and the Top Review (identified as a business unit IT steering committee), this director did not unveil any other structures, processes or relational mechanisms contributing to IT governance. Moreover, one of the reasons for a relatively low level of awareness in the "higher strata" of the organisation, is probably due to *"the rather 'Burgundian' underlying culture typifying many Belgian organisations, as opposed to the more formal Anglo-Saxon culture that is characterised by a transparent top-down stream of information, communication and awareness of important organisational issues,"* argues the IT director.

According to the IT director, *"no explicit IT governance training is provided at this moment."* Yet some of the trainings that are offered to the personnel will probably indirectly contribute to good IT governance. The account managers representing the IT department, for example, receive formal training focusing on their specific role as service providers. The reason for this training was that they didn't clearly understand their role that sometimes led to sub-optimal client interaction and services delivered. *"The ideal IT governance training would start with a definition of the concept and its objectives,"* states the IT director, *"then followed by a comprehensive covering of the business-IT alignment theme including: how to guarantee transparency in terms of value creation and costs, determining and measuring of objectives and realised results, management of resources and risk management in the context just mentioned. All involved parties would be offered the same training, but special attention would be given to all management layers with proper elaborations and detail, as well as adapted examples."*

Knowledge management increasingly becomes part of the Allianz Group agenda. The aim of the group-wide knowledge management initiative does not primarily focus on IT governance, but yet, some IT issues are covered. Knowledge management within the Allianz group primarily includes group-wide principles that should be adhered to. At the time of the case description, the knowledge management system—an Allianz initiative—was still in a start-up phase. However, the classical means of electronic cooperation, such as shared directories, the corporate intranet, shared documents with revision marks and comments are available. For IT specifically, there is no knowledge management system as such. Nonetheless, *"there is a considerable pragmatic evolution in that direction,"* informs the IT director.

Maturity Measurement/Assessment

During the interview protocol the interviewees were asked to assess their organisation's IT governance maturity level using the ITGI (Information Technology Governance Institute) maturity model.

Both the IT manager and the director *non-life* assessed the maturity of AGF at level two—"Repeatable but Intuitive." The IT manager added that "*AGF Belgium is striving to get to the next level, but currently, taking into account the budgetary pressure on the IT department, only small steps of improvement, as opposed to quantum leaps, can be realised.*" The ultimate aim is to achieve maturity level four, "Managed and Measurable." The main motivation for this aim, says the IT director, "*is that level four guarantees that IT governance is measurable and tangible.*"

The assessed maturity level of two can be explained by evaluating the specific requirements for this level (see Figure 18):

1. There is the presence of an IT steering committee both on corporate and business unit level (respectively called Comité Stratégique Information Systems and Top Review). These committees focus often on the management of the tactical client-supplier relationship and not on the operational level (i.e., project management and service level management).

2. A (draft) operational governance charter is in place in the form of a slides presentation outlining the different committees' roles and authority. Surprisingly, the director *non-life* did not seem to be aware of this presentation. Yet, it must be noted that it is the initiative from the IT department, while ideally it should be an initiative by both the business and IT.

3. Several standards and general guidelines for architecture have been put in place. So, the criterion, '*General guidelines are emerging for standards and architecture,*' is complied with.

4. A fourth criterion of maturity level two that is fulfilled in the form of a dialogue between the business and IT during the two annual dialogues: the strategic dialogue and the planning dialogue. The fulfilment of this criterion confirms the growing awareness of the strategic importance of IT for the organisation.

Figure 18. IT governance maturity model (IT Governance Institute): Level two

---

2.   Repeatable but Intuitive

There is **awareness of IT governance objectives**, and practices are developed and applied by individual managers. IT governance activities are becoming established within the organisation's change management process, with active senior management involvement and oversight. Selected IT processes have been identified for improvement that would impact key business processes. IT management is beginning to define standards for processes and technical architectures. **Management has identified basic IT governance measurements**, assessment methods and techniques, but the process has not been adopted across the organisation. There is no formal training and communication on governance standards and responsibilities are left to the individual.

An **IT steering committee** has begun to formalise and establish its roles and responsibilities. There is a **draft governance charter** (e.g., participants, roles, responsibilities, delegated powers, retained powers, shared resources, and policy). Small and pilot governance projects are initiated to see what works and what does not. General guidelines are emerging for **standards** and architecture that make sense for the enterprise and a **dialogue** has started to sell the reasons for their need in the enterprise.

The only criterion that has not been fulfilled yet, is *"Small and pilot governance projects are initiated to see what works and what does not."* Looking at the relatively small size of AGF Belgium, the IT director thinks such pilot projects are not really necessary.

Today's IT governance practice at AGF Belgium is strongly IT-driven. The origin of the emerging IT governance effort is to be found in the management level of the IT department. Consequently, the ambition to reach the next level of maturity will undoubtedly oblige a higher degree of awareness of IT governance at all IT levels, and even more essentially at the business side of the organisation.

Summary of IT Governance Structures, Processes and Relational Mechanisms

Figure 19 summarises the different structures, processes, and relational mechanisms supporting IT governance at AGF Belgium.

The IT function at AGF Belgium is largely centralised, although some standards (e.g., security standards) are imposed by Allianz at group level. There is a direct reporting line between the CIO and the CEO, which reduces the distance between IT and the executive management.

A number of steering committees on different levels have been established to ensure sufficient business and IT involvement in the decision cycles on IT. Next to the executive committee, AGF Belgium has a corporate IT steering committee, IT steering committees at business unit level and a horizontal operational committee which fulfils the role of sounding board.

On the process side, there is the IT strategy planning, which takes place in two consecutive rounds, namely the strategic dialogue followed by the planning dialogue. Projects are prioritised using return on investment (ROI) considerations in combination with cost-benefit analysis expressed in quantitative and qualitative business terms. Rational unified process (RUP) and capability maturity model (CMM) are used as methodologies in the software development process. For the IT operations, ITIL is specifically used for incident and problem management. Some of domains which are actively measured include throughput times, quality of service and cost variability.

An important relational mechanism found at AGF is a tandem account manager (IT)—chief representative for information systems (business unit). Both of them are a member of the business unit's IT steering committee and meet on a regular basis. The main objective for this tandem is the attainment of good communication between IT and the individual business units. IT governance awareness to the organisation is established through the corporate IT steering committee communications, as well as team sessions during which important information is repeated and an exchange of ideas takes place. Furthermore, a knowledge management system was in a start-up phase and although the initiative did not primarily focus on IT governance, some IT issues are covered.

Figure 19. IT governance structures, processes and relational mechanisms at AGF Belgium

Structures		
What?		*How?*
1	Organisational structure of IT function	Ninety percent centralised at AGF Belgium, directly reporting to CEO
2	Committees	Executive committee (ComDir)
		Corporate IT steering committee (Comité Stratégique IT)
		Business unit IT steering committees (Top Review)
		Operational committee (ComInfo)
Processes		
What?		*How?*
1	IT strategy planning	Strategic dialogue and planning dialogue
2	Balanced scorecard technique	Not applied
3	Information economics	Partly applied
4	ROI calculation	Used in combination with cost-benefit analysis
5	Measuring	Throughput times, quality of service and cost variability, development productivity and quality
6	COBIT	In start up
7	ITIL	Specifically used for incident and problem management
8	RUP	Used for software development
9	Gartner Group Publications	Used as inspiration
10	ITGI Publications	Used as inspiration
11	CMM	Used to measure maturity of software development process
Relational Mechanisms		
What?		*How?*
1	Business-IT communication	Tandem account manager (IT)—chief representative for information systems (business unit CIO)
2	Training	No formal 'IT governance awareness training' only for specific IT themes
3	IT governance awareness	Important role of 'IT strategy committee'
		Team sessions
4	Knowledge management	Initiative at Allianz Group level, no specific IT (governance) focus
5	Job rotation	Not systematically applied

Case Study: Vanbreda

Company Introduction

In the 1930s, Bank J. Van Breda & C° was founded in Belgium by Jos and Maurice Van Breda. While they initially focused on bank activities, they evolved over the years into a financial services group with bank and insurance activities. The bank component retained its original name (Bank J. Van Breda & C°), whereas the insurance component operates these days under the name Vanbreda and currently exists of two companies: Vanbreda Risk & Benefits and Vanbreda International. Another part of the group is Informatica J. Van Breda & C°, the IT servicing company of the aforementioned business divisions. As mentioned in the introduction of this book, this case study was described in the period 2003-2005. It should therefore be noted that this case description only describes the IT governance status at that time in the organisation.

Figure 20 illustrates the dependencies between the different Van Breda/Vanbreda companies.

This case description focuses on the Vanbreda insurance branches of which the detailed organisational structure is visualised in Figure 21. Both insur-

Figure 20. Dependencies between the insurance component and the bank

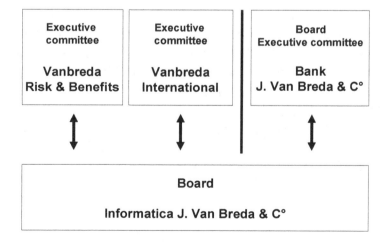

Figure 21. Organisation structure of the insurance component

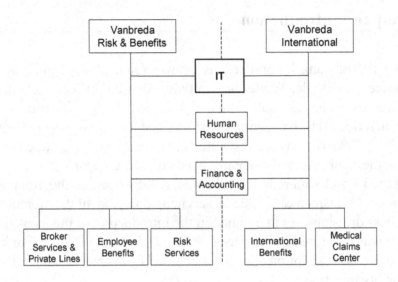

ance companies share a number of functional departments, including systems development. They have a combined turnover of € 75 million with a headcount of 650. Vanbreda Risk & Benefits focuses on insurance brokerage, risk management and employee benefits within Belgium, whereas Vanbreda International is specialised in the area of international employee benefits. The core business of Vanbreda Risk & Benefits is situated in the areas of insurance brokerage, reinsurance brokerage, consultancy, and risk management to enterprises, public authorities, non-profit organisations, and individuals, both domestically and abroad. The core business of Vanbreda International is the design of health plans for international groups and their claims administration. Vanbreda International is also specialised in giving advice on the most efficient funding arrangements for the social security system of their clients and concentrates on medical and dental coverage, long term care, pension plans, and so forth.

IT Governance Context

When asked what is understood by the concept of IT governance within Vanbreda, the financial director answered: "*IT governance indisputably shows some parallels with corporate governance. It is about setting up the right structures distinguishing between operational and strategic IT aspects. It is important that decisions are being taken at the right level and that one has a 'helicopter view' on IT.*"

The importance of setting up clear IT governance structures became clear to the management of Vanbreda when a major project failed. At that time, all IT operations and system development of the group were centralised within Informatica J. Van Breda & C°, partly explaining the project failure because business and IT were drifting apart too much. It was acknowledged that both banking and insurance businesses had need for specific business applications, which led to a new IT governance structure integrating IT development directly into the business and leaving the operational activities within Informatica J. Van Breda & C°. This is a typical example of the federal IT organisation, a model that is wide spread in large organisations. When, recently, this structure was implemented, IT development staff was transferred away from the single IT organisation towards the bank and insurance business entities. By anchoring these IT employees into the business, a better fusion between the business and IT could be achieved. On the other hand, the decision of keeping operations centrally was based on cost efficiency and economic rationality. The entire change is being perceived as a growth process and did not cause substantial problems. The financial director comments: "*The whole process is being experienced as a logical evolution.*"

Asking what the ideal IT governance would look like, the financial director replied: "*We would first have to determine which IT governance model applies to our organisation (i.e., 'which characteristics depicted in the IT governance framework apply to the organisation?'). Next, we can assess the 'as-is' situation. We would then have to determine where we want to be in the future (i.e., the 'to-be' situation). Bridging the gap between as-is and to-be would require clearly defined initiatives and projects that obviously have to be accompanied by the right type and amount of training to all people involved in this effort.*" The IT director senses that most of the educational and training programs currently on the market "*last several days and thus are very time-consuming while they hardly generate anything.*" He asks for an alternative way of training suggesting *"a small team of consultants/trainers visiting the organisation, completing a 5 to 10-day audit and then providing explicit proposals for changes. This form of training would have a minimal cost and maximal output. In addition, it could be interesting to have short sessions from time to time during which a theoretical framework would be outlined and explained, followed by practical questions."*

IT Governance Structures

Organisational Structures

As described in the previous section, a major characteristic of the IT organisation is its federal approach with operations centrally located at Informatica J. Van Breda & C° and systems development within the insurance businesses. The main goal of this structure is to bring IT development closer to the business. Figure 22 portrays the organisation chart of Informatica J. Van Breda & C°. This chart shows a classical organisation of IT operations with production management, systems management, help desk facility, systems architecture, and security. Somewhat specific is document management, containing all activities related to archiving, printing and physical mail, and voice mail (telephony). Informatica J. Van Breda & C° is a separate company

Figure 22. Informatica J. Van Breda & C° organisational structure

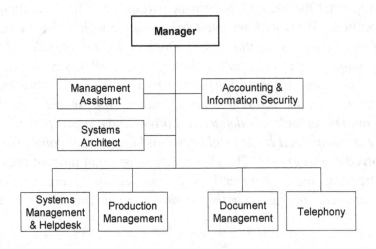

with a turnover of € 6.4 million employing 30 people. The turnover can be considered as the total IT operations budget of the group. Approximately 60 percent of this turnover goes to Vanbreda International and Vanbreda Risk & Benefits.

Figure 23 shows how the IT projects and development department of Vanbreda's insurance business is organised. Within this systems development department, a clear distinction is made between projects and development. The project units form a bridging function, known as account management, between the business and development, whereas the development units include the systems architects and the developers. The IT projects and development department counts 46 people, of which 40 are developers and 6 are account managers. Their IT budget is about € 7.5 million, representing about 10 percent of the turnover, a common percentage in the financial sector.

Individual function descriptions exist at Vanbreda to define the roles and responsibilities of their employees. These descriptions consist of a function name, objectives, a task description, required skills, and the assessors. A typical function description for the IT director is shown in Figure 24. From this description it can be seen that the IT director has complete responsibility over the IT development and implementation activities for the insurance business entities. Currently, this position is taken by a business manager with broad technical expertise which, conform the function description, corresponds with the required skills. The related assessors use a competence matrix to monitor whether the employee has fulfilled his role and taken up his responsibilities.

Figure 23. Organisational structure of IT projects and development

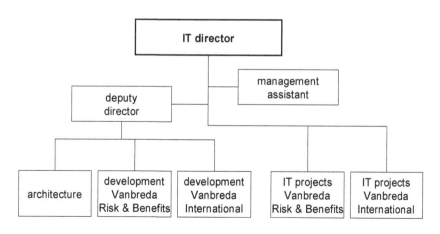

Figure 24. Abstract of an individual function description

Function name:	IT director
Objectives:	He has final responsibility on the IT development for both insurance entities. He is responsible for the continuity and permanent improvement of services. [...]
Task description:	He is responsible for the development of an IT communication strategy that fully supports the business strategy, with an effective and efficient use of specified resources. With strong project organization he needs to deliver high quality applications fast and cost-efficient, respecting the formulated needs and agreed budget and timing. [...] He has to prepare and document strategic IT choices and decisions.
Required skills:	This function requires a broad knowledge of the whole IT area, as well as in-depth knowledge of the different sub domains and good understanding of the business. [...] Furthermore excellent teamwork, communication and leadership skills and focus on efficiency as well as effectiveness and are essential.
Assessment:	This function is to be assessed by the managing director.

The competence matrix covers supervisory or management skills, analysing skills, communicative skills, planning and organisational skills, knowledge, involvement, and personal skills.

Committees Supporting IT Governance

The introductory chapter explains that there are different levels of IT governance responsibility—that is, the strategic level, the management level, and the operational level—and that IT governance should be an integral part of corporate governance. Committees are an excellent way of dealing with the IT governance responsibilities on different levels and at the same time they make it possible to integrate IT governance into corporate governance. As shown in Figure 25, Vanbreda establishes a number of committees for steering IT operations and development within the businesses. Each committee has its specific meeting frequency.

The board of Informatica J. Van Breda & C° is co-chaired by the CEOs of the insurance and banking units. In the context of best governance practices, the board is extended with an independent member. Other members of the board are the IT manager of Informatica and the ICT Director. This specific

Figure 25. Committees supporting IT governance

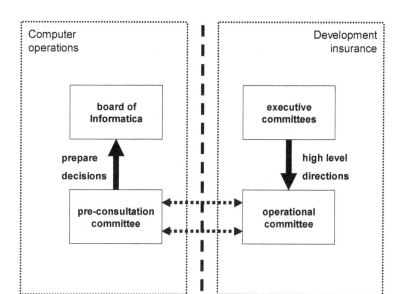

composition implies that the board also acts as an executive committee. Typical issues on the agenda are shown in Figure 26 and encompass for example an overview of the IT projects and the approval of established service level agreements between Informatica and the businesses.

The board is supported by a **pre-consultation committee** having more frequent meetings. This committee has an almost identical composition as the board and is also co-chaired by the CEOs of insurance and the bank. It prepares

Figure 26. Typical agenda of the board of Informatica J. Van Breda & C°

1. Approval and signing of the minutes of the previous Board

2. Overview of the headcount 2004

3. Overview of the projects in 2004

4. SLAs Informatica J. Van Breda & C° (version June 2004)

5. Information Security (version June 2004)

Figure 27. Typical agenda of the operational committee

1. **Report of previous Operational Committee**
2. **Tracking of Projects**
   2.1. **Projects of Vanbreda Risk & Benefits**
      - Planning IT development per 1/09/2004
   2.2. **Projects of Vanbreda International**
      - To be decided: Project E04056 "Translation into English"
      - To be decided: Project E04057 "Translation into English"
      - To be decided: Project E04060 "Split payments"
      - Planning IT development per 1/09/2004
3. **Personnel**
   - New vacancies Vanbreda International
4. **Miscellaneous**
   - Budget 2005 project hours Vanbreda Risk & Benefits
   - Budget 2005 project hours Vanbreda International
   - Capacity IT development 2005

Figure 28. Vanbreda committees, authorities and composition

Name	Authority	Composition	
		IT	**Business**
Board of Informatica J. Van Breda & C°	Aligning operations to business needs, overview of projects, approval of SLAs	IT directors of insurance and the bank, manager of Informatica	the CEOs
Pre-consultation committee	Prepares the board's decisions, discusses operational problems	IT directors of insurance and the bank, manager of Informatica	The CEOs
Executive committee Vanbreda Risk & Benefits	Providing high level directions	The IT director of the insurance units	All the directors of Vanbreda Risk & Benefits
Executive committee Vanbreda International	Providing high level directions	The IT director of the insurance units	All the directors of Vanbreda International
Operational committee	Prioritisation, selection and tracking of projects	The IT director and his deputy director of the insurance units	CEOs of both insurance units

the boards decisions and discusses operational problems. Whereas the board meets four times a year, this committee meets every second week.

The development activities of the insurance business are governed by its **executive committees**, focusing on high level directions, and an **operational committee**, which prioritises, selects and tracks projects in line with these directions. The operational committee is composed of the IT director, his deputy and two CEOs representing their insurance entity. Some typical agenda points of the operational committee (Figure 27), such as project priorities, resource allocation, and budgeting, demonstrate that this committee largely matches with what was defined in the introductory chapter as an IT steering committee.

Figure 28 provides a summary of the different committees having IT influence at Vanbreda, their authority and members within IT and the business.

IT Governance Processes

A formal written IT strategy is not in place for the insurance businesses. However, according to an internal slides presentation, it is the aim of IT projects and development to contribute to the achievement of both insurance entities objectives with a highly qualified team and with the cooperation of specialised partners. Furthermore, they want to realise high-quality applications fast and cost efficient, by means of a strong project organisation, on scope, on budget, and on time. Specific for Informatica J. Van Breda & C°, the IT strategy—which is actually their de facto business strategy—comes down to providing the best infrastructure and maximising the economies of scale in a shared services model.

There is no formal process that supports the IT development strategy, yet the IT strategy is linked pragmatically to the business strategy. The generic business strategies for both insurance entities are: "*maximising the number of clients and keeping current clients*" for Vanbreda International and "*maximising the number of clients and acquiring new clients*" for Vanbreda Risk & Benefits. This difference is translated into a difference in marketing strategy and logically this has an impact on the IT strategy of both insurance entities.

An important instrument supporting strategic decisions for business and IT is the strategic fit matrix as shown in Figure 29. This matrix was first used by the IT director for a large project called 'e-services.' The members of the execu-

Figure 29. Example of a strategic fit matrix

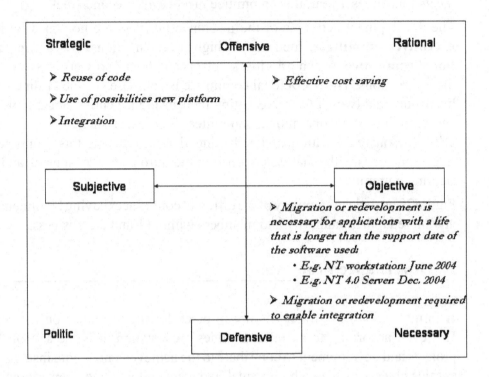

tive committee found that the matrix approach gave them a clear impression of the project and they decided to use it as a standard decision diagram for all projects. At the beginning of every project, the person who is responsible for the project should fill out the matrix by answering the questions: "Does this project have strategic elements that comply with the business strategy?", "What are the costs and benefits of the project?", and "Why is the project necessary?" The fourth quadrant (politic) is not yet in use. These answers place the project into different quadrants (strategic, rational, and necessary) and identify the character of the project (offensive, defensive, subjective, and objective). Figure 29 shows an example of a strategic fit matrix for a specific project, that is, the migration to Windows XP, Office 2003, and .Net.

Another method in use for the strategic evaluation of individual internet based projects is the strategic cross of Groeneveld and Hoogerbrug (2001). The strategic cross represents four different strategic parameters: impact,

Figure 30. Strategic cross

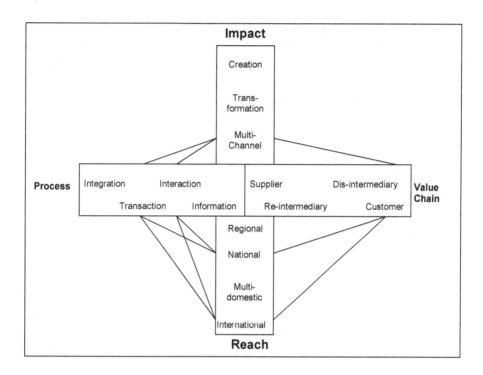

value chain, reach, and process. Each of these strategic parameters has different attributes in a specified interval. Graphically connecting the different parameters' attributes gives a clear indication of the scope and strategic meaning of the project. An illustration of this technique is provided in Figure 30. Following attributes of each parameter are applicable for Vanbreda's major e-strategy project:

- Impact: *Multi-channel*: customers can choose whether or not they want to use the on-line services
- Value Chain: *Customer*: Vanbreda focuses on the customer
- Reach: *National* and *international*
- Process: *Interaction* and *transaction*: there is interaction with the customer plus primary processes are delivered through the internet

For projects that are developed within the IT department the cost is to be calculated by multiplying the estimated number of project hours with an hourly
rate which is determined by the operational committee. The cost estimates
are presented at the committee that will have to decide on the project, that
is, the executive committee in case it is a medium size project (i.e., between
€ 2.500 and 25.000) or the operational committee in case it is a large project
(i.e., over € 25.000). Small projects (i.e., less than € 2.500) can be decided by
the advisor IT projects himself. During this decisional flow some aspects of
the balanced scorecard technique are being used. The information economics method is sometimes used with large projects. Also ROI calculations for
new projects are common practice.

Service level agreements (SLAs) are put in place to guarantee that every piece
of the IT puzzle knows exactly its role and responsibility in particular situa-
tions. The SLAs at Vanbreda are jointly defined by Informatica J. Van Breda
& C° and the business side and focus currently on services such as document
management, production management, system management, data protection
and the help desk (Figure 31). An improvement project is initiated including
the setting up of an automatic monitoring and reporting system. Follow-up
of SLAs takes place during monthly meetings. During these meetings the
measurements performed by Informatica are presented to the IT director and
the IT projects advisors.

Figure 31. Abstract of the help desk SLA of Vanbreda

1. Opening hours
2. Answering of calls
3. Registration of calls
4. Interventions
5. General services
6. Guaranteed hardware and software services
a. Personal computers, screens, portables, printers, modems, network cards and scanners
b. Isabel, Ariane…
c. Vendor website, Vanbreda Online…
7. Guaranteed, but supplementary hardware and software services
8. Other hardware and software services
9. Measurements
10. Appendices

The concepts of COBIT are known within the Informatica and the IT projects and development department but are not applied yet. According to the IT director of the insurance entities COBIT is not implemented because "*all is well as it is, we want to keep the present dynamics at Vanbreda, a relatively small organisation.*" ITIL is used by Informatica for its delivery processes including incident management, problem management and change management. Incident managers are appointed and every two weeks a problem/change meeting takes place.

Relational Mechanisms

Two important functions supporting the IT-business relationship have been identified: the IT project advisor and the account management function within the project and development department. The function description (Figure 32) and the cross-departmental responsibility (Figure 33) of the IT project advisor illustrate that he plays a crucial role in directing the project requests.

IT projects are usually initiated by the business; however Informatica can also initiate project requests whenever they discover new technology opportunities from which the insurance businesses can benefit. All requests are presented to the IT projects advisor who is the linking pin between the project initiator (mostly business) and involved partners including the IT projects and development department, Informatica and third parties. The

Figure 32. Abstract of the function description of the advisor IT projects

Function name:	Advisor IT projects
Objectives:	He is responsible for the delivery of functional specifications and serves as a linking pin for all IT projects of Vanbreda [...]
Task description:	He should give advice on mainframe and personal computer projects, e.g. functional analysis of projects. He monitors the SLA between Vanbreda and Informatica J. Van Breda & C°. He creates a good cooperation with the appointed staff and key users. [...]
Required skills:	Specialist knowledge of mainframe and personal computer systems, showing creativity and cleverness while searching for solutions, fluency and tact in communication, good organizational skills, structured reporting skills [...]
Assessment:	This function is to be assessed by the director IT

Figure 33. The role of the advisor IT projects (linking pin)

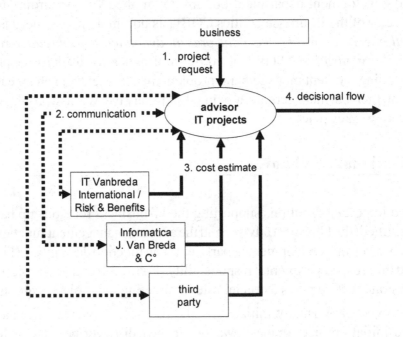

account management function within the projects and development department is seen as an important IT governance mechanism by Vanbreda. Account managers are organised per business unit and separating this function formally from the development group increases the business-IT relationship fundamentally. The account managers also guard the SLAs with the corporate IT department (Informatica).

The relationship between IT and the business was assessed at a rather high level four on a five-point Likert scale by the IT director and the manager of Informatica J. van Breda & C°. When asking the same question, the financial director even attributed a score between four and five, stressing the high degree of satisfaction and the good cooperation between IT and the business. The incorporation of the IT development group into the business unit is seen as the main driver for the optimal relationship between IT and the business group. *"Until the decision to move development towards Vanbreda International and Vanbreda Risk & Benefits was made, there was sometimes a lack of understanding of the business's needs from IT,"* explained the manager of

Informatica J. van Breda & C°. The decentralisation of development activities proves to be very effective. The IT director adds: "*IT can now steer the needs of the business, because IT is much closer to the business. Everything can be captured pretty easily. IT is better aware of technological possibilities and can make suggestions for the business. Compare it to a driver who does not know a convertible car. He will not ask for a convertible as long as he hasn't seen one for the first time when visiting a dealership. Its close position to the business enables IT to anticipate.*" Another factor contributing to the good relationship is "*the presence of the IT director in the insurance executive committees which undeniably contributes to IT being a part of the executive agenda,*" as argued by Informatica's manager.

Job rotation between business and IT and reversely is not a common practice. However, it happens from time to time: recently a business manger changed position and is now responsible for IT security within Informatica. With the integration of systems development in the business, co-location is now realised. The developers share the same work space as the business people and daily contacts are even enforced by the landscape setting of the desks.

No formal initiatives are taken at Vanbreda regarding IT governance training. But "*major IT-enabled projects are being presented to the business in what is called IT road shows,*" argues the IT director of the IT projects and development department. During a road show, the IT director visits the business entities and presents the planned and ongoing IT projects. In the case of a major e-services project, he explained what the objectives were, what the benefits were and what changes it would induce in the daily work. The IT road shows are seen as a mechanism to improve the understanding between IT and the business.

Maturity Measurement/Assessment

The maturity of IT governance has never been measured at the Vanbreda companies before. The interviewees were nonetheless asked to assess their organisation's IT governance maturity level using the ITGI maturity model. As described in the introductory chapter, this model comprises six maturity levels, ranging from zero to five. The rather high self assessment conducted by the IT director and the manager of Informatica resulted in level three ('*Defined Process*'), and maybe even level four ('*Managed and Measurable*').

In essence, maturity level three demands the following: "(1) *The IT steer-ing committee is formalised and operational, with defined participation and responsibilities agreed by all stakeholders, (2) The governance charter and policy is also formalised and documented, and (3) The governance organisa-tion beyond the IT steering committee is established and staffed.*"

Although criteria (1) and (3) seem to be fulfilled, Vanbreda cannot be at-tributed maturity level three. This is because, in order to be at a particular maturity level, all criteria have to be complied with. Vanbreda has many IT governance mechanisms in place, but an exact plan or a 'written down' docu-ment explaining the IT governance initiatives is missing. Consequently, the IT governance maturity at Vanbreda is positioned at level two ('*Repeatable but Intuitive,*' see Figure 34).

Figure 34. IT governance maturity model (IT Governance Institute): Level two

---

2. Repeatable but Intuitive

There is awareness of IT governance objectives, and practices are developed and applied by individual managers. IT governance activities are becoming established within the organisation's change management process, with active senior management involvement and oversight. Selected IT processes have been identified for improvement that would impact key business processes. IT management is beginning to define standards for processes and technical architectures. Management has identified basic IT governance measurements, assessment methods, and techniques, but the process has not been adopted across the organisation. There is no formal training and communication on governance standards and responsibilities are left to the individual.

An IT steering committee has begun to formalise and establish its roles and responsibilities. There is a draft governance charter (e.g., participants, roles, responsibilities, delegated powers, retained powers, shared resources, and policy). Small and pilot governance projects are initiated to see what works and what does not. General guidelines are emerging for standards and architecture that make sense for the enterprise and a dialogue has started to sell the reasons for their need in the enterprise.

Summary of IT Governance Processes, Structures and Relational Mechanisms

From the summary table of IT governance structures, processes, and relational mechanisms (Figure 35), it is clear that Vanbreda carries out a considerable number of efforts relating to IT governance.

First of all, there are the structural components contributing to IT governance. The federal organised IT department contributes to a good IT governance situation. The IT development and projects department of the Vanbreda companies are centralised into the business. IT services, IT operations and IT infrastructure are being provided in a shared services model in which Informatica J. Van Breda & C° plays a crucial role.

Four committees that tackle IT issues are shaped within Vanbreda companies: the board of Informatica J. Van Breda & C° ; the executive committee, which is in fact composed of two separate committees, one for Vanbreda International and one for Vanbreda Risk & Benefits; the operational committee IT, identified as an IT steering committee, and finally the pre-consultation committee. Other structural characteristics of IT governance include clearly defined roles, responsibilities and authorities. A competency matrix and formal job descriptions are specific tools used for this.

The IT strategy is rather straightforward and in operational terms, two tools are being used: the strategic fit evaluation matrix and the strategic cross. For projects, ROI calculation is common practice. In addition, different measuring and monitoring activities take place (e.g., SLAs). The Information Technology Infrastructure Library (ITIL) is being used at Informatica J. Van Breda & C°.

The third tier of the IT governance framework—relational mechanisms—appropriately gets the right attention at Vanbreda companies. The advisors IT projects serve as a single point of contact for streamlining all IT-related project requests.

Business-IT communication takes place in the form of 'road shows' that also enable a higher level of IT awareness at the business side. Job rotation—from IT to the business and possibly the other way around—is not common at Vanbreda companies. Nonetheless, some occurrences of job rotation were conveyed.

Figure 35. IT governance structures, processes and relational mechanisms at Vanbreda companies

Structures		
What?		**How?**
1	Organisational Structure of IT function	Centralised, with shared services from Informatica J. Van Breda & C°
2	Committees	Board of Informatica J. Van Breda & C°
		Executive committee
		Operational committee IT (IT steering committee)
		Pre-consultation committee
3	Roles and responsibilities	Advisor IT-projects: linking pin
		Use of competence matrix
		Job descriptions
Processes		
What?		**How?**
1	IT strategy planning	Strategic fit evaluation matrix
		Strategic cross
2	Balanced scorecard technique	Serves as an inspiration during the decisional flow of projects
3	Information economics	Serves as an inspiration during the decisional flow of large projects
4	ROI calculation	Applied
5	Measuring	Different monitoring and measuring activities (e.g., SLAs)
6	COBIT	Not applied
7	ITIL	Partly implemented at Informatica J. van Breda & C°
Relational Mechanisms		
What?		**How?**
1	Business-IT communication	Good understanding, road shows to present ongoing and future projects
2	Training	No formal IT governance training provided
3	IT governance awareness	Road shows to present ongoing and future projects
5	Job rotation	No common practice

Case Study: CM

Company Introduction

CM (Christian Union) is one of the five Belgian national health insurance unions. In Belgium, every worker pays for compulsory social security via taxes. This includes health insurance, replacement income in case of un-employment, pension or inability to work, child allowance, and additional social assistance benefits. CM is the largest Belgian organisation providing the health insurance part of the social security package. Besides the compulsory health insurance, CM also offers other insurance or health service products, such as hospital plans covering hospitalisation costs. CM counts over 4 million members. As mentioned in the introduction of this book, this case study was described in the period 2003-2005. It should therefore be noted that this case description only describes the IT governance status at that time in the organisation.

CM is the product of a merger of 21 regional entities. Total headcount of national and regional staff is 5,300. The president of CM is elected by the

Figure 36. Organisational structure

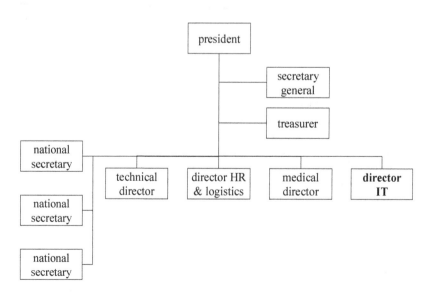

the board of governors. He is supported by a secretary-general, a treasurer, four directors (technical, HR&logistics, medical and IT), and three national secretaries (Figure 36).

The regional entities could be seen as the geographically organised business units of CM having a lot of authority. Besides the organisation of the compulsory health insurance towards their members, they create and offer additional health services. Although synergies are looked after on a national level, the regional entities still have a lot of decision power and decide on the majority of the budget. Further, each of the regional entities has its own human resources, accounting, and marketing department. The IT director comments: *"They have a lot of freedom […], which leads to a lot of tension, for example, when local entities decide to lease personal computers while the central IT department favours the policy of procurement."*

Each of these regional entities has its specific organisational structure. Interviews were conducted with the general director and IT staff of CM Antwerp. The structure of this representative entity will be further used. CM Antwerp

Figure 37. Organisational structure of CM Antwerp

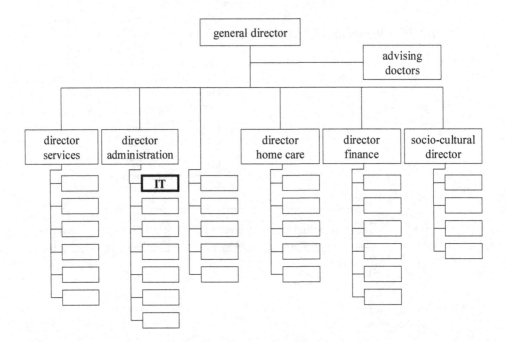

is headed by a general director who is assisted by advising medical doctors and five directors (Figure 37). Each of the directors has a number of responsibilities; the director administration for example is responsible for the IT department.

IT Governance Context

Due to the complex bottom-up structure with a high degree of local authority, it was difficult for the central IT department to formalise its charter. However, in the summer of 2002, the IT director participated in a Gartner conference on IT governance which inspired him to write his charter including CM's IT strategy. This document is written with CM's vision in mind: *"the will to stay a strong player—or even the reference—in the ever changing context of today's social security sector."* The IT governance framework of CM is explained in the IT strategy document, including guidelines on how IT decisions are taken, on who is responsible and accountable, and on which mechanisms and standards will be used. Gartner's IT definition and recommendations were very helpful in establishing the IT governance framework: *"IT is a critical asset that requires effective governance so that decision rights and accountabilities are assigned appropriately. IT governance should leverage and enable business decisions and processes. But one size clearly does not fit all. Shape your IT governance to your business orientation. Act on the experiences of top performers."*

The outcome of the IT governance exercise is a list of seven basic IT governance principles, depicted in Figure 38. The IT governance document was finally accepted by the board in 2003 and was published in the annual report as "Phoenix or the long-term strategic plan of the IT board." This plan is supported by the board because it foresees a more efficient and profitable organisation of the customer services and it guarantees a better alignment between business and IT. This plan, with seven basic IT governance principles, clearly explains the role and responsibilities of the central IT department towards the organisation as a whole and the local IT departments in specific. It defends the advantages of a central IT ("The Power of a centralised internal service entity"), explains its responsibilities ("IT architecture...," "relationship with IT market and partners"), and clarifies its way of working with respect to the budget and investment prioritisation ("strategic and tactical prioritisation"). The next sections will further explain some of these principles.

Figure 38. Seven basic principles of IT governance at CM

1. The power of a centralised internal service entity
2. Maximum alignment with the CM organization,
   taking into account the specific character of IT
3. IT architecture as a standard for the whole organisation
4. A 3-tier IT budget within CM
5. Strategic and tactical prioritisation within IT
6. Cooperation with IT staff of regional business units
7. Relationship with IT market and partners

"These seven basic principles of IT governance at CM are only communicated to the business afterwards," admits the general director of CM Antwerp, *"yet it did not come 'out of the blue' and it answered a lot of questions."* The CM Antwerp IT responsible confirms that now it is commonly accepted that vision and IT strategy are perceived as a central or national issue whereas the local units focus on operations and maintenance.

IT Governance Structures

Organisational Structures

CM employs 5,300 people with an IT headcount of 250 located centrally and 70 operating within the regional entities. The IT development is organised centrally for reasons of economies of scale and standardisation of applications. In this way, an integrated administration for all CM members (i.e., customers) is guaranteed. The regional IT staff mainly concentrates on support and less on development. The central IT department designs the IT architecture compliant with corporate guidelines. This IT architecture is documented in a portfolio of standards, procedures, and guidelines. The IT architecture is clearly communicated to the regional entities that may not make architectural choices that do not comply.

Figure 39. Organisational structure of the IT department

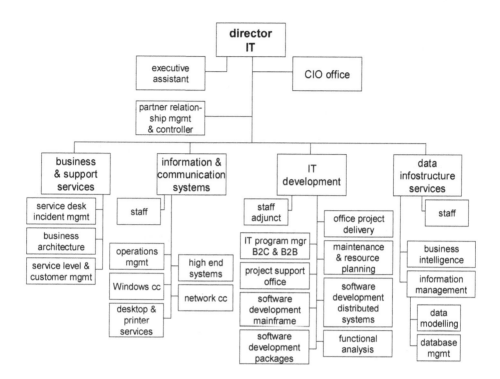

The central IT organisation is headed by the director IT (CIO), who reports directly to the president. The IT director leads four main divisions and is supported by an executive assistant, a controller, and the CIO office (Figure 39). The four main divisions include business support services, information and communication systems, IT development, and data infostructure services. Business support services include the service desk, incident management, business architecture, service level management (SLA), and customer management. Information and communication services contain operations management, services for high end systems, windows and the network infrastructure, and desktop and printer services. IT development includes different development groups, organised per system competency, and supported by functional analyses, project management, maintenance, and resource planning. Data infostructure services cover business intelligence and information management, including data modelling and database management.

Figure 40. Organisational structure CIO office

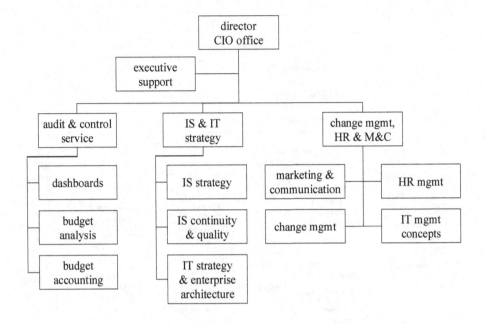

The tasks and responsibilities of the CIO office (Figure 40) directly contribute to the personal accountability of the IT director. They comprise the strategy insight and planning and high-level control of the central IT activities, such as the definition of the overall IT architecture and different audit and control services. Additionally, the CIO office is responsible for internal and external communication, partner relationship management, financial control, and human resources for their department. There is a very close interaction between the IT director and the people of the CIO office.

The central IT department is part of the CM organisation and as such must comply with the organisation's rules and practices. However, due to the specific nature of IT (high tech environment, flexible working schedules, etc.) a specific human resources management, including competitive wages, was put in place in order to retain a high-quality team of IT people.

As aforementioned, each regional entity has its own IT department. Although organisational structures may vary in the different regional entities, in general, these local IT departments are comparable. The IT department of CM Antwerp consists of a department head, an operator, and five analyst-programmers. The IT department head reports to the regional director of administration. He coordinates the regional IT workload and communicates closely with the business. The operator is responsible for the back-ups, printing activities, inventory of computer supplies, and follow-up of contracts. The five analyst-programmers are responsible for the regional helpdesk and the deployment of small regional IT projects.

The total IT budget of CM consists of three parts. The IT budget covering the delivery and development of services within the framework of compulsory insurance business is €35 million, whereas the budget for the non-compulsory insurance amounts to $4 million. The latter budget is managed by a charge-back principle. The regional IT departments have an additional budget funded out of their budget. The allocation of these budgets is not the authority of the central IT director. The IT budget of CM Antwerp for example is € 1,45 million, of which approximately 15 percent is allocated to development and 85 percent to maintenance. From the current central IT budget almost 30 percent is spent on development activities, i.e., about 20,000 persondays. Merely 20 percent of the development is outsourced.

In the past, there was no separate IT budget for the two insurance domains (compulsory and non-compulsory), which was not transparent for project evaluation and prioritisation, causing frustration especially in the non-compulsory insurance business units. The recently introduced charge-back mechanism for the latter business unit seems to work out fine now and provides a transparent overview of their expenses and projects.

CM recently started to formally document roles and responsibilities for their different functions. Individual function descriptions are now being written for both the central and the regional entities. For CM Antwerp most of them are written and approved. Figure 41 shows an example of such an individual function description, that is, of the regional department head responsible for IT. The function description needs further alignment with respect to roles and responsibilities set by the central IT department. Until now, competencies are not being measured because this has not been the company's culture. Yet, in the future, CM is planning to introduce competence measurement. This project is in a start-up phase, meaning that some entities are voluntarily beginning to evaluate individual's competences against their function description. At CM Antwerp competencies are measured during the selection process of every new employee. Then, every year, an evaluation dialogue takes place where it is verified whether the employee, as well as his superior, is satisfied

Figure 41. Extract of an individual function description

Function name:	(Regional) Department head / responsible for IT
Organisation:	Reporting to the (regional) director administration
Objectives:	Take overall responsibility of IT in the regional entity. [...] Organise and follow up of the daily activities in the regional IT department. [...] Coach local IT people. [...] Advice on the IT strategy of the regional entity. [...]Prepare, organise, coordinate and follow up of IT projects [...]
Main tasks:	Participate in the IT strategy process. Make suggestions relating to the choice of technology and architecture, procurement of IT material and introduction of new technologies. Analyzing IT needs and establishing the budget. [...]
Responsibilities:	Proposal of technology and IT architecture, quality of delivered IT services, user-friendly and effective applications, purchase and maintenance of IT material, and, management of IT budget. [...]
Competencies:	University degree with at least one to two years of additional experience. Experience in IT systems, application software and networks. Knowledge of programming languages and database management. [...] Knowledge of CM related business subjects, like the functioning of the regional business units, communication skills. [...]

with the delivered results and new challenges and training opportunities are discussed. *"The next step will introduce a rewarding mechanism not only for performance but also for competences,"* comments the responsible for IT at CM Antwerp.

Committees Supporting IT Governance

At CM, four committees play an important role in the IT governance context: the CM committee, the college of secretaries, the prioritisation committee (PRICO), and regional prioritisation committees (see Figure 42).

The CM committee is composed of the president, vice presidents, the treasurer, the three national secretaries, and representatives of the regional entities. This committee acts as a board and decides on the strategic framework of the organisation and approves major business strategic decisions.

The assembly of secretaries is composed of the members of the CM committee as well as the secretaries of all regional entities. The assembly advices the CM's national executive board regarding new CM services in the space of the compulsory and additional business and coordinates the execution

Figure 42. Committees supporting IT governance

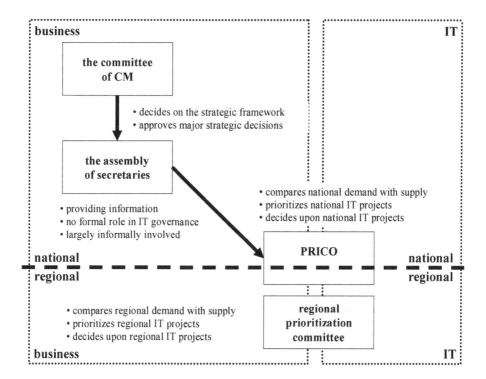

of the strategic decisions within the regional entities. Specific IT issues are seldom explicitly on the agenda, however, this once a month meeting plays an important role in providing useful information on the business needs to the prioritisation committee.

The **PRICO** (prioritisation committee) is trusted with a double task: the preparation of the next annual planning of central IT and the follow up of the actual planning. This committee is composed of representatives of both central IT (advising authority) and the business (deciding authority), and can be seen as an IT steering committee. The business members in this committee represent both the central level and the regional entities. The PRICO analyses supply and demand, prioritises IT projects, and decides upon execution.

On the local level, each region has a **regional prioritisation committee** with as members the general director and the regional directors (Figure 37).

Figure 43. Extract of regional IT projects within CM Antwerp

Category	Project	Requestor	Requested	Approved	Cost
MUST	CRM	[...]	62,00	62,00	€ 16.408
MUST	VPN		9,00	9,00	€ 2.382
A	Education		4,00	4,00	€ 1.059
A	Intranet		20,00	20,00	€ 5.239
B	BIDOC		4,00	4,00	€ 529
B	CM-phone		2,00	2,00	€ 595
BC	Standard letters		4,00	4,00	€ 595
XTRA	Addition to CM-phone		6,10	6,10	€ 1.614
NO	Website		5,00	pilot portal	-
[...]					
MUST	Upgrade network		15,00	postponed	-
[...]					
NO	E-zine		3,00	0,00	-

This committee can be seen as a replica of the PRICO on regional level and decides upon the IT projects on that level. Every year, each regional director has to deliver a list with their IT project requests for the next year. These lists are supplemented with the respective costs and benefits and are then presented in the regional prioritisation committee. The projects are evaluated and ranked into categories ranging from project is a must to project is no immediate need (Figure 43). Projects are basically realised in the reported order. Projects with category 'NO' are not likely to be realised at all (e.g., E-zine) or need to be reshaped for reconsideration (e.g., Web site).

IT Governance Processes

The IT strategy at CM is strictly derived from the strategic choices made by the business. There is no formal business strategy planning process, but both the CM committee and the assembly of secretaries provide directions on the business strategy. Based on these directions, the overall IT priorities are annually set by the prioritisation committee.

In determining the specific IT goals, the *Value Discipline Model* (Treasy & Wiersema, 1995) is used with its tree basic strategies: operational excellence (best total cost), customer intimacy (best total solution), and product leadership (best product). For 2003 and 2004, the focus of CM's central IT department was decided to be operational excellence not excluding techno-logical innovation.

A fixed budget for both businesses—compulsory and non-compulsory ser-vices—is set providing the number of persondays for the development of major projects, service calls, and change requests. The services and their cost are published in a service catalogue, upon which the specific service level agreements will be based. The IT director comments: *"IT has to provide the business with the best service against the best price in a transparent way by means of a well developed service level management."* The outcome of the budgeting exercise is a central IT plan, of which the strategic decisions are taken by the committee of CM, while the tactical decisions are taken by the prioritisation committee. The regional entities also establish their IT plan and the corresponding budget aligned with the local business needs. Although the applied IT governance concepts and the central IT strategy plan are clearly communicated, a proper and systematic alignment between the local and central IT strategy is not yet realised.

The IT processes are being measured on a fairly low level. Yet, the balanced scorecard concepts are applied in about 20 dashboards for specific IT depart-ments. These dashboards are technically oriented and cover amongst others metrics for productivity, up-time, system use, service calls, and budgeting. Every three months, these dashboards are bundled into a management report that is presented by the IT director to the committee of CM. This management report also covers the evolution of the budget, personnel, and the status of the major projects. As illustrated in Figure 43, cost estimations are produced for each major project an on regional level in most cases a cost/benefit analysis is performed for their IT projects.

As aforementioned, the concept of SLA is introduced as an important gov-ernance mechanism. Currently, no SLAs are operational, however several SLAs are written following the template shown in Figure 44. Some SLAs are already approved will become operational in the near future. The SLAs are defined between central IT and the business, both on a national and on a regional level. Regional IT departments will not have their own SLAs, ex-cept for specific maintenance contracts with third parties. Large outsourcing contracts will be steered and managed by the central IT division.

ITIL is used for most operational IT processes and activities. Already imple-mented ITIL processes include incident management, problem management and operations management. In the near future the ITIL processes focusing on the customer/users will be implemented. Besides, the ITIL processes, CM

Figure 44. Template service level agreements

```
1. Introduction
      a.  Objective
      b.  Parties involved
      c.  Validity
      d.  Evolution
2. Scope of the product
3. Scope of the services
      a.  Incident management
      b.  Problem management
      c.  Change request management
      d.  Availability management
      e.  Capacity management
4. Service measurement
      a.  Objective
      b.  Target groups
      c.  Frequency
      d.  Reports
5. Review actions
      a.  Objective
      b.  Frequency
      c.  Escalation
6. Price
7. Payment conditions
```

invested a lot in the systems development process by developing its own project developed methodology supported by the Canadian DMR Consulting firm, now Fujitsu Consulting.

Relational Mechanisms

Two specific relational mechanisms within the CM are identified. On the higher level business and IT people meet and discuss IT issues in the prioritisation committee and the regional IT group is co-located with their business colleagues resulting in a better understanding of the business needs.

The IT director considers the relationship between business and IT as being good. This is somewhat questioned by the general director of CM Antwerp: "*central IT staff and members of the prioritisation committee often think very positive of the business/IT relationship whereas others within the organisation would probably say that the relationship is rather poor."* In order to improve this relationship, the basic IT governance document has been communicated to the business directors and to all employees. The IT governance efforts are perceived as *"being on the right track, but still many things are to be done."*

Maturity Measurement/Assessment

The displayed ITGI maturity level of two "Repeatable but Intuitive" (Figure 45) fits well with the attained level at CM. The prioritisation committee is acting as an IT steering committee, is now operational and its role and responsibilities are defined and agreed upon by stakeholders. An IT governance charter is in place containing the seven principles of IT governance and describing

Figure 45. IT governance maturity model: Level two

---

2. Repeatable but Intuitive

There is **awareness of IT governance objectives**, and practices are developed and applied by individual managers. IT governance activities are becoming established within the organisation's change management process, with active senior management involvement and oversight. Selected IT processes have been identified for improvement that would impact key business processes. IT management is **beginning to define standards for processes and technical architectures**. Management has identified basic IT governance measurements, assessment methods, and techniques, but the process has not been adopted across the organisation. There is **no formal training** and communication on governance standards and responsibilities are left to the individual.

An **IT steering committee** has begun to formalise and establish its roles and responsibilities. There is a **draft governance charter** (e.g., participants, roles, responsibilities, delegated powers, retained powers, shared resources, and policy). Small and pilot governance projects are initiated to see what works and what does not. General guidelines are emerging for standards and architecture that make sense for the enterprise and a dialogue has started to sell the reasons for their need in the enterprise.

---

the responsibilities of the central IT department, its alignment with the business, the IT architecture, the IT budget, the prioritisation mechanisms, and its relationships with the regional IT staff, partners and vendors.

Most of these activities are still in a beginning phase. Today's IT governance practice at CM is strongly IT-driven. The origin of the emerging IT governance effort is with IT management, that is, the initiative coming from the IT director. The ambition to reach the next level of maturity will undoubtedly oblige a higher degree of awareness of IT governance at all IT levels, and even more essentially at the business part of the organisation. The IT director recognises this, but he adds *"as health insurance is situated in the public sector, these evolutions take some more time."*

Summary of IT Governance Structures, Processes and Relational Mechanisms

Based on discussions with executives and inspired by a Gartner conference chaired by Peter Weill, the IT director established the seven basic principles of IT governance at CM. These basic principles cover the organisational structure of IT, its character, the IT architecture, the IT budget, prioritisation, the cooperation with the regional entities, and the relationship with the vendors and partners.

Important IT governance mechanisms are the different established committees: the committee of CM, the assembly of secretaries, the national prioritisation committee (called PRICO), and the regional prioritisation committees. The committee of CM decides on the strategic framework and approves major strategic choices, whereas the assembly of secretaries coordinates the execution of the strategic decisions and provides useful information on the business needs to the other committees. The national and regional prioritisation committees both prioritise IT projects and coordinate their implementation.

On the IT governance processes side, the balanced scorecard concepts have inspired the development and implementation of dashboards. These dashboards typically measure the technical performance of the operational functions. ITIL is currently used for incident, problem and operations management. Further, SLA practices are in place and specific methodologies for project management are used.

A major challenge within CM still is the relationship between business and IT. The development and the communication of the basic IT governance principles was a good start. The established prioritisation committees are very supporting in the prioritisation and coordination of IT projects. However, it is essential that actions are taken to put IT systematically on the agenda of both the CM committee and assembly of secretaries in order to enhance the business/IT fusion on strategic level.

Figure 46. IT governance structures, processes and relational mechanisms at CM

Structures		
What?		**How?**
1	Organisational structure of IT function	Largely centralised, small regional IT departments with strong Local IT power
2	Committees	The committee of CM (board)
		The assembly of secretaries
		PRICO (IT steering committee)
		Regional prioritisation committees
3	Roles and responsibilities	Individual function descriptions are being introduced
		Pilot project for competence measuring within regional entities
Processes		
What?		**How?**
1	IT strategy planning	Yearly project and budget based
2	Balanced scorecard technique	Not strictly, different dashboards are used, bundled and reported to management
3	Information economics	Not used
4	Service Level management	SLAs written and approved
5	COBIT	Not applied
6	ITIL	Used for most operational IT activities
7	Other methodologies	Own project development method
8	Cost-benefit analysis	Used to evaluate regional IT projects
Relational Mechanisms		
What?		**How?**
1	Business-IT communication	Poor to average, substantial distance between regional entities and central IT Improvement is observed, especially during new projects
2	Training	No formal IT governance training
3	Knowledge management	Intranet doesn't cover IT governance issues
4	Job rotation	Not as a career path

Figure 46 summarises the governance structures, processes and relational mechanisms implemented at CM.

Case Study: Huntsman

Company Introduction

Huntsman's roots date back to 1970 with the formation of the Huntsman Container Corporation, which pioneered more than 80 innovative plastic packaging products. The first Huntsman sites were located in California, Ohio, and Tennessee, and in 1976 the first oversees site was built in England. Nowadays, Huntsman has grown to a worldwide supplier of chemicals, polymers, and packaging. Its growth is a result of strategic acquisitions, smart joint ventures, and carefully planned internal expansion. Today, Huntsman companies count approximately 11.300 employees active in manufacturing, research and development, sales, and administration with 57 operations in 22 countries and with 2004 revenue of $11.5 billion. Huntsman, headquartered in Salt Lake City, Utah (U.S.), was the world's largest privately owned chemical company until it went public on the U.S. stock exchange earlier this year. As mentioned in the introduction of this book, this case study was described in the period 2003-2005. It should therefore be noted that this case description only describes the IT governance status at that time in the organisation.

Figure 47 portrays the six Huntsman divisions and appliance industries. This case study focuses on the polyurethanes and the advanced materials divisions.

Polyurethanes play a key role in our daily life: we sit on them, walk on them, and even sleep on them. Huntsman provides as an example seat cushioning for car manufacturers, such as BMW, and soles for different kinds of specialised sports foot wear for Nike, Reebok, and Adidas. Other applications include insulation, mattresses, pillows, video tapes, protective glazing, and even traffic and highway signs. The advanced materials division includes six specialised business units: structural adhesives, electrical insulation materials, printed circuit board technology, structural composites, and surface technologies.

Figure 47. Organisational structure

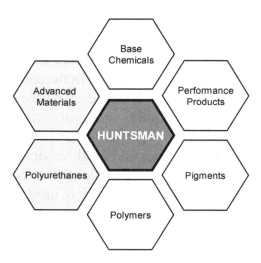

IT Governance Context

The history of IT within the Huntsman organisation is strongly tied to the substantial growth of the company by means of acquisitions each bringing in their own IT organisation. As a consequence, there was a strong delineation of IT with a legacy of disparate systems in the three most important regions: U.S., Europe, and Asia.

The need for a more global enterprise-wide IT organisation was triggered by the Atlas project. This project was aimed at the globalisation of the polyurethanes business that, until then, was mainly run on a regional basis. The project implemented single global business processes underpinned by a single global SAP template. During this project, it became clear that there was a great need for having actual views on the status of the entire organisation's business and that this kind of information was not readily available to the business (it often took days or even weeks to provide it). A new global IT project and consequently new IT structures had to be developed to meet this urgent demand. The executive vice president comments: *"This IT project is doomed for failure if the local entities keep holding on to their legacy systems*

*(mainframe computers, desktops, laptops...). [...] We need global embrace-
ment of the project in order to be successful."*

Nowadays, the IT departments are globalised but with a high business and
application domain orientation. "The last five years, many efforts have been
made in order to create single global platforms, to share the 'nuts-and-bolts'
of IT," said the executive vice president. In the context of a cost optimisation program, it was only a logical step to create one global IT organisation,
responsible for defining enterprise-wide standards and platforms. Within
Huntsman this centralisation is called the 'glocal' approach, combining an
optimal mix of global synergies and local responsiveness offering the required flexibility. Still, it remains a challenge to create the IT globalisation
within Huntsman. As Huntsman is a merger of many previously independent
organisations, it is quite a challenge to transparently depict how one tries to
make IT cohesive across the different businesses.

IT Governance Structures

Organisational Structure

In 2004, it was decided to centralise the different divisional IT departments,
in line with the decision to move towards a Huntsman-wide shared services
model. This global reorganisation of IT is expected to bring increased efficiency and cost savings. Five application-oriented service teams are created:
ERP/data warehouse, global systems, global infrastructure, planning and
security, and purchasing (Figure 48).

The ERP/data warehouse team is responsible for SAP, GMIS (management
information systems), business to business, portals, ERP, data warehousing,
and reporting systems. The ERP/data warehouse section together with the
global systems section deliver and support the applications whereas plan-
ning/security and global infrastructure are responsible for the operations.

Besides the cross-business responsibility for their specific domain, the
service team managers also hold general IT-responsibility for one or more
business units. Figure 49 displays an example of this vertical and horizontal
responsibility. The dotted squares represent the six Huntsman divisions. The
horizontal square represents a specific application domain. This example illustrates that the ERP data warehouse team manager is not only responsible for

Figure 48. Organisational structure of IT

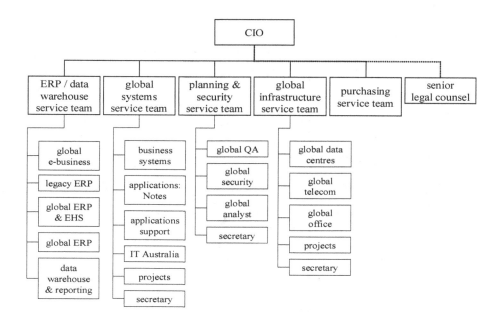

the functional IT strategy and fixed costs control for ERP, data warehousing and e-business throughout all of the divisions, but he is also accountable for the complete IT strategy and fixed costs control for the two business units polyurethanes and advanced materials. The reason for this modus operandi is to ensure that IT is better aligned with the business needs. *"One of the main drivers for this complicated model,"* justified the executive vice president, *"is that IT should not be fully accountable and responsible for business projects. It is the role of the business to assume full ownership."*

Although Huntsman's organisational structure significantly changed during the globalisation process, the existing hierarchical levels largely remained (Figure 50). An important change included the creation of a new group CIO function, which has the same level as a senior vice president. What is new is that all IT directors now report to the CIO, having a more direct link to global executive management. Also, synergies over the different IT departments are encouraged and, where before, IT discussions were budget oriented,

Figure 49. Vertical and horizontal responsibility of the ERP data warehouse team manager

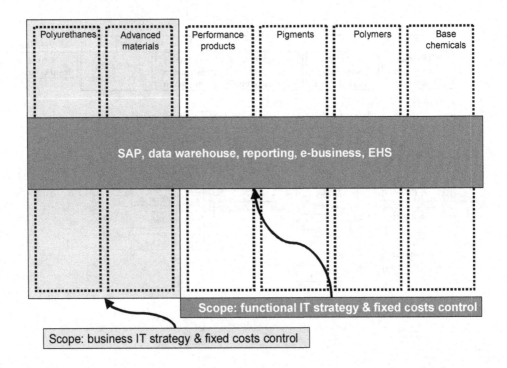

they now focus merely on functional and more technical issues. The role and responsibilities of the IT director remained largely the same. What is important is that the horizontal and vertical responsibilities (Figure 49) are now formalised, whereas, before it was not officially recognised.

The IT function is divided into two domains: systems and development. The system domain groups all aspects related to infrastructure, data management and telecommunication; the development domain groups activities for ERP, portals and other applications. Huntsman and its IT organisations are very flat, which means that there is a relatively small amount of hierarchical levels, enabling team members of for example the ERP/data warehouse service team to directly turn to the team manager in case of any questions or issues.

Figure 50. Old and new IT hierarchy

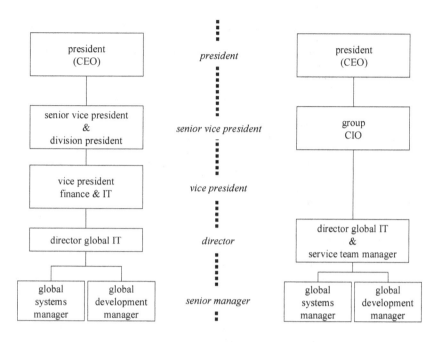

Clear and unambiguous job descriptions contribute to the smooth operation of Huntsman's IT. Figure 51 displays an extract of the individual job description of the ERP/data warehouse service team manager, officially called *director global IT enterprise business systems.*

In the beginning of each year, objectives are set for each IT staff member. This is the basis for the evaluation at the end of the year. For senior management, this evaluation partly determines their bonus while for middle and lower management it may result in an annual salary increase. Overall achievement of business goals (turnover and profit) and accomplishments in the area of environment, health, and safety may also affect IT senior management's bonuses.

Figure 51. Extract of an individual function description

Job title:	director global IT Enterprise Business Systems
Reports to:	CIO
Job purpose:	Lead, direct and develop IT professionals in the development and execution of IT strategies. Develop, coordinate and ensure delivery of IT strategies within the Polyurethanes and Advanced materials businesses. Communicate and embed business plans into IT strategies.
Functional accountabilities:	
	As a member of the IT Leadership Team (ITLT), serve as a senior IT advisor to senior management; provide leadership for development and implementation of IT strategies. Manage deployment of legacy ERP systems. Develop and implement a strategy to migrate business systems to existing ERP platforms. [...]
Business accountabilities (within Polyurethanes and Advanced materials divisions):	
	Manage and coordinate IT activities. Ensure IT business requirements are within IT budgets and coordinated across the function. Ensure IT projects are coordinated consistent with requirements and information is provided to business management as warranted. [...]
Special features:	Ability to interpret technical ERP terms to customers as to transmit meaning and value of program and process to the user. [...] Comprehensive knowledge of all business strategies and key drivers.
Knowledge, experience and skills:	
	At minimum graduate in an appropriate technical discipline with more than 10 years of relevant industrial experience and increasingly challenging technical, managerial and/or IT roles. Being able to bridge geographical and cultural complexities and being able to operate remotely from his manager/supervisor or other supporting functions as the position requires. [...]
Competences:	Strong concern for standards, strong desire to facilitate the work and development of others, high level of self conviction and integrity, good analytical and conceptual thinking, high level of interpersonal skills.

Committees Supporting IT Governance

At Huntsman, there are several committees impacting and directing IT (Figure 52). Cross divisional committees include the board or officers meeting and the IT leadership team (ITLT). Additionally, every division has a committee focusing on the link between IT and the business; within the polyurethanes division it is called the business process steering group (BPSG). An operational IT committee focusing on e-commerce and process optimisation exists within every division.

Members of the officers meeting include all the presidents and some of the senior vice presidents. Since the group CIO has become a member of the officers meeting, IT related topics are on the agenda and as such IT awareness

Figure 52. Committees supporting IT governance

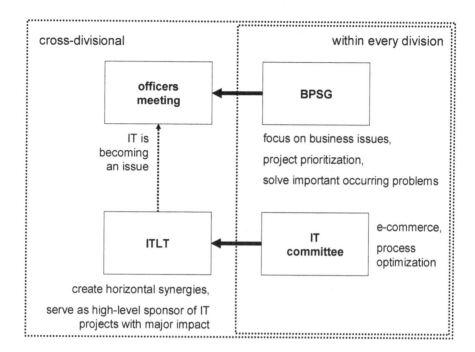

is clearly growing at board level. The IT leadership team is installed to bridge the different company's IT divisions (Figure 48). This committee is composed of the five service team managers and presided by the group CIO.

They meet once a month by means of teleconferencing and have a live meeting once every three months. *"The main objective is to create 'horizontal synergies,"* comments the executive vice president. Moreover, ITLT serves as a high-level sponsor for projects with a major impact such as large ERP-implementations supporting different divisions. Figure 53 pictures an abstract of a typical ITLT agenda. As mentioned before, the CIO can put important IT topics form this meeting on the officers meeting agenda (dotted arrow line in Figure 52).

The BPSG focuses on business issues. This committee gathers a day and a half every two months and is led by finance. The people responsible for the

Figure 53. Typical agenda of ITLT

```
1. HR meeting
      1.1.  Hay Grades meeting
      1.2.  General topics
2. CIO presentations & Topics
      2.1.  State of the Union
      2.2.  Bonus program
      2.3.  HR strategy
      2.4.  Dashboard discussion
3. Office strategy
4. Review new SAP contract
5. Applications strategy
6. Update on project portfolio process and project slate
7. New cost centres
8. KPI scorecard presentation
9. Strategy development
10.  Purchasing strategy
11.  ERP / data warehouse
12.  SOD project
13.  SOX & security
      13.1. Site self-audit data
14.  Coronado project reviews
15.  Current budget reviews
16.  Cap Gemini presentation
```

major business processes, as well as the service team managers, are members of this committee. Apart from their main task, project prioritisation, they also resolve major occurring problems. The outcomes of this steering group meeting provide direct input for the officers meeting.

A divisional IT committee typically focus on e-commerce and process optimisation of the supply chain. This committee is composed of senior business management, such as supply chain managers. The outcomes of this IT committee meeting provide direct input for the ITLT.

Figure 54 provides a summary of the different committees, their authority on IT matters, and their representatives of IT and the business.

Figure 54. Huntsman committees, authorities and composition

Name	Authority	Composition	
		IT	**Business**
The board (officers meeting)	IT sometimes on the agenda	The group CIO	All the presidents and some senior vice presidents
ITLT (Information Technology Leadership Team)	Create horizontal synergies bridge the different IT service teams Serve as high-level sponsor of projects with a major impact	The group CIO and all the IT service team managers	
BPSG (Business Process Steering Group)	Focus on business issues project prioritisation Solve important occurring problems	The service team managers	People responsible for the major business processes
Operational IT committee	E-commerce process optimisation supply chain		Supply chain managers

IT Governance Processes

The executive vice president confirms that *"IT is not a goal, it is a means."* He perceives IT governance as the sum of being compliant with all regulations on the one hand and risk management on the other hand: *"First there is the operational part of IT, answering questions such as 'do we have the right software licenses?' or 'are we complying with the terms and conditions of contracts?' Then there is risk management which implies that as a business, it is our continuous aim to grow in a profitable way whilst mitigating risk."* Further, the vice president comments *"for large projects, the 'techie' part is not the real challenge. The real challenge exists in convincing the organisation to embrace the project, to get organisation-wide buy-in."*

Since 2004, the Huntsman IT mission is formulated as follows "Our primary goal is to provide effective, efficient, high value IT solutions for our businesses. This will be accomplished through a global IT organisation that leverages tools and resources, management of IT resources on a global basis, a strong commitment to personnel development, meaningful interactive stakeholder communication, safe and secure assets, IT projects, initiatives and daily operations, which are measured and aligned with the goals of our customers." Also, a global service proposal template is in place outlining actions to be taken in order to achieve sustained, cost effective services within global IT (Figure 55).

The main objective of IT is to support the business by pro-actively creating effective solutions and measuring the result is therefore important. The balanced scorecard (BSC) technique is applied at Huntsman Polyurethanes. The monitoring of the BSC metrics is performed by both IT and the business. Additionally, the use of the BSC technique should contribute to a higher level of awareness of the IT efforts and contributions to the organisation. The members of the BPSG are always keen to evaluate the monthly scorecard that is used as a snapshot for management actions. It should be noted that the IT balanced scorecard and the different business balanced scorecards are linked in financial terms and their combination offers very valuable information for management (Figure 56).

Figure 55. Global service proposal template

- Balance short term cost savings vs. longer term performance
- Be driven by key business objectives
    - Optimally match IT resources to business requirements
    - Flexibility to scope with ongoing business change
    - Manage IT security & risk to the business
- Focus on value of services provided
    - Eliminate non-value adding activities and processes
    - Re-engineer inefficient activities and processes
    - Optimise business-critical activities and processes
- Manage governance processes to control spending & investment
    - CIO will own IT investment decision processes and all proposals will be governed by these processes
    - Global design authority team to approve new products & projects
    - All projects & services will comply with coordinated implementation processes and operating standards
    - Leverage & utilise global purchasing power, from a rationalised supplier base

Figure 56. Extract of the global business IT team scorecard

Financial Perspective					**Budget**
Region	Actual	Budget		Var	Var%
e.g., America, etc.	*x*	*y*		*y-x*	*(y-x)/y*
E-Commerce					**WOP & B2B**
WOP e.g., Customers live (sold to)		month t-2	month t-1	month t	
B2B: Hauliers, Suppliers					# of XML internet
Customer Perspective					**System avail.**
% uptime exclusive planned interventions	Target	month t-2	month t-1	month t	
e.g., SAP, GMIS, Regional systems, etc.					
Support/Activity Perspective					**Incidents**
	Asia	Europe		Total	Last month
Reported incidents for SAP, GMIS, etc.					
Resolved incidents for SAP, GMIS, etc.					
Organisational Perspective					**Users**
	Asia	Europe		Total	Last month
Staff: Own staff, contractors,					
Supported staff by functional area: for SAP, Lotus Notes, GMIS, etc.					

A global IT KPI scorecard and its reporting process are being developed at Huntsman, by the *planning & security* service team. This process will define Huntsman's key performance areas, identify the key metrics, establish the requirements for data collection and calculations, define a global IT scorecard, and implement a solution to publish the results periodically. A draft proposal has been made to the ITLT outlining a KPI framework (Figure

Figure 57. KPI framework

Cost	Security & Risk Management	Compliance
• Capital spend vs. target • Revenue spend vs. target • Huntsman average cost per seat	• Vulnerability heat scan index • Incidents • % site audits below satisfactory that have been remediated	• Quality of support tickets • Severity 1 problems with root cause analysis • Accuracy of the IT organisational chart • Adherence to the purchasing process • Supplier positioning
Resource, Supplier & Asset Management	**Service**	**Improvements (effectiveness)**
• % of IT personnel with annually updated development plans • % of IT personnel with training objectives met • % of positions that need succession plans without one	• Average time for emergency ticket closure • Unplanned interventions causing downtime (measured against those systems that are in the SOX scope) • Average number of tickets per seat % problem tickets solved by 2nd touch • Server availability (measured against those systems that are in the SOX scope) • % tickets resolved vs. logged	• % completed projects with post event review • % completed projects overrun • % project with project manager assigned • % projects pending approval
Transition		
• % of IT personnel with job specifications • % of IT personnel transitioned to global IT		

57), which describes the key areas that underpin the global IT strategy. The proposed perspectives are *cost, security and risk management, compliance, resource, supplier and asset management, service,* and *improvements.* Simultaneously, some specific short term metrics, monitoring the *transition* process have been defined. Initially the presentation of KPIs will be done via an Excel spreadsheet, but the ultimate goal is to develop *"an intranet application that will generate a traffic light system to indicate the status of global IT performance."*

A formal project approval process is in place at BPSG level (Figure 58). Currently, global IT is developing KPIs to monitor the effectiveness of this process. A formal approval by senior management and the vice president is needed for major projects. Finally, the president has to approve. In order to steer this entire project evaluation or business case process, a workflow

Figure 58. Project prioritisation

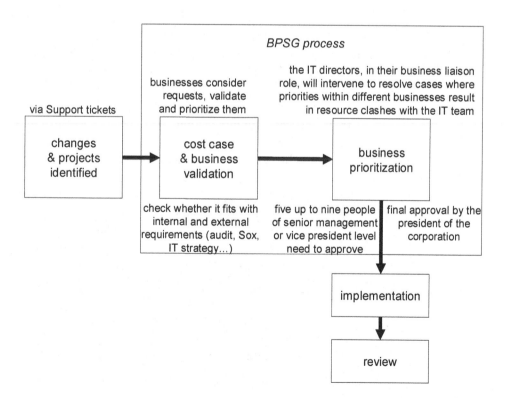

with a number of templates exists. Approval criteria include PB (pay back) and ROI (return on investment) taking into account the limited available budgets. Only projects with a PB period below one year are considered for approval. Additionally, the cash impact of projects is increasingly becoming an essential criterion for project evaluation: recently a project with a better cash impact was preferred over a project with a better ROI. For strategic projects such as an ERP implementations or major upgrade project, the ROI is supplemented with qualitative benefits such as providing access to e-commerce capabilities.

The business case for the 'thin-client' project replacing high-end workstations with cheaper terminals (Figure 59) illustrates some of the aforementioned evaluation criteria, while Figure 60 displays the financial evaluation figures for this project.

Figure 59. The thin-client project

Workstations	Workstations are replaced by Wyse devices which are available at 10 percent of the price of laptops. Moreover, Wyse devices have a lifetime of five years, as opposed to laptops that have only a one to three year lifetime. Wyse devices are used in a server-centric computing architecture. In essence, this architecture hosts applications and data centrally on a server (as opposed to having data and applications on the (fat) client machines) offering more secure, more manageable, more affordable and more reliable solutions. User and corporate needs, as well as priorities, guidelines, and standards have to be balanced in order to determine the right Wyse device (from a wide array) for each company 'worker type.'
Project Build	Standard image will be beamed to the Wyse devices from central servers. This will decrease the need for on-site consultancy. Obviously, more application servers will be needed. Excellent lease ratings with a low buyout clause have been negotiated.
Support	Support is fully outsourced, which leads to a significantly reduced cost compared to the current maintenance cost of hardware and software
Remote Access	Dial-in expenditures will be reduced to approximately 30 percent of current levels.

Figure 60. Financial evaluation of thin-client project

Net Present Value	approx $9 million
Savings	approx $15 million in five years
PayBack Time	14 months (more than threshold of 1 year)
Total Capital	approx $6 million
Phase 1 (Americas) capital request	approx $ 3.5 million

Most business cases are prepared by IT (more specifically the people reporting to a service team manager or the service team manager himself) with the assistance of business colleagues, often the sponsor of the project and the business project manager. For typical IT projects such as infrastructure initiatives, IT is responsible for the business case.

ITIL processes are predominately implemented for change management (Figure 61). A specific characteristic of the Huntsman change management

Figure 61. Change management process

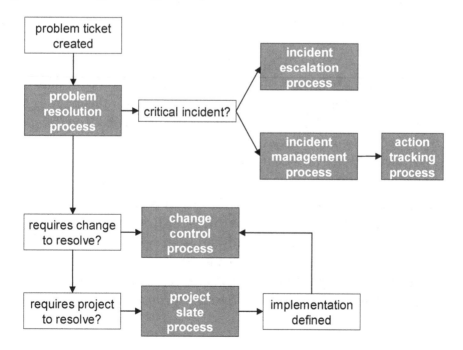

culture is that extensive measuring and documenting is done. Each change request requires a detailed description and appropriate attention is paid to its audit trail. The director global IT enterprise business systems comments: *"No ticket, no cure!"*

The use of weekly updated dashboards is another measuring technique at Huntsman. These dashboards, using traffic light colours, give an indication of how well particular applications or services are performing. Further, when projects are completed, a post evaluation takes place. There is also an annual audit, performed by Deloitte & Touche, covering themes such as disaster recovery, data retention, and security. This audit enhances a guaranteed continuity of IT capabilities.

Relational Mechanisms

In supporting the IT-business relationship, the dual role of the service team managers, who are not only responsible for their domain but also for the IT services for a specific business unit, plays an important role. This dual responsibility brings the IT services manager and his team closer to the business. On project level, the BPSG (project prioritisation committee), where business and IT are discussing the prioritisation of IT projects, enhances a good relationship between both. Further, business and IT are both involved in the evaluating and monitoring activities, using the extensive measuring techniques.

The director global IT enterprise business systems identified a fairly good relationship between the business and IT by attributing a score between 3 and 4 on a 5-point Likert-scale. The main motivation for this score is that *"the relationship between IT on the one hand and the business on the other hand is perfect, as long as IT doesn't touch the fundamental business premises."* The executive vice president acknowledges that IT and the business live in a relationship that could be described as *"a healthy tension."*

A major problem is that by some (business) people IT is still perceived as "something that has to do with computers, be it desktops, notebooks or other thin-client devices." Clearly, hardware is an essential part of IT but at the same time they represent only a minor part of the entire IT puzzle. The director global IT enterprise business systems refers to this problem by saying, *"the IT strategy is not really the business's concern, except when problems arise. There should be an earlier adoption and involvement of IT matters by the business.*"

The goal of IT, explains the director global IT enterprise business systems, should be "*to pro-actively mediate in business issues and in this way to avoid missed opportunities.*" Obviously, pro-activity and missed opportunity management are two sides of the same medal.

Clear communication is an essential issue in the achievement of good relations between IT and business. A formal document and slide presentations explaining the IT strategy is distributed on the different management levels. Substantial progress is made in project management and its communication. For the thin-client project, for instance, subsequent communication and user-acceptance initiatives are being undertaken: getting buy-in from employees, forming key user groups for trials of the new technology (in the office, on the road and at home), global communication by means of a dedicated intranet site and on-site presentations.

The implemented knowledge management system at Huntsman covers a wide area of subjects including IT issues. The 'IT news items,' are presented on the same page on the corporate intranet as the financial results. The "IT news items" cover information about running projects, new emerging technologies, and 'success stories.' An example of a typical success story is displayed in Figure 62.

Another supporting mechanism for a better relationship between IT and business is job-rotation. Huntsman offers its employees the possibility to switch between IT and business jobs and vice versa. This possibility is part of every individual's career planning. The career planning depends, among other factors, on the annual performance review, personal preferences, geographical preferences, and the match with existing opportunities within the organisation. In practice, employees do take the opportunity to widen their knowledge and rotate between different IT and business functions. The relational mechanism of job-rotation contributes to an increased mutual insight in the business and IT.

The business's awareness of the IT governance and strategy issues would ideally be at a much higher level within Huntsman. Three reasons for the "*not-high-enough*" level of awareness can be identified: (1) IT is still not sufficiently the business's concern, (2) the business is often only present (at meetings, committees, etc.) to listen to IT and not so much to jointly search for potential areas for cooperation, and (3) the business still tends to turn to IT only in case of (serious) problems.

Figure 62. Example of a 'News Story' published in the knowledge management system

> *Thanks to the recently implemented thin-clients, a potentially major production problem could relatively easily be dealt with. On a given Sunday afternoon, Huntsman staff succeeded in solving a production problem after logging in by means of their thin-clients at their homes. Only 15 minutes after logging in, Huntsman staff had fixed the problem and the production was restarted. Clearly, losses of great consequence that might have been caused by a longer idle-time were avoided.*

Maturity Measurement/Assessment

The maturity level of IT governance at Huntsman is clearly level 2. Elements that are applicable are highlighted in bold (Figure 63) and are based on:

- A variety of IT governance structures, processes, and relational mechanisms are in place.
- Active senior management involvement: the group CIO presides the ITLT and is a member of the board (officers meeting). The Group CIO has the level of a senior vice president.
- Standards for processes and technical architectures are in place.
- Start up of communication activities.

The executive vice president's assessment was level four, "*Manage and Measurable,*" based on the following arguments: clear understanding of who the customer is, process ownership, extensive monitor and measure activities and follow up, risk awareness, defined tolerances, action, and root cause analysis. However, other elements of level four, such as formal IT governance training and the evolution of IT governance into an enterprise-wide process, are not yet achieved.

Figure 63. IT governance maturity model (IT Governance Institute): Level two

---

2. Repeatable but Intuitive

There is awareness of IT governance objectives, and practices are developed and applied by individual managers. **IT governance activities** are becoming established within the **organisation's change management process**, with **active senior management involvement** and oversight. Selected IT processes have been identified for improvement that would impact key business processes. IT management is beginning to define **standards for processes and technical architectures**. Management has identified basic IT governance measurements, assessment methods and techniques, but the process has not been adopted across the organisation. There is **no formal training and communication** on governance standards and responsibilities are left to the individual.

An **IT steering committee** has begun to formalise and establish its roles and responsibilities. There is a **draft governance charter** (e.g., participants, roles, responsibilities, delegated powers, retained powers, shared resources, and policy). Small and pilot governance projects are initiated to see what works and what does not. General guidelines are emerging for **standards and architecture** that make sense for the enterprise and a dialogue has started to sell the reasons for their need in the enterprise.

Summary of IT Governance Structures, Processes and Relational Mechanisms

As recapitulated in Figure 64, quite some structures, processes and relational mechanisms are in place at Huntsman.

The organisational structure of IT is somewhat complex. It can be seen as a virtual matrix structure where every service team manager has full command over particular applications and platforms, and at the same time has IT responsibility for a specific business division. Other structural elements of IT governance comprise the existence of IT committees. Three specific committees were identified: the ITLT, the BPSG, and the operational IT committee. Furthermore, roles and responsibilities are clearly defined using unambiguous job descriptions. With the CIO residing in the board of directors, IT governance issues are more regularly on the board's agenda.

Figure 64. IT governance structures, processes and relational mechanisms at Huntsman

Structures		
What?		**How?**
1	Organisational structure of IT function	Virtual matrix organisation, mix of application domain and business responsibility
2	Committees	Information Technology Leadership Team (ITLT)
		Business Process Steering Group (BPSG)
		Operational IT committee
3	Roles and responsibilities	Clear and unambiguous job descriptions
Processes		
What?		**How?**
1	Balanced scorecard technique	Global business IT team scorecard (monthly)
2	Information economics	Not used as such
3	ROI calculation	Common practice
4	Pay back time	Threshold: 1 year
5	Net present value	For all projects
6	KPI framework	KPIs defined for different domains
7	Measuring	Dashboards
		Project after-calculation
		audit: disaster recovery, data retention and security
8	COBIT	Not used
9	ITIL	Strict implementation, especially for change management
Relational Mechanisms		
What?		**How?**
1	IT business relationship	Project-related (via BPSG)
		dual responsibility of IT service managers
2	Training	Not formally
3	IT governance awareness	Intranet and on-site presentations
4	Knowledge management	Corporate intranet with IT pages
5	Job rotation	Part of career path planning

IT governance related processes at Huntsman include the use of the balanced scorecard, as well as different measuring and monitoring techniques: ROI calculation, payback time, net present value, dashboards, and project after-calculation. A global KPI framework is being developed, where besides financial indicators, indicators in the domains of *security and risk management, resource management, and service quality* are also measured. On top of this, an annual audit covering disaster recovery, data retention and security takes place. Further, ITIL processes are extensively implemented.

As for the relational mechanisms, both the dual role of the IT service managers, the BPSG committee and different project teams contribute to a good IT-business relationship. Communication over the IT strategy and the different projects is a regular practice by means of the corporate intranet and on-site presentations. Job rotation from IT to the business and the other way around is an opportunity in the career path planning of staff.

Case Study: Sidmar – Arcelor

Company Introduction

This case study describes the IT governance practices within Sidmar, a leading steel producer with headquarters in Ghent, Belgium. The company was founded in 1962 as a daughter of the Luxembourgian steel group Arbed, and is located on a site east of the Gent-Terneuzen sea canal. This location was chosen because of the direct connection with the sea, which also gave the name to the company: Sidmar short for "Sidérurgie Maritime." Sidmar produces flat steel with its major clients being car manufacturers. In 2002, Sidmar became part of the Arcelor group due to the merger of Arbed with the Spanish steel group Aceralia and the French Usinor (Figure 65). This steel group is the largest steel producer in the world with a turnover of € 26 billion and a workforce of more than 100.000. As mentioned in the introduction of this book, this case study was described in the period 2003-2005. It should therefore be noted that this case description only describes the IT governance status at that time in the organisation.

Sidmar still uniquely focuses on activities in the flat steel sector. It has a crude steel capacity of five million tons and produces mainly for the automotive, construction, household appliances, and general industry, as well as for the packaging industry. One car out of two in Europe contains parts produced by Sidmar. Sidmar employs approximately 5600 people and realises a turnover of € 2 billion. Sidmar's strategy is well defined by one of its directors: "Sidmar is one of four coastal steel plants in which Arcelor intends to concentrate its flat steel production in the coming years. Sidmar is Europe's most completely integrated plant—from raw material processing until production of tailor-welded blanks for the automotive industry all on one site. Thanks to this, Sidmar is the cost-leader in Europe. Arcelor wants to further strengthen this position by in-depth investments in Europe and by expanding in 'new' countries such as Brazil, Russia, India, China, Eastern Europe and Turkey. Sidmar has state-of-the-art production facilities and is very well placed to develop new steel products (e.g., high strength steels for the automotive industry). Additionally, a lot of effort is done with regard to sustainable development (environmental care, safety and health of employees, social responsibility)." Figure 66 displays the organisational structure of Sidmar with a senior vice president responsible for IT.

Figure 65. Organisation structure of Arcelor

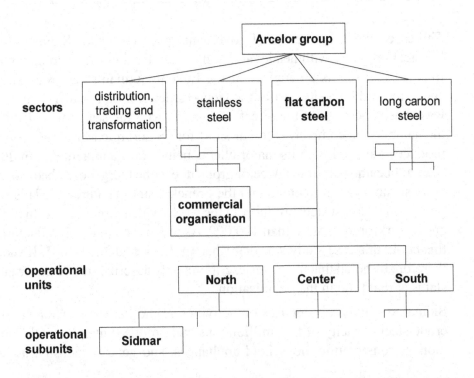

Figure 66. Organisation structure of Sidmar

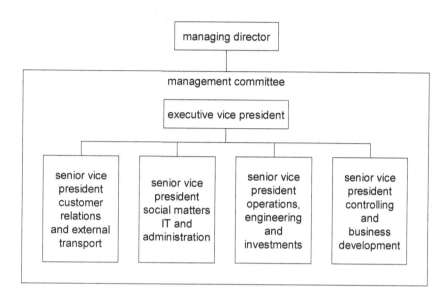

IT Governance Context

Although the term "IT governance' is not explicitly used within Sidmar and its IT department, it is clear that the organisation and processes for a good alignment between IT and business have been initiated and matured since a couple of years. It is the Sidmar controller's perception that Sidmar has been successful in the areas of productivity and efficiency and that this is mainly because of a good functioning IT department. This is also acknowledged by the Arcelor group in the sense that Sidmar's IT department was chosen to provide IT services to the group commercial department.

The IT department is centralised and its strategy and processes are well communicated throughout the company. The mission and value statement of IT is clear and simple: *"Supply and support Sidmar and the Sector Flat products with all needed IT-systems and related services, in order to enable all business processes at all levels (strategic, tactical and operational) to be executed in an integrated and efficient way."*

During the last 10 years, the expenditure of the IT department has known a continuous growth. From 1996 to 2001, this growth was rather strong due to a heavy investment program at the Sidmar plant and the delivery of solutions towards the commercial organization of the flat carbon steel sector. Since 2001, the IT budget is frozen and now that Sidmar is part of Arcelor, the budget is expected to stay under pressure.

On business governance level, Sidmar introduced in 2004 a company-wide process-based management system. This is know under the name ICE, standing for integral company excellence. ICE actually brought existing individual components of process management together into one structured whole, covering all levels at Sidmar and describing strategic, tactical, operational and supporting processes.

One of the 22 ICE processes is P23: *Management of Information Systems*, under responsibility of the IT department and its director. The process clearly defines ins and outs, different sub-processes, and its activities, the interdependencies with other processes, measurements (KPIs), and a reporting and evaluation structure.

IT Governance Structures

Organisational Structures

The centrally located IT department of Sidmar does not exclusively provide services to its own organisation; it also partly supports the commercial organisation of the flat carbon steel sector (Figure 67). Approximately 15 to 20 percent of the total IT budget is being spent for the commercial organisation. Over time a further integration and alignment with the global IT department of the Arcelor group is expected.

The IT department counts approximately 170 internal and 90 external employees, divided into three main groups (Figure 68). A first group is responsible for the development and architecture of applications, a second group deals with infrastructure and networks, and a third group supervises the operations including logistics, administration and helpdesk.

The application development and architecture team is seen as the most important player in the IT governance organisation. They have the prime contact

Figure 67. Sidmar's IT budget

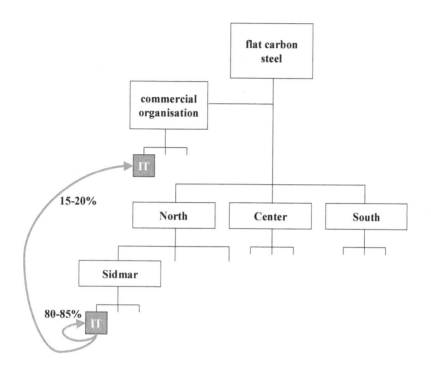

with the business when it comes to fulfilling their needs by means of new projects or improving functions into existing applications. The structure of the application development team (Figure 69) is business-oriented, contrary to the former technology-oriented structure. They represent the largest group with about 155 people, from which 56 are external. Together they stand for a capacity of 35.000 persondays, divided over new projects (60 percent) and maintenance (40 percent).

As aforementioned, the IT budget will continue to stay under pressure, but it is the intention that savings on the IT budget will not be at the expense of new projects. A better internal efficiency especially for the infrastructure and maintenance must lead to the optimisation of the IT budget.

Roles and responsibilities (especially of senior management) are clearly documented at Sidmar. Individual function descriptions consisting of a function name and a well-defined task description are being used. An abstract

Figure 68. Organisational structure of the IT department

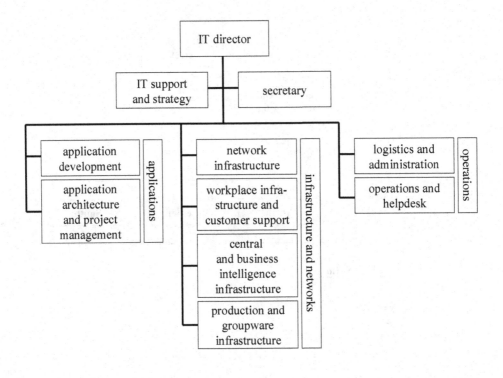

Figure 69. Organisation structure of the application development team

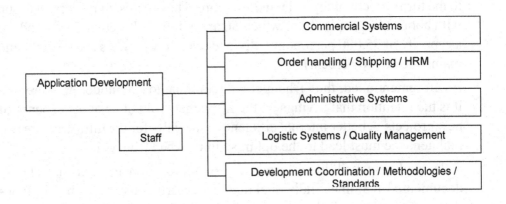

Figure 70. Abstract of an individual function description

Function name:	Information architect
Task description:	Control of project team. Planning, coordination and follow up of the activities of the IT department in consultation with the users. [...] Pre-studies and specifications for new systems. [...] Acting as an internal consultant for IT staff in the field of systems architecture. Active follow up of recent IT developments.

of a typical IT function description is shown in Figure 70. Regular dialogue between IT staff and his hierarchical director contributes to a good follow up of roles and responsibilities. In order to monitor whether employees have fulfilled their roles and taken up their responsibilities, an official evaluation by the hierarchical director takes place once a year. This evaluation is an open discussion with the employee in person, during which the objectives set in the previous year are evaluated and new or adapted objectives are agreed upon. This evaluation does not have an immediate effect on the remuneration of senior management, yet it can have an indirect impact on the evolution of their salary and/or exceptional bonuses.

Committees Supporting IT Governance

From the introductory chapter, it became clear that there are different levels of IT governance responsibility and that IT governance should be an integral part of corporate governance. Setting up different committees is an excellent way of dealing with the IT governance responsibilities on different levels and at the same time they make it possible to integrate IT governance into corporate governance. As shown in Figure 71, Sidmar has established three committees playing an important role in the IT governance context: the board of directors, the corporate IT committee, and the IBO (information management and organisation) committees at business unit level.

The board of directors is composed of business people focusing on strategic projects and IT governance issues are covered in an informative way. IT is represented by the vice president of social affairs, information technology and administration. The IT director has only access to the board through this vice president.

The IT steering committee (IT committee) has meetings at least twice a year, during which all new IT projects are discussed as well as IT projects that need to be revisited. It is composed of the five members of the management committee, the controller, the IT director and the applications director. Figure 72 shows a typical agenda of the IT committee. The IT committee prioritises the different IT projects and decides upon necessary resources. All decisions taken by the IT committee have to be unanimous.

Business unit committees (IBO committees) capture and discuss the local needs of the business units. They decide on maintenance and small enhancements and therefore have their own IBO budget. They also inform the IT committee on smaller projects where an evaluation of the benefits is required as well as a prioritisation schemes within the IBO budget. The IBO budget

Figure 71. Committees supporting IT governance

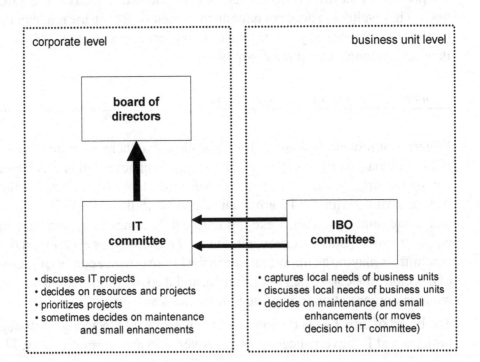

Figure 72. Typical agenda of the IT committee

1. Overview of capacities
    1.1. Capacity of previous year in terms of man days
        –   Project capacity is total capacity minus maintenance and extensions
    1.2. Capacity of this year in terms of man days with constant staffing
        –   Project capacity is total capacity minus maintenance and extensions
2. Presentation of projects
    2.1. New projects
    2.2. Revised projects
    2.3. Pilot projects
3. Evaluation of projects
    3.1. Cost benefit evaluation
    3.2. Evaluation of basic criteria
        –   Profitability: pay back time
        –   Competitive advantage: improvement of performance
        –   Operational urgency
        –   Decision support
    3.3. Calculating scores of projects
4. Rating of projects according to priority (five priority classes: A-B-C-D-E)
5. Allocation of projects (next year's capacity is not fully allocated in order to keep flexibility)
6. Miscellaneous
    6.1. Raise or lower staff number

covers the cost of small projects and enhancements that are approved by the department head.

Figure 73 provides a summary of the different committees at Sidmar, their authority on IT matters and their representatives of IT and the business.

IT Governance Processes

The IT strategy of Sidmar comes down to supplying and supporting the business with all needed IT systems and related services, in order to enable all business processes at all levels, that is, strategic, tactical, and operational, to be executed in an integrated and efficient way. As described previously, the IT strategy is completely comprised in the formalised ICE process for management of information systems.

Figure 73. Sidmar committees, authorities and composition

Name	Authority	Composition	
		IT	**Business**
Board of directors	Covers IT mainly in an informative way Gives advice on strategic projects	Vice president social affairs IT and administration	General director Vice president customer relations (and external transport), Vice president production engineering and investments, Vice president controlling and business development
IT committee	Discusses IT projects Decides on resources and projects Sometimes decides on maintenance and small enhancements Prioritises projects	IT director Applications director	Direction committee Controller
IBO committees	Captures and discusses local needs of business units Decides on maintenance Small enhancements and projects Prioritises small projects within the IBO budget		Several business people from a certain business unit

Collaboration, internally as well as with all customers and suppliers, is seen as one of the main critical success factors. Other critical success factors are the active participation and full involvement of the complete IT staff from early project phases on and the continuous improvement actions to obtain a high quality level of service. Furthermore, the IT department chooses an architecture where integration with existing systems is key, above a strategy based on best of breed products. As an example, after Sidmar chose SAP as their ERP standard, they favoured the implementation of additional SAP modules (covering the business needs) over a 'new,' maybe better application package.

A clear decision making process for IT projects is in place. Because this process is one of the key elements in a good working business-IT alignment, it is described in more detail. This process makes a distinction between small IT projects and enhancements (less than 100 persondays), and large IT projects (more than 100 persondays). All projects originate from ideas generated in the business units. For smaller projects, the decision power and the execution lies in the hands of the individual business unit, and is covered by their IBO budget. Large projects are always handled by IT and follow a strict decision and prioritisation path before the project can be initiated (Figure 74). New opportunities often surface at a fairly low level. In that case, the section head communicates this idea to his division head who in turn communicates it to the department director. The department director will propose the project in the IT committee and will act as a sponsor for the project. An architect will be assigned to conduct a feasibility study focusing on the costs and benefits. IT and business people will be involved in this study respectively responsible for the cost estimation and benefits evaluation. The ultimate decision will be taken by the IT committee based on the figures provided by the feasibility study.

The IT committee prioritises IT projects on the basis of the size of the projects and four criteria: profitability, competitive advantage, operational urgency, and decision support (Figure 75). A decision grid, as shown in Figure 76, is used to score IT projects. Each project can score up to five points per quadrant, so the total score per project varies between four and 20 points. (A small project (class L) at the lowest level for all basic criteria will only have a score of 4).

Based on the calculated scores, the projects get a priority class assigned following the set priority classes of Figure 77. Typically projects with a priority

Figure 74. Project initiation

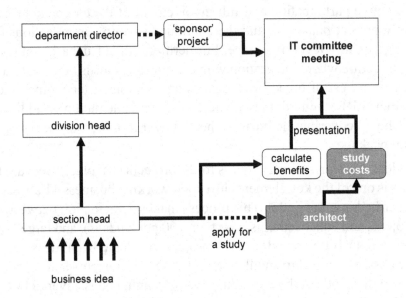

class A or B are accepted, while projects with a class C or D are less likely to be implemented. If the project is accepted it will be planned taking into account the available resource capacity. If needed, the IT Committee can decide to bring in new internal and/or external resources. This prioritisation method proved to be very effective and both IT and the business are satisfied with this way of working. The method is a specific application of the information economics approach.

As explained earlier, a company-wide process management system is implemented within Sidmar. These 22 processes are also formally measured by means of defined KPIs. For process P23: management of information systems, a KPI scorecard is developed. This scorecard is available online and reports indicators such as percentage of support problems solved within the same day against the 85 percent set objective. This system has been recently set up and the indicators still have to evolve from rather technical towards more customer oriented parameters.

A start is made with the implementation of ITIL processes. *"COBIT is*

Figure 75. Project class and basic criteria

	Project Class	Basic Criteria			
	Number of planned man days	Profitability: Pay back time (years)	Competitive Advantage	Operational Urgency	Decision Support
High	> 2000	< 1.5	Improve performance significantly on customer key buying factors for strategic segments	Direct reaction on extreme operational risk, changed legal or operational environment, extreme maintenance risk	High impact support for key decision makers
Medium high	1000 - 2000	1.5 – 2.5	Improve performance significantly on customer key buying factors for other segments	Eliminate critical operational handicaps	Other support for key decision makers
Medium	500 - 1000	2.5 – 4	Improve performance slightly on customer key buying factors	Reduce week points in current operations	High impact for other management
Medium low	200 - 500	4 – 6	Improve performance on other buying factors	Avoid small problems in operational usage	Ongoing support for other management
Low	< 200	> 6	No impact on competitive position	No urgency	No impact on management effectiveness

definitely something for the future," says the IT director. He is convinced that both—ITIL and COBIT—have potential at Sidmar and is planning to use them in order to structure its process P23 ('management of information systems') into sub processes.

Figure 76. Decision grid

Project class	L	ML	M	MH	H
H	1	1	2	2	3
MH	1	1	2	3	4
M	1	2	3	3	4
ML	1	2	3	4	5
L	1	2	3	4	5
	L	ML	M	MH	H
	Profitablity				

Project class	L	ML	M	MH	H
H	1	1	1	2	3
MH	1	1	2	3	4
M	1	1	2	4	4
ML	1	1	3	4	5
L	1	2	4	5	5
	L	ML	M	MH	H
	Competitive advantage				

Project class	L	ML	M	MH	H
H	1	1	1	2	5
MH	1	1	2	3	5
M	1	1	2	3	5
ML	1	1	3	4	5
L	1	2	3	4	5
	L	ML	M	MH	H
	Operational urgency				

Project class	L	ML	M	MH	H
H	1	1	1	1	1
MH	1	1	1	1	2
M	1	1	1	2	3
ML	1	1	2	3	4
L	1	2	3	4	5
	L	ML	M	MH	H
	Decision support				

Figure 77. Priority classes

Priority classes

A   5 points on at least one criterion

   Accept, high priority

B   4 points on profitability or 3 points on at least two criteria

   Accept

C   3 points on profitability or total of 7 points

   Accept if resources available

D   3 points on one criterion

   Accept only if subcontractable

E   All other projects

   Decline

Relational Mechanisms

The IT architect and the IBO committee play both an important role in building and maintaining a good IT-business relationship. For each project, an architect is assigned who coordinates the project in close relationship with the responsible business people. The IT architect is already involved in the project initiation. The IT director emphasises *"The overlap between business and IT is the most important enabler of alignment. It is around this overlap that the main task of the architects is situated since they know the business as well as its processes. The ten architects within Sidmar have three major roles:* project management, technology and business process development, and maintaining the link between the business and IT."

The relationship between business and IT is perceived good to excellent by the controller and by the director IT. *"One of the reasons for this good relationship,"* explains the director IT, *"are the IBO committees where the needs of the business are captured and discussed and translated into IT projects and enhancements."* A somewhat specific governance mechanism comprises the informal lunches where the IT director and the business unit managers discuss IT issues.

Maturity Measurement/Assessment

The maturity level of IT governance at Sidmar results in level 2, based on following elements:

- A wide set of processes and mechanisms are in place, including detailed measurement tools, which are needed in the higher maturity levels
- IT committees exist, where all directors are involved, implicating that IT is highly visible with senior management
- Standards for processes an architecture exist

Figure 78 displays the IT governance elements (highlighted in bold) that are applicable at Sidmar.

The controller assessed the maturity of Sidmar at level three—"Defined Process" with even arguments in favour of level four—"Managed and Mea-

Figure 78. IT governance maturity model (IT Governance Institute): Level two

---

2. Repeatable but Intuitive

There is awareness of IT governance objectives, and practices are developed and applied by individual managers. **IT governance activities** are becoming established within the organisation's change management process, with **active senior management involvement** and oversight. Selected **IT processes** have been **identified for improvement** that would impact key business processes. IT management is beginning to define **standards for processes and technical architectures.** Management has identified **basic IT governance measurements, assessment methods and techniques,** but the process has not been adopted across the organisation. There is **no formal training and communication** on governance standards and responsibilities are left to the individual.

An **IT steering committee** has begun to formalise and establish its roles and responsibilities. There is a draft governance charter (e.g., participants, roles, responsibilities, delegated powers, retained powers, shared resources, and policy). Small and pilot governance projects are initiated to see what works and what does not. General guidelines are emerging for standards and architecture that make sense for the enterprise and a dialogue has started to sell the reasons for their need in the enterprise.

---

surable." Both the controller and the IT director agreed that the ultimate goal is the achievement of maturity level four, "Managed and Measurable." The main motivation for this, says the IT director, *"is that level four guarantees that IT governance is measurable and tangible."* Although the basics are in place, the IT governance charter and policy is not formally documented, which finally results in maturity level 2.

Summary of IT Governance Structures, Processes and Relational Mechanisms

Figure 79 summarises the IT governance structures, processes and relational mechanisms that are in place within Sidmar.

Figure 79. IT governance structures, processes and relational mechanisms at Sidmar

Structures		
What?		**How?**
1	Organisational structure of IT function	Centralised, IT department provides services to commercial organisation of the entire flat carbon steel sector as well
2	Committees	Board of directors
		IT steering committee on corporate level
		Business unit IT steering committees (IBO committees)
Processes		
What?		**How?**
1	IT strategy planning	A highly structured project prioritisation and decision Making process exists,
2	Balanced scorecard technique	Not applied
3	Information economics	Served as an inspiration for Sidmar's decision grid
4	Decision grid	Used in combination with cost-benefit analysis, study on competitive advantages, operational urgency and decision support during the decision making process
5	KPIs	For P23: *Management of Information Systems* as part of the company-wide process management system
6	Measuring	Continuous monitoring of maintenance activities
		Evaluation criteria for IT projects
7	COBIT and ITIL	Are being studied, there are plans to use it in the near future
Relational Mechanisms		
What?		**How?**
1	Business-IT relationship	Role IT architects function of IBO committee
2	Training	No specific 'IT governance awareness training'
3	IT governance awareness	Collective lunches for business and IT people
4	Knowledge management	No specific IT governance focus, yet initiatives include project briefing and information on changes in infrastructure, architecture and staff
5	Job rotation	As part of the career path

The IT function at Sidmar is centralised providing services to its own organisation, as well as to the group commercial department. The IT committee at corporate level and the IBO committees at business unit level play an important role in the IT governance process. An important mechanism in this context is the well defined prioritisation process scoring IT projects on the basis of their profitability, competitive advantage, operational excellence and decision support capacity. Another important mechanism is the specific role of the IT architects which primarily focuses on building a close relationship between IT and business people. Further, a start is made by development KPIs for IT.

Conclusion Pilot Studies

From these pilot case studies, different drivers for adopting IT governance were identified. An important one was certainly the need to comply with Sarbanes-Oxley requirements, which impacts heavily on the control environment in IT. Although this is in the first place a US regulation, some of the pilot companies studied, felt the need to comply because their US mother company needed to comply or because customers/suppliers were requiring it. Other important drivers for IT governance were the pressure to achieve economies of scales after mergers and acquisitions and budget pressure, resulting in a smaller IT budgets for new projects. The challenge, of course, is then to optimally assign the remaining budget to projects and activities that are delivering value to the business. Finally, some pilot case companies mentioned that the IT governance project was more an effort of formalizing and structuring existing structures and processes that were applied already. Although the aforementioned IT governance definitions stated that IT governance is a primary responsibility of the board of directors, it appeared from the pilot cases that IT governance efforts are mostly not driven by business strategic level management. The board was seldom involved in IT governance and as a result, IT governance often had a rather operational focus. In all cases, IT governance was mostly an initiative of the IT department.

From these six pilot cases, it is tentatively concluded that organisations are indeed applying a mix of structures, practices, and relational mechanisms to build up an IT governance framework. The IT department of these case companies was mostly organised using a centralized or federal model. In the federal model, operations are centralized to achieve economies of scale while development is decentralized to stay closer to the business needs. IT steering committees are common practice and are used under many different names. IT strategy committees are on the other hand not common practice, which again is an indication of the low board involvement in IT governance. Yet, the CIO in many cases was reporting to the CEO or another executive committee member. Regarding IT governance processes, the BSC and COBIT are not (or merely) used, while processes found in ITIL such as SLA are more popular. Many prioritization methods and processes were identified, based on information economics (IE) or other frameworks accompanied with ROI type of measures. Finally, many relational mechanisms were used in the domains of shared understanding of business/IT objectives, active conflict resolution, cross-functional business/IT training and business/IT job rotation. In many cases, these mechanisms were rather informally organized.

An important observation was that the proposed practices can work on one or more levels in the organisation. Some of the practices will work on one specific level; other practices can be applied at many levels. For example, the IT strategy committee can only be applied at strategic level (as it is defined by the IT Governance Institute (2003) as a board committee). The BSC or COBIT however can be applied at strategic level, but also at management and operational level.

Also, some new practices, which were not yet covered, were identified. Examples include activity-based costing (ABC), which is certainly an important alignment mechanism as it enables the business to fully understand the cost consequences of the taken decisions and more detailed frameworks such as CMM and RUP.

From the pilot case (KBC), clear indications were found that working in the finance industry, heavily dependent upon IT and going through a mergers and acquisitions period, requires a rather complex IT governance framework, in which many different committees need to play an important role. During these cases, an initial view about the governance outcome was given, using the maturity model of the IT Governance Institute (ITGI, 2005), which provides a maturity scale from 0 (non-existent) to 5 (optimised) for the maturity of the governance framework. All interviewees were asked to make a self-assessment, and the scores of these interviewees ranged from 2 to 4, with the member of the board of directors assigning the highest score. The argument for the lowest score was that probably not all involved people in the model completely passed the 'awareness' phase and clearly understand their role. However, giving the fact that a member of the board of directors assigns such a high score provides an intuitive feeling that this board member perceives IT as being reasonable aligned to the business.

References

Benbasat, I., Goldstein, D., & Mead, M. (1987). The case research strategy in studies of information systems. *MIS Quarterly*, *11*(3), 368-386.

Carnegie Mellon Software engineering Institute. *Capability Maturity Model (CMM)*. Retrieved from www.sei.cmu.edu/cmmi/

Henderson, J.C., & Venkatraman, N. (1993). Strategic alignment: Leveraging information technology for transforming organizations. *IBM Systems Journal*, *32*(1).

IBM. *Rational Unified Process (RUP)*. Retrieved from www.ibm.com

ITGI (2003). *Board briefing on IT governance* (2nd ed.). Retrieved from www.itgi.org

ITGI (2005). *COBIT 4.0*. Retrieved from www.itgi.org

Luftman, J. (2002). Achieving Alignment Détente. *CIO Insight*, *July*. Retrieved from http://www.cioinsight.com/article2/0,3959,325354,00.asp

Microsoft. *Microsoft Operations Framework (MOF)*. Retrieved from www.microsoft.com/mof

Parker, M. (1995). *Strategic transformation and information technology*. London: Prentice Hall.

Patel, N.V. (2003). An emerging strategy for e-business IT governance. In W. Van Grembergen (Ed.), *Strategies for information technology governance*. Hershey, PA: Idea Group Publishing.

Peterson, R. R. (2003). Information strategies and tactics for information technology governance. In W. Van Grembergen (Ed.), *Strategies for information technology governance*. Hershey, PA: Idea Group Publishing.

Ribbers, P., Peterson, R., & Parker, M. (2002). *Designing Information Technology Governance Processes: Diagnosing Contemporary Practises and Competing Theories.* Proceedings of the 35th Hawaii International Conference on System Sciences (HICSS).

Romano, P. L. (Ed.). (1994). *Activity-based management in action.* Montvale, 160.

Van Grembergen, W., De Haes, S., & Guldentops, E. (2003). Structures, processes and relational mechanisms for IT governance. In W. Van Grembergen (Ed.), *Strategies for information technology governance.* Hershey, PA: Idea Group Publishing.

Van Grembergen, W., Saull, R., & De Haes, S. (2003). Linking the IT balanced scorecard to the business objectives at a major Canadian financial group. *Journal for Information Technology Cases and Applications (JITCA)*, 5(1).

Weill, P., & Woodham, R. (2002). *Don't just lead, govern: Implementing effective IT governance.* (CISR WP No. 326). Cambridge, MA: MIT Sloan School of management.

Chapter V

IT Governance Implementation Guide

Introduction

There is no real "silver bullet" (the ideal way) for implementing and maintaining good IT governance within an organization. Organizations differ in culture and size, they operate in different sectors, and they may own a different market position resulting in different business strategies. These different contingencies have a direct impact on the organizational structure and processes, and as such have a direct impact on the IT governance mechanisms.

Striving for better IT governance is a continuous process, which most probably will never be completed. Indeed, as the company, the marketplace, and people are constantly changing, it is important to closely monitor the company's structures, processes, and mechanisms and to adapt and fine-tune them to the new situation. (The same is true for IT governance.)

Based on earlier research and completed with best practices captured from the case study research, a set of guidelines and ideas was compiled which should help your organization in achieving better IT governance. From this collection of practical guidelines and best practices you can pick those that best suit your environment. Some have sense to follow in a more chronological order (i.e., first determine business goals and IT goals and then optimise the IT processes), while others just provide an overview of mechanisms and practical guidelines that can be used in a best-practice set-up.

Most organisations already have IT governance elements in place or are in the process of implementing others. So how do you best start?

A logical first step is to inform you about the different aspects of IT governance, its mechanisms, processes, and frameworks. Not only you, but all people, responsible for driving the overall IT governance initiative should be educated on this topic by means of literature, best practices, seminars, trainings, and others. Next, a status of the current situation in the company related to IT governance should be made. The IT governance maturity models (2005) are a useful instrument for this purpose. By analysing the current IT governance status and the desired IT governance status, gaps can be identified and a company-specific IT-governance implementation plan can be set up. This is a process that must be adopted both by IT people and people from the business, and should be executed at all levels in the organisation. As confirmed by the case studies, most of the IT governance initiatives are driven (mainly) by IT. Although a lot of these initiatives may be good, they have the intrinsic danger that they are not easily adopted by the business people because they were not involved. Involvement of the business, as early as possible, is therefore crucial for a successful IT governance implantation.

Below listed guidelines can assist in finding elements that may suit your situation and as such may complete your plan.

Nine Guidelines for Better IT Governance

1. Define Business Goals and IT Goals

Achieving better IT governance starts with the business, and more specifically with understanding its strategy and goals. Each organization should own clear business goals and a related business strategy, communicated to and adopted by the entire organization. In earlier research on aligning IT and business goals (2005) it was confirmed that in practice this is not always the case. Business strategy and goals are not always formally written out and if so, people throughout the organization are not always aware of them. Preferably, IT management should be involved early in the business strategy definition process, especially in those companies that are highly dependent on IT.

The IT goals should be aligned to the business goals. A good exercise may be to write out the business and IT goals and put them into a matrix indicating whether the IT goal is of primary (P), secondary (S), or of no importance in achieving the business goal. While doing this exercise, gaps may be identified or IT goals may be reviewed in order to better align with the business goals. Figure 1 shows an example of such a linking exercise for the financial sector.

Most IT departments from the case research did own a 'clear' IT strategy. The mapping to the business strategy though was less straightforward. Ideally, the IT strategy should be an IT blueprint of the business strategy plan. The IT goals, set out in the IT strategy plan should clearly support the achievement of one or more business goals. It is the responsibility of the board and senior management to ensure that the IT strategy is aligned with the business strategy.

Figure 1. Example linking business goals to IT goals (Van Grembergen, De Haes, & Moons, 2005)

Business Goals	Developing innovative IT services with a focus on	Information security	Fulfilling SLA's with business departments	Increasing IT department efficiency	Integration and consolidation of different IT departments	IT disaster recovery and business continuity	IT governance / IT strategic alignment	IT measures to satisfy Basel II requirements	Lowering cost of transaction processing	Making IT measurable	Optimizing the IT infrastructure	Rapid development of new IT services	Reducing external staff	Standardising IT systems
Achieving compliance with Basel II regulations					S	S	P							
Improving competitiveness through IT	P					P				S	P			
Improving customer orientation and service	P		S	P	S	S		P	S		S	S		
Post-merger integration and consolidation				P		S				S		S	S	
Reducing operational cost			P	P	S	S	P	P	P		P	P		
Reducing transaction cost			P	S		S	P	P	S				S	
Risk management	S	P	S	S	P	P	S				P	S		
Shortening service development lifecycle						S		S		P				
Tailoring solutions for different target groups	P					S								

- Clear business goals, communicated to the entire organisation
- Early involvement of IT in business strategy process
- Align IT goals to business goals
- Derive IT strategy from business strategy

2. Define the Right IT Governance Processes

Whenever the business goals and the IT goals are aligned, it is important for IT to organise itself around a set of efficient and effective IT processes. The COBIT framework provides a set of 34 generally accepted IT processes. Each process is well-documented with clear control objectives, management guidelines and metrics (KGIs and KPIs). Dependent on the business/IT strategy and its goals, an organisation may start developing those processes that are of high importance for supporting the IT goals. Assign a process owner and clearly define the scope and control objectives of the process. By linking a process to other processes, clear inputs and deliverables can be defined. In addition, the different responsibilities and accountabilities (the RACI diagrams can provide guidance here. ITGI, 2005) must be identified. A process can only be identified as effective when some clear metrics are set up. Both KGIs and KPIs mutual relationship must be set on different levels. Finally, the maturity models, offer a comprehensible method for measuring the progress of the process itself. The current (as-is) situation can be placed against the desirable (to-be) situation and the gap between both can be identified and necessary actions can be set up.

- Select most important IT processes
- Assign process owners
- Develop metrics
- Measure the progress (maturity models)

3. Set Up a Clear IT Organisation and Decision Structure

As described before in this book, effective IT governance is also determined by the way the IT function is organised and where the IT decision-making authority is located within the organisation. From the case studies, the federal organising structure for the IT function is confirmed to be the most popular. The federal structure is merely a hybrid design of centralised infrastructure control and decentralised application control. Cost optimisation and economies of scale are the main reasons for centralising IT responsibilities. Especially in large organisations, post-acquisitions, and merger there is a pressure towards centralisation, particularly in the areas of infrastructure and global standardisation. Development activities or the decision rights over IT development projects, including budgets are typically kept close to the business units. Some calls this the "glocal" approach, combining an optimal mix of global synergies and local responsiveness offering the required flexibility. Others explicitly see the application development and architecture teams as the most important player in the IT organisation because of their close relationship with the business units.

A short distance between IT management (CIO) and executive management (CEO) is favoured. A CIO reporting directly to the CEO is a straightforward solution but other set-ups where for example the CIO sits down with the CEO on a regular basis or where IT management is involved in executive committees may imply similar positive results. Today, a number of IT departments still report into an overall financial department possibly resulting in a financially oriented approach, which may be too unilateral for the IT function.

A specific HR management may be adopted for the IT departments, in order to attract and retain highly qualified people (especially in governmental organisations). Also, high-availability requirements may ask for a specific HR management in the IT department.

- Federal structure for IT organisations are most popular and are seen as most effective
    - Candidates for centralised approach: global infrastructure, group-wide standards for IT purchases, security
    - Candidates for decentralised approach: business applications, decision for business specific IT projects (applications)
- Strive for a short distance between IT management and corporate management
- A specific HR management for the IT department may be required

---

4. Involve Executive Management and the Board of Directors

The examples from our case studies confirm the fact that IT governance initia-tives are initiated by IT and are in some cases still exclusively in the hands of IT. Adoption from the business is important but maybe even more important is that executive management is aware of it and is actively participating in the existing IT governance activities.

As observed during the case study research, different structures exist on project (execution) level to involve IT into the business and vice versa; but on executive level IT and business are not always well aligned. A mechanism that encourages higher executive involvement in IT consists of an IT strategy committee, where executive management is involved and plays an active role in the decision taking process around the IT strategy and the alignment of that strategy with the corporate strategy. Also, an organizational structure, where the CIO reports directly to executive management favours a better execute involvement in IT governance.

IT topics should regularly appear and be discussed in executive committees or on board level, especially in those organisations where IT plays a crucial role in keeping the business running. Even when the CIO is not a part of the executive committees, he should be represented by another executive member or he/she could be invited whenever an IT related topic is handled.

• Establish an IT strategy committee
• Involve the board
• Establish an IT governance team with executive and business involvement
• Invite IT Director to executive committee
• CIO close to board of directors

5. Manage Roles and Responsibilities

As described before, IT governance structures involve the organisation, the location of the IT function, the existence of clearly defined roles and responsibilities and a diversity of IT/business committees. Most case study companies did define or are in the process of defining formal roles and responsibilities documents. Defining these responsibilities and writing them down in documents is one thing, acting upon them is of course more important. All (IT) people, working in an IT governance context should have, besides their IT specific responsibilities, clear responsibilities defined towards the business they work for, and this throughout all levels, including the CIO and IT management. To make sure individuals adopt and execute upon their roles and responsibilities, a process of 'formal' evaluation and review is a good mechanism. Typically a person and his/her manager review and evaluate the defined roles and responsibilities against the delivered activities. This way each individual is formally informed about their function. Roles and responsibilities should also be communicated throughout the organisation or at least within functional teams, so expectations are set clear.

It is the responsibility of the board and executive management to communicate these roles and responsibilities and to make sure that they are clearly understood throughout the whole organisation.

- Define clear roles and responsibilities for all functions on all levels
- Include business responsibilities for IT people
- Communicate to individuals
- Communicate throughout the organisation
- Review and evaluate

6. Install IT Steering and IT Strategy Committees

Good working (IT) committees play an important role in establishing a good IT/business alignment. As described earlier in this book, IT steering committees and IT strategy committees are both important IT governance structures. While the IT strategy committee operates at the board level, the IT steering committee is situated at executive level, which implies that they have different responsibility, authority and membership. In practice most companies are well organised with IT steering committees, while IT strategy committees are still scarce. However, having a type of IT strategy committee in place does bring value to the IT governance set-up. IT issues and projects are discussed on executive level and management is much earlier involved and better informed in IT related matters.

In practice, the IT steering, and in some cases the IT strategy committee, may exist in different forms and they all carry different names. Important is that those IT committees exist on different levels and that they are composed of business and IT people.

> • Setup IT strategy committee
> • IT steering committees

7. Manage and Align the IT Investment Portfolio

Results from the case study research show that a lot of the IT-business inter-action occurs around "projects." In essence this is the tactical and tangible ('pragmatic') way of translating specific business needs into supporting applications and infrastructure. Also, more successful IT governance com-panies held a clear project evaluation and prioritization methodology, where both IT and business people were closely involved. Prioritisation methods where not only financial aspects, such as costs, ROI, NVP play a role but also other factors like quality of service, customer satisfaction and competi-tive advantage are seen as useful. In one particular case, for each project IT was responsible for calculating the costs of a project, while business was responsible for analyzing the anticipated benefits.

Good working project-related committees, where both IT and business are represented play a crucial role. In addition, formal tandems of IT people (e.g., IT architect) and responsible business people were created. Also, early involvement in the project cycle of both IT and business owners, provides a good base for successful completion.

Different methods exist for evaluating and prioritising a project and managing the complete project portfolio. Methods based on the information econom-ics methodology seem to work well. It is important to note that whatever method is used, the decision process and the different criteria used should be transparent and well explained. People throughout the organisation, and particularly those involved in projects, should have a clear view on the status of the projects and the project portfolio and a transparent decision process needs to be present to give insight as to why selected projects are executed and others are not.

- Adopt a project evaluation method

  Incorporate financial parameters (ROI, NVP, …)

  Incorporate non financial parameters such as:
  - Strategic value
  - Customer satisfaction
- Adopt a project prioritisation method

  Make sure this is used consequently

  Make sure everybody is aware of this methodology in use
- Involvement of both business and IT people from early project phase on

8. Use Performance Measurement Tools

Measuring and monitoring the different IT processes on different levels is very important. It is important to identify per domain or per process those metrics that support the related goals. Using the balanced scorecard technique gives the possibility to not only use financial metrics, but also metrics that refer to for example end-user satisfaction, corporate contribution and training. Metrics should be 'measurable,' preferably quantified and should be placed against a target to be achieved within a given timeframe, for example, 15 IT developers trained by end of the calendar year. Each metric should have a responsible person or team of persons. Some successful performance monitoring, done by both IT and the business, were identified during the case study. Relationships between metrics are also important elements in measuring performance. Different scorecards may be built and maintained per application domain, like more operational oriented scorecards for the different application development domains. Ideally, those scorecards are rolled up and/or aggregated into one overall scorecard, containing the most important and crucial metrics. The IT scorecard can in turn be linked to the business scorecard.

If scorecards are shared amongst the organisation, by means of easy accessible intranets or knowledge management systems, it may contribute to higher awareness of the IT efforts and their contribution to the organisation. It is also confirmed that scorecards are interesting monitoring tools for management, especially when they can be rolled up into a corporate scorecard.

9. Set Up and Support Communication and Awareness Mechanisms

Companies, who score better in IT/business relationship, also have a good communication 'infrastructure' in place in order to encourage the relationship between business and IT. Good communication mechanisms come in different forms.

There is nothing more effective than people having a direct dialogue. In order to encourage such a direct communication between business and IT people different mechanisms can be implemented. During the case studies some good functioning mechanisms were identified, like tandem functions (see point 7) and the role of an IT steering committee (see point 5) where both business people are represented. Of course good communication must be established between different levels of the organization and additional attention should be given to the higher levels of the organisational structure (see executive involvement). Tandem functions, where IT people have a direct counterpart in the business come in different roles and positions. These functions do exist on project levels; that is, during the course of a project an IT person is appointed, who has a business-specific responsibility and talks to business people. A more structural approach is where specific IT people do have long-term responsibilities for a specific business unit. A commonly used name is 'account manager.'

But good communication is more than having the right people 'around the table.' Speaking the same language, where both parties (business and IT) understand each other, is important. IT people must be informed about the business, its specific terminology, its way of working, and its processes in place. But in order to encourage qualitative communication, business people should also be aware of (at least) basic IT terminology. Providing the necessary training to educate both is a first instrument. But co-location, meaning physically placing the IT people's workplace into the business department, and job-ration can also encourage a better integration of IT responsibles with the business unit(s). In one particular case, the incorporation of the IT development group into the business unit was seen as the main driver for the optimal relationship between IT and the business group. The developers share the same work space as the business people and daily contacts are enforced by the physical landscape of the working environment.

The language used in general is an important attention point as well. IT people should ensure that they do not to use too many technical terms. Any problem, proposition, or communication in general should be understandable by business people.

Other tools that may help raise the awareness of IT and IT governance towards the business, include good working intranet sites or knowledge managements systems. One example from the case studies used the corporate intranet site for publishing success stories. In addition, all relevant measurement and monitoring tools together with the reporting on the statuses of running projects are considered good candidates for internal publishing as it assists in keeping business people aware of actual IT activities.

- 'Formal' tandem functions business-IT people
  - Project based
  - Business unit based
- Train IT people on business topics
- Train business people on IT topics
- Co-location
- Job-ration
- Knowledge management systems / Intranet sites
  - Publish success stories
  - Project status overview
  - Scorecards
- Informal meeting points

References

ITGI (2005). *COBIT 4.0*. Retrieved from www.itgi.org

Van Grembergen, W., De Haes, S., & Moons, J. (2005). IT governance: Linking business goals to IT goals and COBIT processes. *Information Systems Control Journal, 4*.

About the Authors

Professor Dr. Wim Van Grembergen – wim.vangrembergen@ua.ac.be
Vlasrootstraat 56
9170 Sint-Pauwels
Belgium

Wim Van Grembergen is professor at the Economics and Management Faculty of the University of Antwerp (UA) and executive professor at the University of Antwerp Management School (UAMS). He was previously a guest professor at the University of Leuven (KUL) and had teaching assignments at the University of Stellenbosch in South Africa, at the Institute of Business Studies in Moscow and the Queensland University of Technology in Australia. He teaches information systems at the bachelor's, master's, and executive level, and researches in business transformations through information technology, audit of information systems, IT performance management and IT governance. From 1989 to 1995 he served as academic director of the MBA program of UFSIA (now UA) and presently he is academic coordinator of an IT-audit master program and an e-business master program. Dr. Van Grembergen presented at the European Conference on Information Systems (ECIS), at the Information Resources Management Association (IRMA) Conference and at the Hawaii International Conference on Systems Sciences (HICSS). He was track chair on IT evaluation for the IRMA-conference (2000-2003) and is minitrack chair "IT governance and its mechanisms" for the HICSS-conference since 2002. He published articles in journals such as *Journal of Strategic Information Systems, Journal of Corporate Transformation, Journal of Information on Technology Cases and Applications, Journal of Information Systems Control* and *EDP Auditing (Auerbach).* He has several publications in leading Belgian and Dutch journals, has published a book in 1997 on business process reengineering in Belgian organizations, and in 1998 a book on the IT balanced scorecard. He edited a book entitled *IT Evaluation Methods and Management,* which was published in 2001 by IGI Global (formerly Idea Group Publishing), and in 2002 *Information Systems Evaluation Management* also published by IGP. In 2003, he published a book titled *Strategies for Information Technology Governance.* Professor Van Grembergen serves on the editorial boards of *Journal of Global Information Technology Management (JGITM), Journal of Information Technology Cases and Applications (JITCA), Annals of Cases on Information Technology and Management in Organizations.* Professor Van Grembergen is engaged in the continuous development of the CobiT framework and has presented papers and conducted workshops at ISACA (Information Systems Audit and Control Association) international conferences. He is also member of the Academic Relations Task Force of ISACA and is currently conducting research projects for ISACA on IT Governance. Dr. Van Grembergen is a frequent speaker at academic and professional meetings and conferences and has served in a consulting capacity to a number of firms. He is a member of the board of directors of IT companies including an IT consultancy firm and an IT firm servicing a Belgian financial group. Recently he established at UAMS the ITAG Research Institute that aims to contribute to the understanding of IT Alignment and Governance through research and dissemination of the knowledge via publications, conferences and seminars (www.uams.be/itag).

Steven De Haes – steven.dehaes@ua.ac.be
Merksplassebaan 19
2390 Malle
Belgium

Steven De Haes is responsible for the information systems management executive programs and research at the University of Antwerp Management School (UAMS), including the master's program in e-business and the masters program in computer auditing. He has teaching assignments in many executive programs in the domain of IT governance, IT assurance, strategic alignment, IT performance measurement, and so forth. He is also actively engaged in applied research in the domain of IT governance and strategic alignment. He performs research and project management assignments for the IT Governance Institute (ITGI) in the domain of IT governance, COBIT, VAL IT, and so forth. He is the chair of the Belgian COBIT Development Group and contributed many publications issued by the IT Governance Institute (COBIT 4, COBIT Quickstart, IT Assurance Guide) Currently, he is preparing a PhD on the practices and mechanisms of IT governance and their impact on strategic alignment. He has several publications on IT governance primarily in the *Information Systems Control Journal* and the *Journal for Information Technology Case Studies and Applications (JITCA)*. He presented papers at leading conferences such as the *Hawaiian International Conference on System Sciences (HICSS)* and the *Information Resources Management Association (IRMA) Conference*. He also contributed to the book titled *Strategies for Information Technology Governance,* published in 2003 *(Ed. Van Grembergen)*. He acted as speaker and facilitator in many international conferences and CIO networks. Recently he established together with Professor Van Grembergen the ITAG Research Institute that aims to contribute to the understanding of IT alignment and governance through research and dissemination of the knowledge via publications, conferences, and seminars (www.uams.be/itag).

John Thorp, CMC, I.S.P.
President, The Thorp Network Inc.
Consulting Fellow, Fujitsu Consulting

John Thorp is an internationally sought-after management consultant with close to 45 years experience in the information management field. Author of "The Information Paradox," John's focus is on helping organizations realize the benefits of IT-enabled change. Over the last five years, John's work has extended beyond IT to the broader issues of enterprise value management and strategic governance. He is currently working with the IT Governance Institute (ITGI) to research, develop and promote Val IT™, an open internationally accepted standard of best practices for optimising the value of IT-enabled change building on their existing COBIT™ framework.

Index

A

AGF Belgium, case study 145
alignment instrument 101
application manager 141
applications 80
availability 77
awareness mechanisms 247

B

balanced scorecard (BSC) 1, 39, 139
    technique 206
better IT governance 239
    guidelines 239
business-IT communication 179
business/IS planning alignment 18
    critical success factors 18
business/IT alignment 116
business analyst 141
business architect 141
business balanced scorecard 77
    customer perspective 77
    financial perspective 77

internal perspective 77
learning and growth perspective 79
business goals 78, 239

C

capability maturity model (CMM) 161
capital investments 3
case studies 125
    overview 127
    AGF Belgium 145
    CM 181
    Huntsman 196
    KBC 127
    Sidmar – Arcelor 217
    Vanbreda 163
change management 148
    process 211
CM, case study 181
COBIT (control objectives for information
    and related technology) 1, 48
    and compliancy for Sarbanes-Oxley
    96
    complementary frameworks 48

control objectives 83
development 77
framework 76, 80, 82
goals and metrics 90
management guidelines 86
maturity models 93
process, inputs/outputs 89
COBIT 4.0 76
acquisition and implementation (AI)
81
application controls 85
delivery and support 81
goals and metrics 91
management guidelines 88
monitor and evaluate (ME) 81
planning and organisation (PO) 81
process controls 84
ComInfo 152
Committee of Sponsoring Organisations of
the Treadway Commission (COSO)
96
communication mechanisms 247
competitive advantage 3
competitive costs 118
competitive potential alignment 15
compliance 77
confidentiality 77
corporate contribution 108
corecard 115, 117
corporate governance 8
cost management 116
customer orientation 108
scorecard 118, 119
customer satisfaction 118
Cybrary 122

D

decision grid 230
decision structure 241
development process performance 121
development services performance 118

E

effectiveness 76
efficiency 76

employee satisfaction 122
enterprise architecture management 121
ERP data warehouse team manager 200
executive management 243

F

functional integration 12
future orientation 108
perspective 121
scorecard 62, 122

G

global business IT team scorecard 207
global service proposal template 206
Great-West Life Assurance Company 102

H

hardware 149
human resource management 122
Huntsman, case study 196

I

information 79
information economics 44
information security 77
information services division (ISD) 106
Information Systems Audit and Control
Association (ISACA) 48
information technology (IT) 1
infrastructure 80
integrity 77
Investors Group 102
IT
pervasiveness of 2
strategic use of 19
IT/business steering committee (IBSC)
133
IT architect 141
IT balanced scorecard 101
as alignment instrument 101
at KBC 139
IT BSC 106
case, lessons learned 113
maturity of 108

Project 104
Project, organization 104
IT budget composition 134
IT charter 141
IT concerns 105
IT dependency 3
IT division
    service provider 107
    strategic partner 107
IT goals 78, 79, 239
IT governance 1, 8, 10, 179
    context 129, 147, 165, 183, 197,
    219
    definition 5
    executive committee 37
    explained 1
    focus areas of 7
    goal of 12
    implementation framework 24
    implementation guide 238
    implementation status 64
    in practice 125
    management committee 37
    maturity evaluation 60
    maturity models 61, 160, 178, 193,
    215, 232, 239
    models 1
    processes 1, 24, 37, 53, 135, 144,
    153, 161, 171, 179, 190, 194, 205,
    215, 227, 234, 241
    relational mechanisms 24, 51
    scorecard perspectives 54
    standards/guidance 49
    strategies 1
    vs. corporate governance 8
    vs. IT management 10
IT governance balanced scorecard 53
    metrics for 54
IT governance framework 76, 126
    COBIT 4.0 76
    necessary elements 25
    necessary framework 126
IT governance structures 1, 24, 26, 131,
    144, 149, 161, 166, 179, 184, 194,
    198, 215, 220, 234
    organizational 131, 149, 166, 184,
    198, 220

IT hierarchy 201
IT investment portfolio 245
IT management 10
    business literacy 19
IT organisation 241
    structure 29, 132
IT processes 79
IT project life cycle 135
IT steering committees 34, 244
    critical success factors 36
IT strategic scorecard 108, 115
    framework 109
    measures of 115
IT strategy 179
    committees 34, 244

K

KBC, case study 127
knowledge-based economy 3
knowledge management 122
KPI framework 208

L

London Life 102

M

maturity measurement/assessment 143,
    159, 177, 193, 214, 231

O

operational excellence 108
    perspective 58
    scorecard 120
operational process performance 121
operational service performance 119
organisational structure 131, 146, 149,
    166, 184, 197, 198, 220
    CIO office 186
    of Arcelor 218
    of CM Antwerp 182
    of IT 199
    of IT projects and development 167
    of Sidmar 219
    of the application development team
    222

of the insurance component 164
of the IT department 150, 185, 222

P

people 80
performance management 7
    tool 246
pervasiveness of IT 2
portfolio management 44
priority classes 230
process manager 141
process maturity 121
product manager 141
project class and basic criteria 229
project initiation 228
project prioritisation 209

R

RACI Diagram 89
rational unified process (RUP) 161
relational mechanisms 140, 144, 157, 161,
    175, 179, 192, 194, 212, 215, 231,
    234
reliability 77
resource management 7
return on investment (ROI) 161
risk management 7, 116

S

Sarbanes-Oxley (SOX) law 96
service level agreements (SLAs) 47
service level management (SLM) 47
shared domain knowledge 51
Sidmar – Arcelor, case study 217
Sidmar's IT budget 221
stakeholders
    concerns 105
    needs 56
    perspective 56
    satisfaction 56
strategic alignment 7, 12
    domains 14
    enablers 18
    inhibitors 18
    maturity levels of Luftman 22

maturity model of Duffy 23
maturity models of 21
strategic alignment model (SAM) 12
    extensions to 15
    important contributions to 16
    interpretations of 15
strategic cross 173
strategic decision making 24
strategic fit 12
strategic information systems planning
    (SISP) 24, 37
strategic use of IT 19
synergy achievement 116

T

technology 148
technology transformation alignment 14
template service level agreements 192
thin-client project 210
    financial evaluation 211
Tri-Company 101
    IT Merger 102

V

VALIT framework 45
value chain 173
value delivery 7, 116
Vanbreda, case study 163